D1637454

Mastering Celtx™

Terry Borst

Course Technology PTR
A part of Cengage Learning

COURSE TECHNOLOGY
CENGAGE Learning

Australia • Brazil • Japan • Korea • Mexico • Singapore • Spain • United Kingdom • United States

COURSE TECHNOLOGY
CENGAGE Learning™

Mastering Celtx™
Terry Borst

Publisher and General Manager, Course Technology PTR: Stacy L. Hiquet

Associate Director of Marketing: Sarah Panella

Manager of Editorial Services: Heather Talbot

Marketing Manager: Mark Hughes

Senior Acquisitions Editor: Mitzi Koontz

Project/Copy Editor: Karen A. Gill

Technical Reviewer: Keith Davenport

Interior Layout Tech: MPS Limited, a Macmillan Company

Cover Designer: Luke Fletcher

Indexer: Larry Sweazy

Proofreader: Laura R. Gabler

For product information and technology assistance, contact us at **Cengage Learning Customer & Sales Support, 1-800-354-9706.**

For permission to use material from this text or product, submit all requests online at **cengage.com/permissions.**
Further permissions questions can be emailed to **permissionrequest@cengage.com.**

Celtx is a trademark of Celtx Studios.

All other trademarks are the property of their respective owners.

All images © Cengage Learning unless otherwise noted. Figure 1.1 is courtesy of Bruce Damer and DigiBarn. Figure 1.2 is courtesy of Tanana Rivera.

Library of Congress Control Number: 2011923929

ISBN-13: 978-1-4354-5901-4

ISBN-10: 1-4354-5901-6

Course Technology, a part of Cengage Learning
20 Channel Center Street
Boston, MA 02210
USA

Cengage Learning is a leading provider of customized learning solutions with office locations around the globe, including Singapore, the United Kingdom, Australia, Mexico, Brazil, and Japan. Locate your local office at: **international.cengage.com/region.**

Cengage Learning products are represented in Canada by Nelson Education, Ltd.

For your lifelong learning solutions, visit **courseptr.com.**

Visit our corporate Web site at **cengage.com.**

Printed in the United States of America
1 2 3 4 5 6 7 13 12 11

This book is dedicated to Carolyn.

Acknowledgments

The author gratefully acknowledges the aid of many individuals in rounding out the content of *Mastering Celtx*.

The Celtx team: Sheila Crosbie, Steve Pick, Laurie Clouston, Ryan FitzGerald, Simon Andrews, Lez Cuff, Greg Dawson, Tony Goold, Chad House, and Mark Kennedy.

Matthew Page, owner of Riffraff New Media (riffraffnm.com), for his generous donation of the award-winning short film *Delivery Date* script and storyboards, as well as for his time mapping shot sketches and discussing his own storyboard usage.

Sean Hannon, professional actor and 3D animator, for his generous donation of storyboard images from the award-winning film *Deja Vu* to illustrate the use of storyboard features in Celtx.

Matt Denoma and Brad Wolfley, for loan of their mobile devices for photography in Chapter 1.

Tanana Rivera, for her photography in Chapter 1.

Patty Barrue-Coffman and Katelyn Peer, for helping demonstrate Celtx Studios chat features.

Peter McCarthy, director and producer whose credits include the groundbreaking films *Sid and Nancy* and *Repo Man*, for his generous insights into the usage of call sheets and schedules.

Karen Gill, for her tireless copyediting and wrangling of screenshots, callouts, and last-minute text revisions.

About the Author

Terry Borst is a member of the Writers Guild of America and has been a working screenwriter since the 1980s.

His screen credits include feature films, TV movies, globally syndicated episodic television, and award-winning video games. For more than a decade, he wrote *alt.screenwriters*, a monthly column about screenwriting and new technology for the Writers Guild's trade magazine *Written By*. He also coauthored two books on the process of conceptualizing and creating media content for video games and virtual simulations.

Borst currently teaches screenwriting at Santa Fe University of Art and Design and has lectured and given workshops at numerous colleges and conferences across North America. He consults on cutting-edge media convergence and artificial intelligence projects, exploring the continued evolution of storytelling in the twenty-first century.

You can find out more about him at terryborst.com.

Contents

Chapter 3
Project Navigation, Library, Notes, and Media   31

Chapter 4
Creating and Editing Production Film Scripts   49

Chapter 5
Script Breakdowns and Catalogs   67

Chapter 6
Reinventing Project Scripting I   85

Chapter 7
Reports   93

Chapter 8
Storyboards   103

Chapter 9
Sketches   **115**

Chapter 10
Reinventing Project Scripting II   **131**

Chapter 11
Calendaring and Scheduling   **139**

Chapter 12
Exploring Celtx's Built-In Sample Projects   **171**

Chapter 13
Celtx Script   181

Chapter 14
Celtx Studios: Creation and Administration   201

Chapter 15
Celtx Studios: User Interaction   215

Chapter 16
Celtx Add-Ons, Utilities, and Sketch Images   245

Chapter 17
The Celtx Community   259

Appendix A
Understanding Script Formats   263

Appendix B
Script Template Typeset/PDF Format Options   273

Appendix C
Breakdown Item Data Fields   283

Appendix D
Menu Bars and Icon Toolbar   295

Appendix E
Keyboard Shortcuts   299

Appendix F
Setting Up Linux for Celtx Studios and Celtx Add-Ons   303

Glossary   305

Index   307

Introduction

Until recently, available screenwriting tools—built around traditional discrete roles and tethered to paper output—have struggled to keep up with the rapid changes in industry practices and needs. However, a new tool called Celtx (pronounced *kel-tx*) has embraced the industry's evolution and created a pre-production workspace that erases the boundaries between different conceptualizing and narrative-building tasks, such as storyboarding, outlining, media asset management, and scriptwriting.

Who This Book Is For

This book—the first comprehensive overview of Celtx (including version 2.9, released early in 2011)—is designed for small-shop media professionals; independent video- and filmmakers; media arts professors and students; ad-hoc media production teams (48-hour film jams and game jams; in-house organizations creating training or promotional videos; and so on); "pro-am" media creators; and anyone interested in exploring his or her creativity as a screenwriter, storyboard artist, or comic book creator.

Readers will be introduced to the essential Celtx toolset (as well as to the Celtx Script app, Celtx Studio, and Celtx add-ons) and will learn how to apply Celtx to a variety of projects and workflows.

The only assumption made is that readers will already have some experience using a text-editing program like Microsoft Word, OpenOffice, or Google Docs. Cutting, copying, and pasting text should be something you've done before.

How This Book Is Organized

Celtx has already been adopted by hundreds of thousands of users, but few have fully exploited Celtx's potential. This book unlocks the door to true Celtx mastery.

- Chapter 1 provides a brief background on how media pre-production evolved out of the silent film era into the twenty-first century, and how Celtx was born out of the changes digital media has brought about. If you're not worried about how Celtx got here but are just raring to go use Celtx, skip this chapter and move on to Chapter 2.

- Chapters 2–7 introduce you to the basics of Celtx usage, including script composition, annotating and cataloging, creating production revisions, breaking down the script, and generating script reports.

- Chapters 8–10 explore Celtx's storyboard and sketch features.

- Chapter 11 explores Celtx's calendaring and scheduling features, including the production of call sheets and other key production documents.

- Chapter 12 explores Celtx's sample projects, which will further review the features introduced in Chapters 2–11.

- Chapter 13 introduces you to the Celtx Script app, for use on iPhones, iPod Touches, and iPads.

- Chapters 14–15 explore Celtx Studios: a platform for integrated project management, project sharing, and "cloud" storage of projects.

- Chapter 16 looks at low-cost Celtx add-ons and additional art packs that can enhance and expand the use of Celtx.

- Chapter 17 explores how the Celtx community, help forums, and other support mechanisms can broaden your uses of Celtx.

- Appendixes provide reference sections for script formats and format options, breakdown form data fields, and further Celtx usage and installation information.

Terminology

In this era of media convergence, the traditional terminology applied to media often falls short of adequately describing the process and product. For example, "films" were time-based media shot on film stock, and "videos" were created using video cameras. But now a majority of films are shot in digital video (DV)—yet we resist calling these "videos." We can now create machinima projects using computer-generated animations built into game engines, and other animated "films" using Flash and Maya, among other software tools.

Time-based media projects can now be distributed via netbook computers, set-top television boxes, Xboxes, iPhones, iPads, and Chumbys. Are these films? Videos? Interstitials? Video game cut scenes? For our purposes in this text, we'll often use the generic term *film*—but always realize that this can be applied to 15-second commercials, 2-minute animated promotions, 15-hour interactive training videos, and just about anything that can fit under the umbrella of "time-based audio/visual media."

Companion Website Downloads

At various times, you'll need to download files to help with the book's walk-through of Celtx features. You'll find all of these companion files at www.courseptr.com/downloads. Locate *Mastering Celtx* on the site, and you'll find the complete Online Companion for the book.

1 The Evolution of Pre-Production

The role of the content developer in time-based media production has changed more in the last 10 years than in the previous 100. Who exactly is the media "content developer," and why is this largely an unrecognized job title? For that answer, it's necessary to go back to the industrial production model developed in the early years of the twentieth century by the movie business.

The earliest silent films, created by the Lumiere Brothers and others, were "documentaries" capturing everyday life—and their makers produced, directed, shot, minimally edited, and even ran craft services. Even the first breakthrough fictional film—*The Great Train Robbery*, running 12 minutes—was edited, shot, written, directed, and produced by its creator, Edwin Porter. (Craft services and transportation may have been farmed out to the actors.)

But as films became longer and equipment and moviemaking elements (such as editing, lighting and set design) became more complex, job tasks began to differentiate and become increasingly specialized. Moviemakers migrated to Southern California for climate, zoning, and tax reasons, and Hollywood soon became known as the Dream Factory, adopting a factory-like industrial model of film creation not unlike Henry Ford's Model-T production line.

Screenwriters wrote film scripts, artists drew storyboards, unit production managers built budgets, casting directors selected the actors, design shops built the sets, lighting directors lit the sets, assistant directors made out call sheets, sound technicians operated booms, cinematographers shot film, directors blocked actors, editors cut film, and so on. Camera work became so specialized that even loading the camera became a unionized position.

Part of the reason for the division of labor was the cost, complexity, or scarcity of operating equipment and real estate. 35-millimeter film cameras were phenomenally expensive to rent, let alone own. Edit bays, projection facilities, and film storage vaults were run by studios, not individuals. Set lights were cumbersome, costly to store, and usually not available to "practice" on.

Because the very means of production were scarce (and impossibly expensive), developing proficiency in *both* editing and film shooting was nearly impossible for an individual.

This industrialized labor model (prizing specialization in the factory assembly line) was largely carried over into documentary filmmaking and so-called "industrial" filmmaking (promotional, training, and other purpose-driven movies). Giant corporations like General Telephone and IBM once maintained vast media operations for studio-like production.

And when television came along, the broadcast networks largely adopted the same industrial model (adding new positions like technical director).

However, the digitalization of media—along with the explosion of possible distribution channels—has resulted in a democratization of production and participation. And with the Internet, YouTube, and Facebook ubiquitous on televisions, computers, and handheld devices, the creation of media has become more urgent and necessary than ever—whether to produce pure entertainment, advertise products and services, persuade voters, train employees, or inform the public. As the cost and size of cameras, microphones, lights, editing equipment, and media storage have decreased, projects have become easier to conceive and execute—with fewer personnel than was previously necessary.

Because of the widespread availability and low cost of equipment and production, almost anybody can create media. (YouTube offers considerable evidence for this.) It is much easier now to gain proficiency in multiple job tasks, which seemed at one time to require a lifetime of specialization.

In the most rarified of commercial realms, it's not at all unusual for filmmaker Jim Cameron (*Avatar*, *Titanic*) to write, direct, and wield a state-of-the-art camera when he needs to. Robert Rodriguez (*Spy Kids*, *Sin City*) often writes, directs, shoots, and edits his own films.

And in the day-to-day trenches of media making for clients in corporate, government, and non-profit spaces, small shops consisting of just a few film school graduates are able to create sophisticated linear and interactive videos: products that once belonged solely to Hollywood studios and massive in-house corporate video departments.

Tagging today's creative media professional as a director, *or* writer, *or* editor seems quite inadequate. He or she is a content developer, wearing multiple hats.

Computers Transform the Factory Assembly Line

Interestingly, two tasks at nearly opposite ends of the production timeline may have been among the first to adopt digital tools. Non-linear editing (NLE) first became available in the mid- to late-1980s with the EditDroid and other laserdisc-based systems, and by the end of the decade, Avid had begun its invasion of studios and post-production shops.

But in the early 1980s, a few pioneering professional screenwriters began turning to home computers for composition, revision, and production of their scripts. This wasn't quite as radical a break as it may seem now: IBM Selectrics had been in use for nearly two decades, and some professionals were already using electronic typewriters capable of small amounts of data storage (boilerplate text, character names). In addition, staggeringly expensive dedicated word processing systems such as IBM Displaywriters and Wangwriters had been available since the start of the decade.

The first home computer systems churning out scripts were truly jerry-rigged contraptions, such as an Atari 800 connected to an IBM Selectric as a printer. But soon after, Osborne Is and Kaypro IIs became available for less than $2,000—and these "portable" systems, connected to thousand-dollar daisy-wheel printers, were producing Hollywood scripts. (Figure 1.1 shows the Osborne I in its glory.) There was no turning back. The IBM PC and later the Apple Macintosh quickly became standard equipment in production offices.

Photo courtesy of Bruce Damer and DigiBarn.

Figure 1.1   An Osborne I computer, at one time the state-of-the-art device for creating scripts.

As illustration software (Illustrator and Photoshop), 3D modeling, digital video, digital audio, and digital media storage became available, nearly every creative aspect of media production was turned over to computer technology.

Those first computer-composed scripts used whatever generic word processing software was handy. Screenwriters struggled setting WordStar "dot" commands, opening WordPerfect menus, and creating Microsoft Word styles to achieve the precise text formatting and page layouts demanded by master scene and audio/visual (A/V) screenplays. Sophisticated screenwriters developed their own customized document templates for scripts. They often dreaded rewrite assignments, because the previous screenwriter may have used his software more like an old-fashioned typewriter (tapping space-space-space-space-space to indent a script element), making revisions on a document draft arduous.

By the mid-1980s, dedicated scriptwriting programs began to appear, easing script composition (no more need to master styles and templates). They were pretty expensive but achieved their goal of generating a beautifully printed screenplay manuscript—fitting perfectly into the traditional industrial model of production.

Scripts, however, are only one step on the factory assembly line (although many argue they're the most important step)—and although their composition had now gone digital, the next steps for that script remained as they had for more than half a century. Scripts had to be distributed on paper (a boon for Hollywood copy shops), and when they received a "green light" for production (and sometimes before), they had to be "broken down"—budgeted and scheduled for production.

Dedicated production budgeting and scheduling applications began being developed, and after a while, they were more or less able to parse a digital screenplay. The process tended to be a little clunky, but it beat the days of handwritten breakdown forms, electronic calculators, and typed-up ledgers. (The cost of these different dedicated software packages was no small thing, of course, especially for independent filmmakers, nonprofit organizations, and other media production entities who are continually strapped for funds.)

Distribution began to evolve from paper to PDFs; screenwriting teams began to be interested in both synchronous and asynchronous collaborations; and script versioning and project management became increasingly urgent (in an era where dozens of screenwriters might work on a feature film). Meanwhile, animation was becoming so important to film production that the ability to easily link up storyboards and script segments became increasingly essential.

At all levels of media production, the multihyphenated content developer was beginning to redefine the very definition of screenwriting. The Writers Guild of America, the union of professional film and television screenwriters, began recruiting reality TV show video editors, arguing that the sequencing of images often constituted the "writing" (certainly the narrative construction) for a project.

Modern digital production was being done ever more rapidly—often by ad-hoc production teams in different locations whose individual members could be working on several different projects (with different ad-hoc teams) simultaneously. (One example of this was a campaign that award-winning advertising agency Wieden+Kennedy executed in 2010, shooting more than 60 thirty-second Old Spice commercials in a single day.)

Dedicated screenwriting programs have done their best in trying to keep up with these changes in the production workflow and even the conceptualization of screenwriting—but their roots remain in the industrial assembly line that defined twentieth century media production.

Today's media pre-production—which blurs the boundaries between job tasks and requires much greater flexibility in collaboration, distribution, and transmedia flexibility—is looking for new tools designed from the ground up to facilitate workflow. Enter Celtx.

The History and Philosophy of Celtx

Several years ago, an eclectic group of software developers and media professionals banded together as Greyfirst Corporation in Newfoundland, with a goal of building a new, more complete tool for the digital media age. Using the Mozilla/Firefox framework, they created an open source application—and after a long period of beta testing, rolled out Celtx version 1.0 in 2008.

The creators of Celtx believe that the discrete job tasks of old (outlining, scriptwriting, storyboarding, production budgeting, and scheduling) have increasingly blurred together. Rather than thinking about individual job tasks in a traditional waterfall hierarchy of project management, a media production team should be looking at the totality of pre-production with a more agile project management approach.

Storyboarding can now lead to scripting as easily as the other way around. Sometimes, character development (backstory, sketches, actor headshots) may be the springboard to scenes and acts. Or, all of these tasks may be done simultaneously and continuously iterated to bring the project to life. In sum, the media team should be able to dictate workflow, rather than the other way around.

In addition, a team should be able to aggregate pre-production tasks in a single software system. Team members should be able to annotate and comment upon each other's work, and revisions should be easily made and tracked. Team members should be able to work together simultaneously within the pre-production system, even if they're in different locations.

The project should be adaptable to different venues and distribution systems—a transmedia approach where the film script can be converted to a comic book or stage script, or the reverse. And the project should be easily synced between the array of devices we might use today, which Figure 1.2 illustrates (Windows netbook, Mac desktop, iPhone, iPad).

Finally, the base pre-production system should be free of charge—while various add-ons and the project management component (Celtx Studios) should be low cost options.

As Adobe's Creative Suite integrates various production and post-production art tasks, so should Celtx integrate pre-production tasks (both the creative and the logistical) into a single environment.

The term *paradigm shift* is too frequently used, but Celtx is the first software package to catch up to the realities of today's media production environment and the needs of today's media creators.

The remainder of this book describes how you can maximize the usage of Celtx for your own media projects. It covers Celtx's version 2.9 (newly released in early 2011) and should serve as a resource even when Celtx moves into version 3.x. Most of the book also applies to versions 2.7 and 2.5, but because Celtx is free, there is no reason for you to delay downloading the current Celtx version.

Figure 1.2 It's not unusual for an individual to use an array of devices while composing a script.

By the book's conclusion, you should no longer have to think about the toolbox but should instead be thinking of what you can dream and how you can communicate.

Summary

Screenwriting and pre-production practices evolved out of the movie studio industrial model employed for most of the twentieth century. However, the development of digital media has changed how media professionals create projects and collaborate.

Celtx—created from the ground up in the twenty-first century—is an open source software tool suite that integrates a variety of scripting and pre-production tasks. Its affordability, instant accessibility on the Internet, and collaborative features make it an excellent choice for any creators of time-based media, whether they're students, professionals, or serious hobbyists.

2 Getting Familiar with Celtx

Celtx provides a complete pre-production solution for scripting, storyboarding, scheduling, and other essential tasks. However, some users will look to Celtx solely as a dedicated screenwriting tool—and there's nothing wrong with that! This chapter focuses on setup and initial use of Celtx, and on script composition and use of the script editor.

Getting Celtx on Your System

Downloading and installing Celtx takes only a few minutes, and it's possible even on a system where you don't have administrative or installation privileges. (Chapter 13, "Celtx Script," discusses using Celtx on your iPhone, iPod Touch, or iPad.)

Celtx.com

The hub of Celtx access, support, and community is http://celtx.com. A visit to the home page provides all this:

- An overview of the tool

- Free downloadable executables for Windows, Mac, and Linux systems

- Support, including links to the Celtx wiki, blog, and user forums

- Entry to Celtx Studio

- Information about and links to Celtx add-ons

- Information about and links to Celtx's mobile screenwriting app (for iPads and iPhones)

Head to the Download page to get started with Celtx.

Note: Your school lab or job site may already have Celtx installed—in which case, you can skip to the later section titled "Starting Celtx and Selecting a Project Template."

Downloading Celtx

The Celtx user community has contributed to localizing Celtx in dozens of languages, and the software tool is available for Windows, Mac, and Linux platforms.

Figure 2.1 shows a typical download page, where you can select the package that's right for you and download it to your local system. The Celtx installable and Celtx itself require little hard disk storage space and can run on desktops, laptops, and netbooks. (See Chapter 13 for a discussion of the Celtx Script app, which runs on iPhones and iPads.)

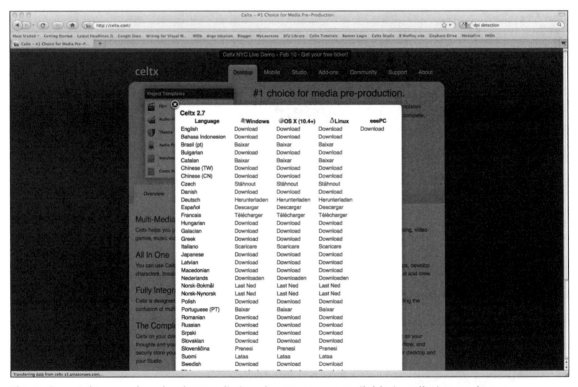

Figure 2.1   Celtx.com download page, listing the numerous available installation packages.

Installing Celtx

Installation should take just a few minutes, and for most systems you should be able to accept the defaults and be up and running before you know it. The installer unpacks the necessary files and runs a standard installation wizard. Depending on the operating system you're using, you end up with a Celtx shortcut on the desktop (Windows) or a Celtx icon in the Applications folder (Mac).

Tip: Although Celtx doesn't officially support running the application from a flash drive or memory card, you can, in fact, elect to have your own "portable Celtx" that can be used on any operating system–compatible system. (For example, a flash drive with the Mac version of Celtx lets you run Celtx on any Mac.)

This may be particularly handy if you're a student rotating between campus computer labs, or you work for an agency or organization that doesn't allow local installations. Be sure to test this way of using Celtx before applying it to "mission-critical" work.

Starting Celtx and Selecting a Project Template

Celtx refers to its data files as projects—and in theory, one project file should be all you need for the script composition and revision process (and all the other pre-production tasks you or your team choose to undertake, including script breakdowns, scheduling, location stills management, and more).

Figure 2.2 shows the Celtx splash screen, where you're asked to select a template for the type of project you want to create.

Figure 2.2   Celtx splash screen, with template selection and sample project scroll-down list boxes, along with Celtx Studio News and Community News.

A project selection list box on the left of the start-up screen includes the following:

- Film (which will include most episodic TV shows)
- Audio Visual (aka A/V)

- Theatre
- Audio Play
- Storyboard
- Comic Book
- Novel

The right side of the screen offers sample projects for each available template. These are well worth extensive exploration (and Chapter 12, "Exploring Celtx's Built-in Sample Projects," covers them), but for now, let's forge bravely ahead!

The good news is that your selection of a template isn't a life-and-death choice here. You won't "lose work" if the project evolves or you change your mind about the template; you can choose a different template for your work at any time. You might start your project as a comic book and decide to convert it to a film script—or you may decide that the audio script you were writing for a podcast can be extended visually (perhaps to a screencast).

Note: If you're launching Celtx on a system where you or other users have previously used the software, you're likely to see Recent Projects on the right side of the screen. However, notice that the right side also contains a link to Samples. Click that link to see the sample project files, which will be discussed in Chapter 12.

What Scripts Do Media scripts typically have two separate (and equally important) tasks.

1. Conveying the "look and feel" of the finished project

    Clients, producers, executives, and investors are some of the potential first readers of scripts, and in this capacity, the script operates as a selling tool to convey a vivid impression of what the finished project will be like.

    Hollywood script readers often talk about whether they can "see the movie" when they read the screenplay. In the best screenplays, readers begin to forget that they're reading words on a page, and instead "project" (or in the case of an audio-only piece, "listen to") the finished work in their own minds. The paradox of any script is that it is a textual experience conveying a nontextual experience!

    Ideally, finished scripts also serve to attract talent to the project: actors, set designers, cinematographers, and so on. Again, the words on the page should morph into an audio/visual experience that the reader understands. However, at this juncture, the script begins a second task…

2.   Providing a database and set of execution instructions

Simultaneous to step 1, scripts function as databases and catalogs and are sets of instructions. They are specially formatted and contain content to help creative principals (such as the director and the cinematographer), cast, and crew execute their jobs and create the finished product.

What props are in this scene? How many actors are in this scene? How many scenes is this actor or prop in? Where should the camera be placed? What kind of special effects might be needed?

These are just a few of the hundreds of production questions that the script must answer. (See Appendix A, "Understanding Script Formats," for examples of how professionals use scripts and why scripts are formatted the way they are. The Appendix also reviews script elements for each type of Celtx script template.)

For practice here, go ahead and select Film from the Project Templates list, which launches Celtx's script editing screen.

Script Composition

Figure 2.3 shows Celtx's script editing screen. The script editor window occupies the center of the screen; the left sidebar contains the Project Library and Scene list windows; and the right sidebar provides a number of features to be discussed in future chapters.

You'll also see a typical horizontal icon toolbar above the main window and sidebars, to be discussed later in this chapter. The horizontal status bar at the bottom of the window contains a link to Celtx community news on the left side; the right side provides Celtx Studios features, to be discussed in Chapter 16, "Add-Ons, Utilities, and Sketch Images."

Tip: Some users find the left and right sidebars distracting as they compose or revise. You can minimize either sidebar at any time by clicking once on its sizing bar. You can bring either sidebar back at any time by toggling (clicking again) the sizing bar. A button on the right side of the editing toolbar also controls the visibility of the right sidebar, as does the Script, Sidebar menu selection.

To best focus on script composition in the practice session, minimize both the left and right sidebars.

Project library and navigation sidebar   Main script editing window   Notes/media/breakdown sidebar

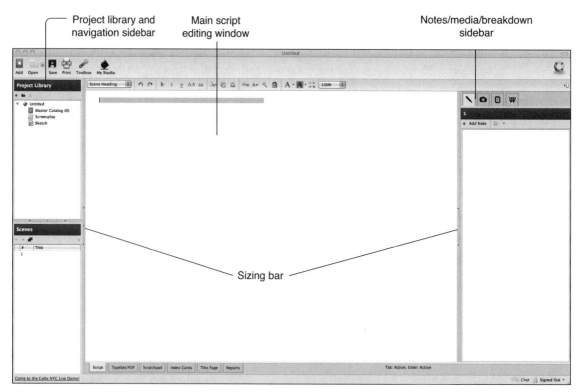

Sizing bar

Figure 2.3   Celtx film script editing screen, showing the script editing window, sidebars, and sizing bars.

Above the editing window is a typical word processing editing toolbar, and of course, a menu bar at the top of the Celtx window. The editing window also contains a number of subtabs at the bottom—but let's ignore those for now, and start a script!

Tip: Undo is a critical feature in text editing; it is always at your disposal, whether via the menu (Edit, Undo), the editing toolbar, or the Ctrl+Z or Cmd+Z keyboard shortcut. Redo allows you to toggle back and forth between two versions of your current edit.

Throughout this chapter are sidebars discussing the layout elements used for any kind of script. Notice that the editing toolbar has a drop-down list box of script elements at its left edge; Scene Heading is currently selected. Celtx knows that you probably want to start with a scene heading, because film scripts are built around the scene. For the practice script, input the following:

`int. restaurant entrance- night`

Scene headings use all uppercase, but notice that you don't need to worry about that: Celtx formats the text. Once you press the Enter key, the editor double spaces and is ready for some action. (The element selector automatically changes to Action in the editing toolbar.

Input what follows:

```
CHAD (30s, handsome) arrives: well-dressed, clean shaven, hair with
product,
looking good. He approaches the HOST (40s, snooty) who is studying the list
of reservations. [ENTER]
```

> **Tip:** Keyboard shortcuts for selecting elements are displayed in the lower-right corner of the status bar/tab bar. This makes it easy to stay on the keyboard while composing your script.

You can continue inputting action paragraphs, of course, but now's a good time to put in some dialog. Start by indicating who's speaking. Click on the drop-down element list box and choose Character. Then input the next line:

```
chad[ENTER]
```

Notice that the script editor automatically capitalizes this element for you. The editor also knows that dialog will immediately follow, and it has automatically changed the element for you to Dialog. Input this:

```
Good evening.[ENTER]
```

The editor automatically double spaces and is prepared for a response from another character; the character name element is already selected. You could select the Action element if you wanted to indicate some action, but instead have Host respond to Chad. Input this:

```
host[ENTER]
```

The editor has automatically changed the element to Dialog, but indicate here how the actor should read the following line. Input an open parenthesis keyboard character:

```
(
```

This adjusts the element to Parenthetical and automatically indents the element. Input the following:

```
raised eyebrow[ENTER]
```

The editor knows that dialog must follow a parenthetical indicator and has already changed to this element. Now input this line:

```
Oui, Monsieur.[ENTER]
```

Finally, end the abbreviated scene with a transition. Select Transition from the element drop-down list box, and then input the following:

cut to:

You've written your first scene.

Note: This initial script composition tutorial has skipped using the Shot element, but see an example of its use in Figure 2.4.

It's also skipped using the Celtx-specific Text element, which is not really an established screenplay format element but can be used as necessary for nonformatted paragraphs, headings, or transitions. For example, try typing FADE IN: at the beginning of your script.

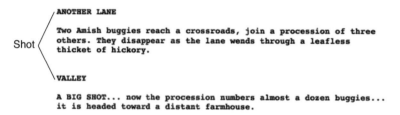

Figure 2.4 A brief excerpt from the screenplay *Witness*, illustrating use of the Shot element.

Tip: There is a long tradition in screenwriting of writing FADE IN: at the top of a script, but it's completely unnecessary. The same can be said of FADE OUT as a final transition, at the end of a screenplay. Put them in if you'd like to, but they won't really make you more professional or improve the quality of your screenplay!

Basic Editing

Monsieur is a French word and should be italicized. Highlight the word, and choose the italic *i* in the editing toolbar. *Oui* is also a French word that should be italicized; follow the same steps.

The editing toolbar in Celtx operates just like the editing toolbar in Microsoft Word and nearly any text editor: Figure 2.5 shows the left side of the editing toolbar. It includes the element selector and buttons for boldfacing, italicizing, underlining, cutting, copying, pasting, changing case, and undo/redo.

Caution: Text in screenplays is rarely bolded or underlined. (See David Trottier's *The Screenwriter's Bible* for a comprehensive discussion about formatting.)

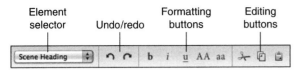

Figure 2.5   Left half of the editing toolbar, for standard editing tasks.

With the short scene you've written, experiment with cutting and pasting. (See if you can reverse the order of dialogs, for example.)

Celtx works like any standard text editor in the highlighting, addition, or deletion of text. (For example, double-clicking a word highlights it, and triple-clicking within a paragraph highlights the paragraph, just like in Microsoft Word.)

See if you can revise this scene to duplicate the scene shown in Figure 2.6.

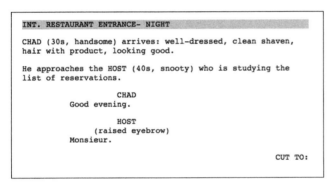

Figure 2.6   Partial first scene of *Delivery Date* practice script.

Tip: The script editor enables drag-and-drop cutting and pasting. Simply highlight a block of text, and then drag it to its new location. Standard menu selections (Edit, Cut; Edit, Copy; Edit, Paste) apply for editing, as well as standard keyboard shortcuts for these operations.

Experiment with changing case, underlining, bolding, and undoing your changes until you're comfortable with using these formatting features.

It's time to save the project. Click on the Save icon, input a project name, and select a folder to put it in.

Tip: Project names like `script` and `practice` aren't very useful—in *any* application. You can call this first project `Delivery Date Sample`.

Editing Toolbar—Other Features

Figure 2.7 displays the right side of the editing toolbar.

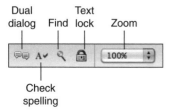

Figure 2.7   Right side of Celtx's editing toolbar.

Working from the right edge of the editing toolbar:

- Try out the zoom control drop-down list box to see which setting is most comfortable for your script composition.

- Text Lock locks the text, preventing editing. This might be useful when having someone else review your script onscreen, or if you'd like to turn off your own compulsive need to edit for a while!

- The Find button works like any standard find-and-replace text editing feature.

- The Check Spelling button works like any standard spell checker text editing feature. You can add new words to the dictionary if necessary. In this sample, you'll find that *oui* is not in the dictionary. Choosing to "ignore all" instances of this word is probably the best selection here.

- Finally, Dual Dialog allows you to create side-by-side dialog, representing times when two characters are speaking simultaneously. For practice, select the following dialog, and then click on the Dual Dialog button, as Figure 2.8 shows. This places dual dialog buttons on both blocks of dialog. You'll see how this looks in a printout or PDF shortly.

Caution: Dual dialog should be used sparingly in a screenplay.

Subtabs in Celtx Each script template has its own set of subtabs at the bottom of the main editing/viewing window. For the most part, subtabs offer similar features across templates (index cards, reports, title pages, and so on), but Theatre (also known as Stageplay) and Audio Play templates also include a cast subtab, and the novel template includes a smaller set of subtabs.

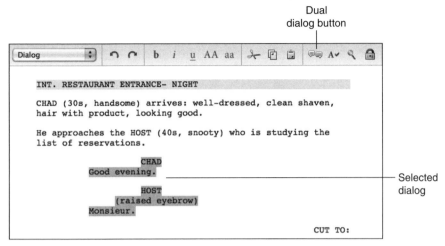

Figure 2.8   Applying the Dual Dialog setting to selected dialog.

Title Page

Now that the script is well underway, it won't hurt to set up your title page. Click on the Title Page subtab at the bottom of the editor window.

The Title Page window opens, and as Figure 2.9 shows, you can now fill in the fields for title, author, preexisting source material (if any), copyright/registration information, and contact information.

The title for this sample is Delivery Date Sample. For practice, include your own name as the author, and include some contact information.

Previewing and Distributing the Script

The script editing window is a good indication of how your script will look—but it's designed to let you focus on composition and revision, and it doesn't fully duplicate script layout.

Ideally, the hour will come when you're fully ready to distribute your script, either on paper or electronically via a PDF file. (The PDF file will guarantee consistency in page breaks, fonts and overall format on any screen or printout.) But you can preview the look of your script, from the title page to the final line, at any time.

Previewing

Click on the Typeset/PDF subtab to preview your sample script and ready it for distribution.

Caution: The Typeset/PDF feature requires an active Internet connection to properly work. If you're not currently connected to the Internet, you need to wait until you can connect again to view your formatted script; in the meantime, you can continue to compose or edit your script.

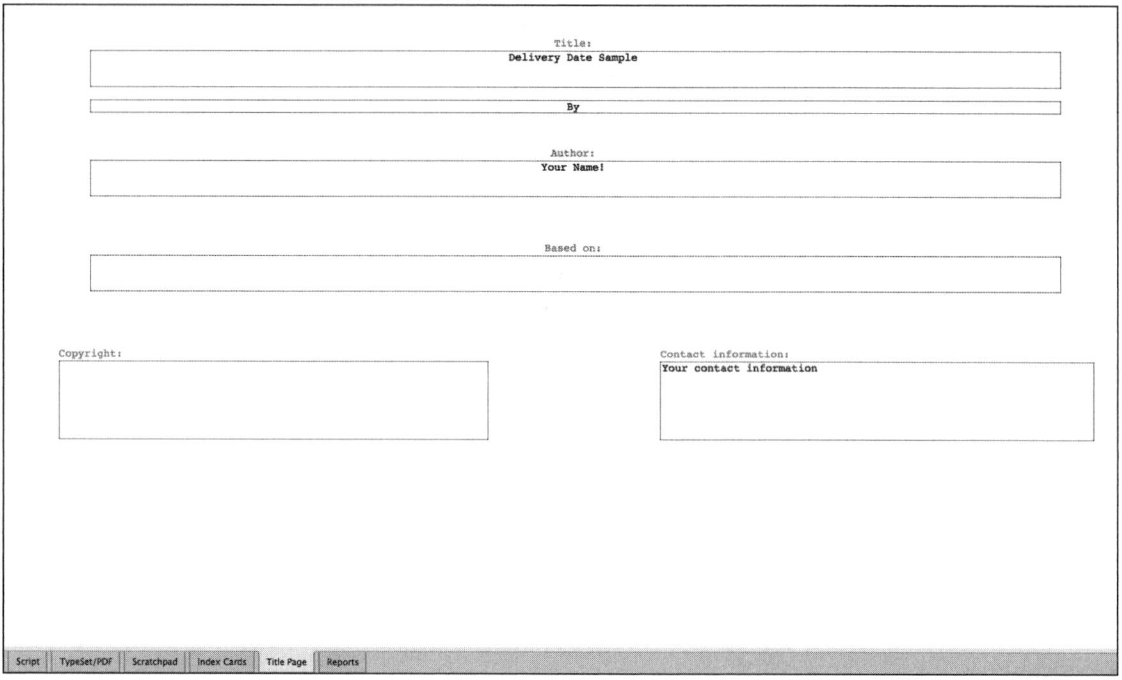

Figure 2.9 Using the Title Page Editor.

As Figure 2.10 shows, your script is now rendered fully formatted. The first page onscreen is your title page, and as you scroll down the screen, you see the first (and currently only) page of your script, including the dual dialog set up earlier.

Note: You may need to scroll to the top of the script to view it from the beginning.

To demonstrate how easy it is to toggle back and forth between editing and typeset modes, try out these steps:

1. Click on the Script window subtab.

2. Highlight the two dialog blocks previously designated as dual dialog.

3. Click the dual dialog button. (This button works just like italic, underlining, and bold buttons, toggling the setting for highlighted text.)

4. Click on the Typeset/PDF subtab.

The dialog is now properly sequential.

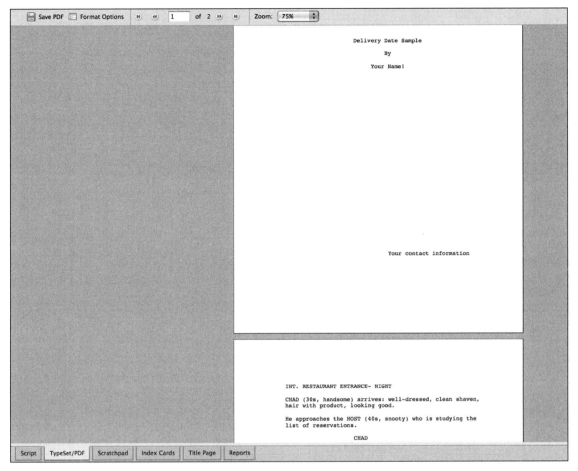

Figure 2.10   Celtx's Typeset/PDF window, using 75% zoom view.

Typeset/PDF Format Options

At the top of the viewing window is a navigation toolbar allowing you to easily move from page to page within the script, as well as a zoom menu.

In addition, you see the Format Options button. Click this button to examine the options.

The Format Options window contains two tabbed dialog boxes. Figure 2.11 displays the following options in the General dialog box:

- **Paper Size.** Choose North American letter size or European A4 size paper.

- **Show Scene Numbers.** This is normally toggled on only when your script is "locked" and headed for pre-production. We'll discuss the formatting of production scripts in Chapter 4, "Creating and Editing Production Film Scripts." The default setting during script composition is None.

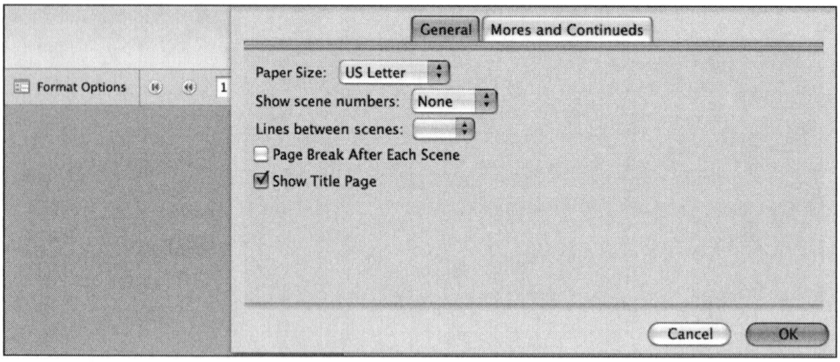

Figure 2.11   The Format Options window, with the General tab active.

- **Lines Between Scenes.** You can increase or decrease the number of blank lines between scenes. Some screenwriters prefer 1, whereas others prefer 2. A setting of 3 is rarely used.

- **Page Break After Each Scene.** This is normally not used, unless you're printing out "sides" for auditioning actors.

- **Show Title Page.** This controls whether the title page is displayed in a printout or PDF.

Figure 2.12 displays the Format Options window when the Mores and Continueds dialog box is activated.

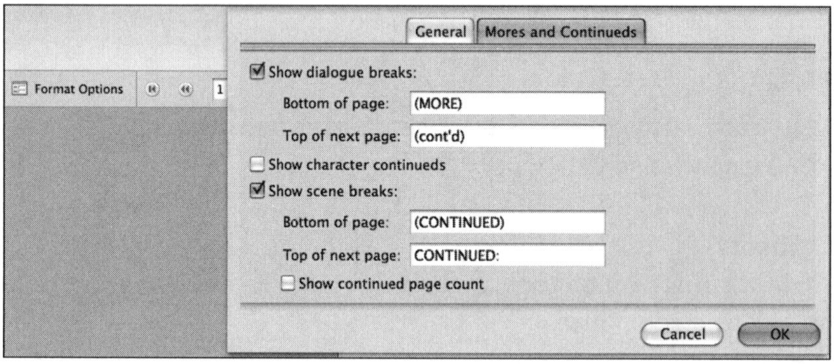

Figure 2.12   The Format Options window, with the Mores and Continueds dialog box active.

The Mores and Continueds dialog box provides a number of options, as indicated in the list that follows. These all need to be turned on when scripts go to production—but they aren't really necessary for script composition and revision, and you can safely uncheck all the options if you find that they clutter the script page while writing.

- Show Dialogue Breaks
- Show Character Continueds

- Show Scene Breaks

- Show Continued Page Count

Caution: Leave the More and Continued text layouts alone, as Celtx follows standard conventions for these indicators (to be discussed more in Chapter 4).

Click OK or Cancel when you're finished with the Format Options window.

Format Options—Different Script Templates The contents of the Format Options dialog box in the Typeset/PDF window change depending on the type of script you're composing. Looking ahead to distribution, different types of scripts require different layouts and additional information or options in their layouts. For example:

- A/V scripts typically need headers further identifying the project and its participants.

- Stageplays typically need cast lists as a separate page following the title page.

- Audio plays may need BBC-customized features. (Worldwide, the BBC is probably the largest distributor of audio plays.)

Appendix B, "Script Template Typeset/PDF Format Options," reviews the dialog box tabs and format options for each Celtx script template.

Distributing the Script

As Figure 2.13 shows, you can now print your script by clicking the Print icon, or you can produce a PDF for electronic distribution by clicking the Save PDF button.

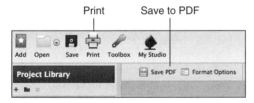

Figure 2.13   Celtx provides two options for immediate distribution: print and save to PDF.

Scratchpad

Click on the Scratchpad subtab to activate the scratchpad.

Figure 2.14 shows the scratchpad, which you can use to make temporary notes or play around with versions of dialog or description. This subtab, when activated, splits the editing window by showing you the script in the top half and the scratchpad in the bottom half.

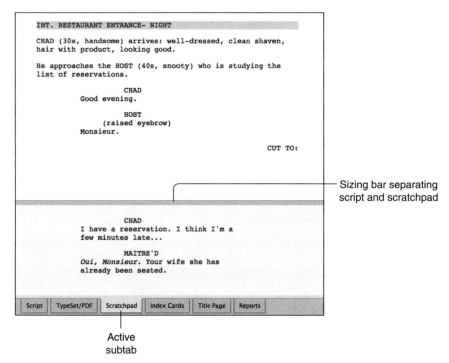

Figure 2.14   The Scratchpad window.

The scratchpad can be easily toggled on and off by clicking the scratchpad sizing bar.

Reports

The Reports subtab and all of its features are discussed in Chapter 7, "Reports."

Index Cards

Despite all the digital tools at their disposal, professional screenwriters often use 3×5 index cards to outline, reorder, and keep track of scenes. Celtx offers electronic index cards for similar use.

Figure 2.15 shows the Index Cards window after the subtab has been activated.

Although you've already begun your script, read on for how you can build out and extend its structure using index cards.

Tip: The walk-through on index cards looks at their use with the film script template; however, all project templates in Celtx include an index card feature. You'll find that using index cards is valuable whether you're writing an A/V script, a novel, or even a comic book!

Creating Cards

A single card is set up for you to enter data in. Figure 2.16 shows how you can fill out this card just by clicking in the scene heading and scene description fields.

Index card toolbar

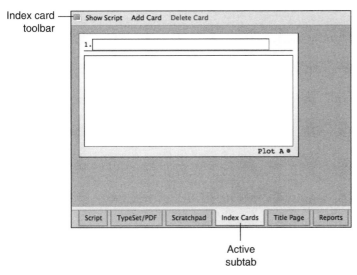

Active subtab

Figure 2.15 The Index Cards window.

Scene heading

Scene description

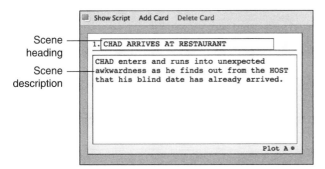

Figure 2.16 The Index Cards window with a first card filled out.

If you've filled out the first card like Figure 2.16 displays, click the Add Card button in the Index Card toolbar and start a second card. Figure 2.17 shows three cards filled out, representing the first part of an outline for the entire script.

Cards are easily dragged and dropped, and they're easily deleted using the Delete Card button in the toolbar.

Keeping Track of Multiple Storylines (Plots and Subplots)

In the lower-right corner of each card, you'll see Plot A currently indicated. Click on this label. You pull up a window where you can designate a scene as belonging to an A storyline, a B storyline, and so on.

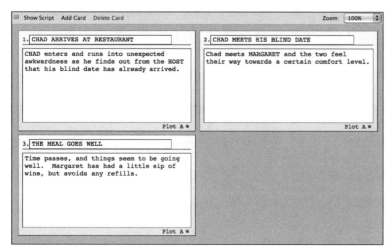

Figure 2.17   The Index Cards window with three cards filled out.

Note: Syd Field's *Screenplay*, Linda Seger's *Making a Good Script Great*, and numerous other books discuss the use of plots (A lines) and subplots (B lines, C lines, and so on).

You can change the label to anything you want. For example, you can track (and color-code) key characters or key locations using the labels, or you can label scenes as "action" or "romance."

Most short scripts have only storyline, so you can ignore these labels when you don't need them.

Toggling Between Cards and Script

Figure 2.18 shows use of the Show Script button.

When selected, the Show Script button displays the script in an index card view, and the button toggles to Show Notes. Clicking the Show button allows you to easily switch back and forth between script and cards.

Tip: You can outline your script by composing index cards first, quickly roughing out scenes without worrying about writing dialog or determining exact locations. Then, when you're ready to compose your script, you can copy and paste from an index card to a scene, all in the Index Card window.

Zoom Views

Figure 2.19 shows the Zoom drop-down list box, tucked into the right corner of the Index Card toolbar.

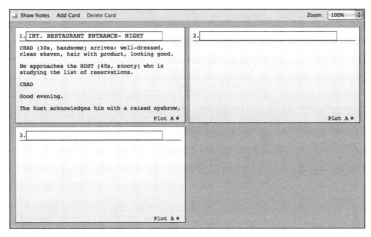

Figure 2.18   The Index Cards window with the current script displayed in an index card view.

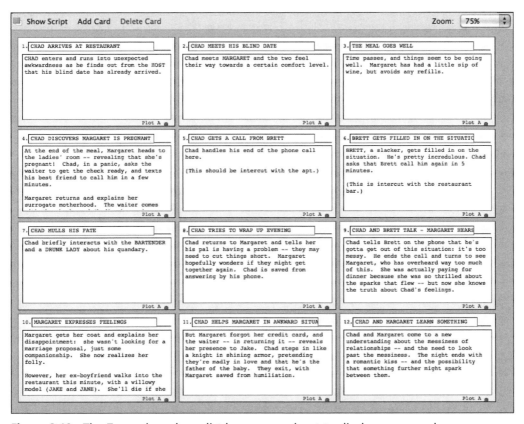

Figure 2.19   The Zoom drop-down list box, zoomed out to display many cards.

Although relatively unnecessary when you have just a few cards, zooming out to a 75% or 50% view can be handy when you have a dozen or more cards. Chapter 3, "Project Navigation, Library, Notes, and Media," gives you more of an opportunity to use this feature.

Printing Cards

When you're ready to print your cards, be sure that the index cards are displaying onscreen. Click the Print icon. As Figure 2.20 shows, you have the option of printing background card colors (if you've used them, as discussed earlier in the chapter) and printing card borders. You can then either cancel or OK the printout.

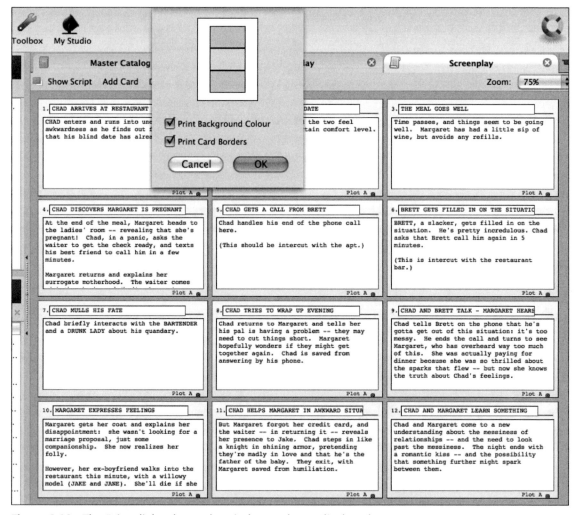

Figure 2.20 The Print dialog box, when index cards are displayed onscreen.

If you use perforated index card sheets, you'll produce instant index cards—but at worst, you'll just need a scissors to separate your cards and post them on a bulletin board or lay them out on the floor.

Tip: Printing on a heavier stock paper (28–70 pounds) creates more durable index cards.

The Icons Toolbar

Celtx's icon toolbar has some standard functions (Open, Save, Print), and as Figure 2.21 shows, several are specific to Celtx:

- **Add.** This is to be discussed beginning in Chapter 3.

- **Open Recent Project drop-down arrow.** This is appended to the Open icon.

- **Toolbox.** This is to be discussed in Chapter 16.

- **My Studio.** This is to be discussed in Chapters 14, "Celtx Studios: Creation and Administration," and 15, "Celtx Studios: User Interaction."

- **Help.** A red life raft (right edge of the toolbar) connects you to Celtx's online support page.

Changing the Type of Script

Sometimes projects change course midstream. A film script might become a theater script; a comic book might be adapted into a film script; a TV commercial might become a continuous narrative piece rather than the pastiche of sound and image it was planned to be.

Celtx allows you to change the type of script you're creating at any time, doing all the hard work of reformatting.

Let's say you started your script with the intention to shoot it on video—but you decide that you'd like to produce it on stage first.

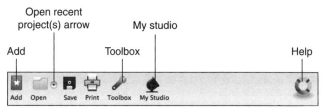

Figure 2.21 Unique Celtx toolbar functions.

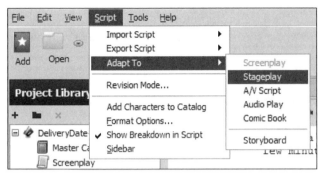

Figure 2.22   Pulling down the Script menu and selecting Adapt To, Stageplay.

Pull down the Script menu, and select Adapt To. You have all of Celtx's script templates to choose from. Select Stageplay. (Figure 2.22 demonstrates this selection.)

Celtx automatically reformats your script. To fully appreciate this, select the Typeset/PDF sub-tab to see the distributable script. It's a play!

Notice that you now have two tabs displaying above the editing frame: Screenplay and Stage-play. Chapter 3 discusses these tabs, including renaming them.

You can adapt your script to any template, although most of them (for example, the A/V Script or Comic Book) aren't really appropriate here.

Adapting to Storyboard can be useful, as Chapter 8, "Storyboards," discusses.

Script Import and Export

The Script menu allows you to import an existing script or outline and export the project script to a non-Celtx data file.

- **Import Script.** Celtx can import any ASCII (text) file. If the text file has been formatted with a script layout, Celtx is generally good at importing the script and assigning script elements properly. (You still need to check the formatting, and you may need to reassign some elements.) Final Draft and Movie Magic Screenwriter allow you to save a script to a formatted text file. If composition has been done initially in Microsoft Word, OpenOffice, or Google Docs, you can save out to a formatted text file and then import the script into Celtx. (Note that if you have the Celtx Script app, you can also import from your iPhone or iPad. Celtx Script is covered in Chapter 13.)

- **Export Script.** Celtx exports the project script to a formatted ASCII (text) file. Final Draft and Movie Magic Screenwriter can then import the formatted text file and render it as a script. Virtually any word processing program can read the exported file. Chapter 4 further discusses script exporting. (Note that if you have Celtx Script, you can import from your iPhone or iPad. Again, Celtx Script is discussed in Chapter 13.)

Note: Celtx projects are saved, closed, and opened just like any data file in any application. You can open multiple instances of Celtx or multiple projects simultaneously. But one of Celtx's achievements is consolidating the proliferation of pre-production files, as you'll see in the chapters ahead.

Importing from Final Draft and Movie Magic Screenwriter To practice importing a script composed in Final Draft, go to the book's Online Companion website (www.courseptr. com/downloads) and find the file named LeadersChapterExcerpt-FD-export. Download the file to your local hard drive or flash drive. (Note that this process works identically for a script composed in Movie Magic Screenwriter and exported to a text format.)

As the file name suggests, this is a script excerpt originally composed in Final Draft and then exported to a text file.

Open Celtx and choose the Film Template. (Or, if you're already in Celtx, pull down the File menu and select New Project. Then choose Film from the Create Project dialog box.)

To import a text file that has been exported from Final Draft or Movie Magic Screenwriter, follow these steps:

1. Pull down the Script menu and select Import Script. (Note that if the Celtx Script app—to be discussed in Chapter 13—is already installed, two import options are presented. Choose From Text if this is the case.)

2. Browse to the location of the downloaded script excerpt and open it.

The script file has now been converted to Celtx format. As you scroll through, notice that Scene Heading, Shot, Character, and Dialog elements have been accurately captured. You can now save the script just like any other Celtx project.

Although a small amount of cleanup may sometimes be necessary for a lengthy imported script, you can easily import any script originally composed in Final Draft or Movie Magic Screenwriter and continue composition and revision in Celtx.

Launching Celtx Once You've Created a Project

Existing Celtx project files are like any other file—easily launched with a double-click or via a context menu.

But you may decide to launch Celtx from the dock or taskbar, a desktop shortcut, or a recently used apps list. You'll then find a Welcome to Celtx splash screen that offers the following:

- A Project Templates window on the left

- A Recent Projects window on the right

- A link to project samples in the Recent Projects title bar (Chapter 12 looks at some of Celtx's built-in samples)

- A Browse button to find other Celtx files not in the Recent Projects list

- An Open From Studio button for launching projects from Celtx Studios (to be discussed in Chapter 15)

This welcome splash screen makes it easy to accomplish four things:

- Start from scratch in creating a new project

- Resume work on a recent (or older) project

- Study the samples to learn more about certain features

- Retrieve a project from the "cloud" storage that Celtx Studios provides

---

Tip: You can bring up the splash screen any time while working in Celtx to get access to templates or sample project files. On a Mac, pull down the Window menu, and choose Splash Screen. Using Windows, pull down the Help menu, and choose Splash Screen.

Summary

This chapter has explored the basic script composition features in Celtx. In the next chapter, you'll begin to see how to use the sidebars to navigate, annotate, and catalog your script.

This chapter covered the following:

- Downloading and installing Celtx

- Selecting and modifying the script template

- Composing the script

- Preparing the script for distribution via print or electronic means

- Using the scratchpad to aid editing

- Creating and editing index cards

- Importing and exporting the script

- Launching Celtx in subsequent uses to start new projects or open old ones

3 Project Navigation, Library, Notes, and Media

Chapter 2, "Getting Familiar with Celtx," explored the basics of script composition, editing, and distribution in Celtx—and recommended that you ignore the left and right sidebars that typically bracket the script editing window.

This chapter gets rid of the blinders and explores Celtx's navigation, library, markup, and cataloging features—all of them accessible through the left and right sidebars.

The walk-throughs will use a complete screenplay, which you can download from the book's Online Companion website at www.courseptr.com/downloads. The screenplay project is titled DeliveryDate-Complete. Also download DD-Synopsis, a small Microsoft Word file (it can be viewed and edited using OpenOffice or other Word-compatible text editors) that you'll use later in the chapter. Save these files to a folder called DeliveryDate. You can place the folder on your desktop, in your Documents folder, or wherever you can easily access the folder.

Figure 3.1 displays the complete *Delivery Date* screenplay, with both left and right sidebars in view. *Delivery Date* is an award-winning short film, written and directed by Matthew Page of RiffRaff Entertainment.

Note: If you make the Typeset/PDF subtab active and scroll through the complete script, you'll see that Celtx has automatically page-numbered your distributable version, placing the page number in the top-right corner per industry convention.

As discussed in Chapter 2, scenes are not currently numbered, as you are still in the composition phase rather than the production phase of media creation. Scene numbering is discussed in Chapter 4, "Creating and Editing Production Film Scripts."

Left Sidebar

The left sidebar contains two windows: one for scene navigation, and the other for the Project Library.

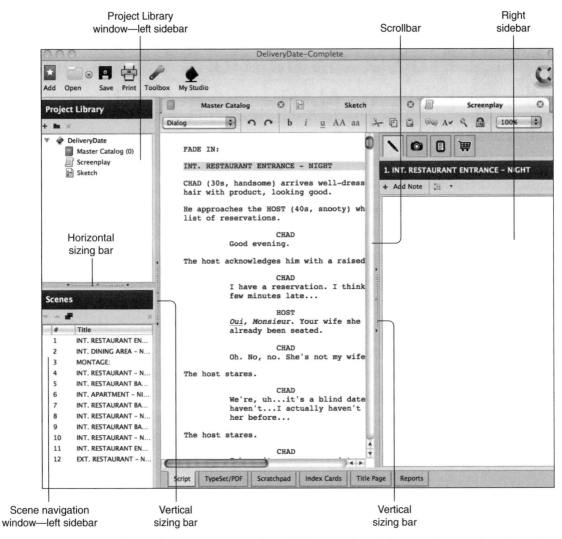

Figure 3.1 The Complete *Delivery Date* screenplay, with both left and right sidebars in view. Note that you can always reveal or hide either sidebar by clicking once on the vertical sizing bar.

Caution: For practice and illustration of features throughout this chapter, you should have the Script subtab active in Delivery Date—unless otherwise indicated.

Tip: The horizontal sizing bar separating the Project Library and the Scene Navigator allows you to resize or hide each window. As this chapter will show, there may be times when you'd like to focus solely on the Project Library, and other times when you'd like to focus solely on the Scene Navigator. You can choose how much screen real estate each window gets.

Scene Navigator

The lower window in the left sidebar is the Scene Navigator. You should see 12 scenes listed. (You may need to use the scrollbar to get to the last scenes.) Double-click on any of the scene headings to navigate immediately to that scene. This expedites quick edits or reviews of any of your scenes.

Figure 3.2 shows the Move Down and Move Up buttons, which allow you to quickly alter the order of your scenes. Try moving the first scene down several scenes and then moving it back up.

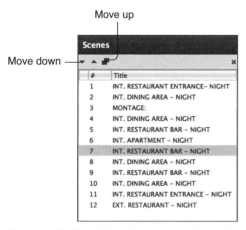

Figure 3.2   The Move Down and Move Up buttons in the Scene Navigator.

You can also drag and drop scene headings to reorder scenes.

As Figure 3.3 shows, Celtx allows you to toggle between Scene Headings and Index Card Headings in the Scene Navigator, simply by clicking the Display Headings button.

As with scenes, it's easy to 1) navigate quickly to a scene by double-clicking its heading, and 2) move around index cards using the Move Up and Move Down buttons, or drag-and-drop index card headings to reorder the cards. (You can also drag and drop the onscreen cards themselves, as discussed in Chapter 2.)

Tip: Chapter 2 discussed the Show Script/Show Notes toggle button and the Zoom drop-down list box in the index card function ribbon. Now that you're working with a complete screenplay running almost 20 pages, you can see the full value of both features.

Display
headings button

Current navigation
mode (index cards)

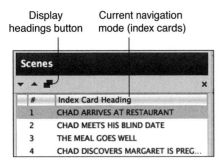

Figure 3.3 The Display Headings button in the Scene Navigator (with the Index Card Heading currently active in the sidebar).

You can use the Scene Navigator in both the Script window and the Typeset/PDF window. Return to the script editing window when you've finished exploring these features.

Note: The Scene Navigator becomes the Page Navigator when using the Comic Book template and becomes the Chapter Navigator when using the Novel template. Navigation features function identically regardless of which template you use.

Project Library

Figure 3.4 focuses on the Project Library window, where you'll see three default entries for your project: Master Catalog, Screenplay, and Sketch.

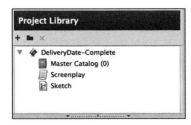

Figure 3.4 The default entries in the Project Library when a project is initially created. One of the entries will be for the script template you started with (Screenplay, A/V Script, Comic Book, and so on).

The Project Library allows you to keep track of—and navigate between—all kinds of script formats, production catalogs, and other material in your project. Double-clicking on any of the entries takes you immediately to the selection.

- The Master Catalog keeps track of your script breakdown catalogs. At this point, you haven't established any, but in Chapter 5, "Script Breakdowns and Catalogs," you'll begin filling out the Master Catalog as you execute a script breakdown.

- Sketch is a mini-application designed for quick sketch-ups of blocking, mise-en-scene, and so on. A full discussion of the sketch toolset is in Chapter 9, "Sketches."

To practice using the Project Manager, you'll adapt the complete *Delivery Date* script to a stageplay format. Select Script, Adapt To from the main menu, and choose Stageplay. (See Figure 2.20 in Chapter 2 for a depiction.)

Stageplay will now be added to the Project Library.

Note: If you look at the Scene Navigator, you see that the stageplay scenes are organized by theatrical act. In this instance, of course, there is only one act.

The index cards are carried over from the screenplay and can be edited so that the content differs from the index cards attached to the screenplay.

Tip: New format options are also available for the stageplay version of this project, as discussed in a sidebar in Chapter 2, and in Appendix B, "Script Template Typeset/PDF Format Options."

You can add materials to your project. Perhaps you'd like to include a synopsis that already exists as a Word or an OpenOffice file. Click on the Add icon. Figure 3.5 shows the Select Item dialog box.

Figure 3.5 The Select Item dialog box, with File selected and the Browse button available for use.

Tip: The Project Library toolbar has a shortcut to the Add Item feature: just click the plus (+) button. This shortcut may be especially useful if you choose to streamline your workspace by hiding the main toolbar (View, Toolbars, None).

A long list of potential item types is presented. Select File, and then click on the Browse button. The file browser works like any typical file browser, allowing you to "attach" any file you'd like to the project. Locate the DD-Synopsis file you downloaded earlier in the chapter, and select it; then click on OK.

Figure 3.6 shows DD-Synopsis listed in the Project Library. You can open the file by double-clicking on the file icon, or you can edit or expand it as necessary.

Figure 3.6 *Delivery Date* synopsis added to Project Library.

Using Celtx Project Libraries as "Binders"
Celtx's ability to add any file means you can use a Project Library as a "binder" for all the different application files you might have. For example, you may have a spreadsheet with a proposed budget, a PowerPoint presentation for meetings with clients or investors, and a Photoshop mock-up of a splash screen or design logo. You can add all these files to a Celtx project and launch them directly from the Project Library.

For further practice, add a bookmark to the Project Library. Perhaps you're already thinking ahead to raising funds for your film: you'll add a bookmark for IndieVest, a film financing company.

Click on the Add icon, select Bookmark from the Select Item dialog box, and input the following as the item name:

IndieVest website

The URL to input is this:

http://www.indievest.com/

Figure 3.7 shows your project as it now stands.

You can use the Project Library window to navigate between different sections of your project. Double-click the Stageplay item, and the Stageplay window becomes active. Double-click the IndieVest bookmark, and you immediately launch the bookmarked website. Return to the Celtx project, and double-click on the Screenplay item. This makes the Screenplay editing window active.

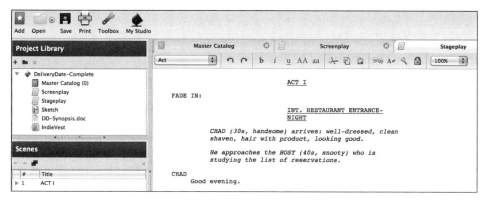

Figure 3.7 *Delivery Date* project with stageplay, synopsis, and bookmark added to library.

Tip: Notice that a drop-down menu arrow resides on the right edge where all tabbed catalog windows (Screenplay, Stageplay, Sketch, and so on) line up. Clicking the arrow lists all the open catalog windows, making it easy to select your preferred window.

Items in the library can also be manipulated via the item's context menu (invoked with a right-click in Windows or a Ctrl-click on the Mac). Figure 3.8 displays the library item context menu, with choices to duplicate, rename, or delete the selected library item (in this case, the bookmark for IndieVest).

Figure 3.8   Invoking the context menu for Project Library items.

For practice, use the context menu to delete the bookmark. Then rename the DD-Synopsis item to Synopsis.

Note: Renaming the attached file library item for the synopsis won't rename the original Word-formatted file.

You may have noticed two other buttons on the Project Library toolbar: Add Folder, which allows you to begin organizing sections and catalogs into folders you create (using standard drag-and-drop technique), and Delete Item (X) button.

This book will continue exploring use and expansion of the Project Library.

Creating Your Own Templates

The tutorials in this chapter have explored usage of the Film and Stageplay templates. Both Chapter 12, "Exploring Celtx's Built-In Sample Projects," and Appendix B further discuss the use of Celtx's templates.

You may eventually decide you'd like to create your own customized template. The template could contain a standard set of links in the Project Library, and perhaps a standard set of legal and production documents.

To set up a customized template:

1.   Create and edit a project file that contains all the items you require.

2.   Pull down the File menu and choose Create Template.

3.   Give the template a name in the dialog box, and click OK.

The next time you start up Celtx and get the Welcome splash screen (or the next time you invoke the splash screen from the window bar), you see your template listed and available for selection.

Right Sidebar

The right sidebar includes tabs for Notes, Media, Breakdown, and the Celtx Store, as Figure 3.9 shows. This chapter explores the first two of these.

Notes

Sooner or later, most scriptwriters and project developers seek feedback on their work. Celtx's Notes feature allows the reader to interact with the script and leave onscreen "sticky notes" for the writer. Of course, script writers can also leave notes for themselves.

Note: In case you'd like to start with a fresh version of the project file you've been maintaining, download and open `DeliveryDate-Complete-ProjLibrary` from the book's Online Companion website: www.courseptr.com/downloads. If you've followed the walk-throughs throughout this chapter, keep working with the same open project file.

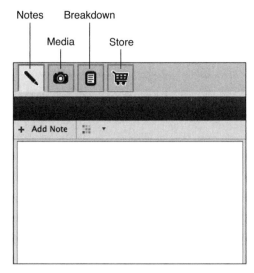

Figure 3.9   The right sidebar with tabs for Notes, Media, Breakdown, and Store.

Creating and Locating Notes

Make sure that Script is the active subtab on the *Delivery Date* script, and be sure you're at the beginning of the screenplay. Perhaps you're of the opinion that Chad should be in his 20s rather than in his 30s. Click after "30s" in the script's action, and then click on the Add Note button.

Now input this:

Does this play better if Chad is in his 20s?

A note has now been attached (or "stuck") to the protagonist's age (or wherever your cursor position is within the script text). The note is even time-stamped.

Scroll down to the bottom of the scene and click at the end of the last sentence. Click on the Add Note button in the right sidebar, and input the following:

Is this shot needed?

Figure 3.10 shows the *Delivery Date* project with a couple of notes attached.

Although the default color for notes is yellow (emulating the "sticky" note), you can assign any color to a note. This can be useful for designating note priorities (red might be top-priority items, whereas yellow would be average priority) or for visually designating who's made a note (a reader might make yellow notes, whereas the author could choose blue for personal notes).

To change the color of the second note, select the note, and then click on the color selector in the Notes toolbar.

Notes can be scrolled through in the Notes sidebar, and the sidebar can be resized via the sizing bar. Note icons can be dragged and dropped anywhere within the script text itself—try it!

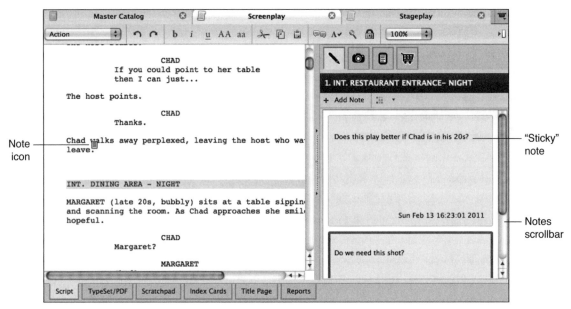

Figure 3.10   *Delivery Date* script and notes.

Tip: When you first open a Celtx project, you might not see notes appear in the Notes window. The Notes sidebar is context-sensitive and displays notes for the scene your pointer is currently positioned in. For your project script, scroll to the top and click the mouse anywhere within the first few lines. That reorients the pointer, and the script notes (which are in the first scene) should appear.

Tip: Click on any note icon within the script, and the contents of the note are immediately displayed in the Notes window.

Editing and Deleting Notes

As you've probably already discovered, editing notes is just like editing any onscreen text. Text in notes can't be italicized, bolded, or otherwise enhanced (except for the use of all uppercase). It's best to think of these notes as sticky notes—nothing fancy, but capable of immediately grabbing your attention and reminding you of questions, reorganization, further research, and so on.

Notes deletion is also an intuitive process. For practice, you'll delete the note about Chad's age. Locate the note onscreen, and as Figure 3.11 demonstrates, click on the note's delete (X) button.

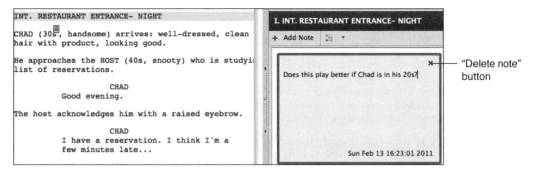

Figure 3.11 Deletion of note.

Tip: If you prefer, right-click or Ctrl-click on the note icon in the script text, and the context menu allows you to *cut* the note out (which effectively serves as a deletion). However, this action also allows you to paste the note elsewhere, if you prefer this technique to dragging and dropping.

Tip: An impulsive note deletion can, of course, be immediately undone, just like any other text editing action.

Printing Notes

A printed script with notes is one of the many reports available from the Reports sheet, which is covered in Chapter 7, "Reports."

Tip: Notes are not printed in the Typeset/PDF rendering of your script. This means that you can annotate your script (or have a colleague annotate the script) to your heart's content—but you can distribute a "clean" version of the script any time you'd like.

Saving Your Script with Notes

Pull down the File menu and choose Save Project As. You can save the project file as DeliveryDate-CompleteWithNote to your local drive.

Copying Partial or Full Scripts or Outlines Between Projects

Celtx makes it easy to copy material from one project file to another. The process is identical to copying material from one Word file to another, or one Final Draft file to another.

To demonstrate this, open the file `DeliveryDate-CompleteWithNote` from your local drive. (You may already have this project file open if you've been working continuously through the chapter.) The file is also downloadable from the book's Online Companion website: www.courseptr.com/downloads.

Follow these steps to copy material between projects:

1. Once the file is open, select the first two scenes of the script and copy them. The copy action includes the script note added in this chapter's tutorial.

2. Pull down the File menu and choose New Project.

3. The Create Project dialog box opens. Select the Film template.

4. You are automatically placed in a script editing window. Paste the copied scenes into the window.

The two copied scenes appear, and you see that the note exists in the Notes sidebar. (You may need to navigate to the first scene to see it.)

You can copy any kind of text between files, regardless of whether the text is contained in text pages, script pages, index cards, or notes in different files.

You won't need this new file for any of the future walk-throughs in this book, but you may want to save it to experiment with it outside of your exercises.

Media

Virtually all dedicated screenwriting programs offer the capability of annotating scripts. But the Media sidebar in Celtx begins to expand what you can do with a film script, a play script, or another project.

Throughout the composition of the script (and through the production revisions, as discussed in Chapter 4), you can attach media—still photos, audio, or even video—to the text.

This may be useful if you have particular locations or props already in mind, or if you just want to give some reference ideas to a storyboard artist, casting director, or set designer. (Note that storyboarding in Celtx is discussed in Chapter 8, "Storyboards.")

To practice using this feature, the next section assumes you've already gone out to scout a few possible locations and have taken a few reference stills.

Media You've Captured

For this tutorial, download and uncompress or unarchive `ReferenceImagesChapter3.zip`—a file you can download from the book's Online Companion website: www.courseptr.com/

downloads. Place the uncompressed image files in a folder. (You can name it something like `Delivery Date Reference Images`.)

If you've been working straight through this chapter, you can continue to use the project file you have open—but if you're starting again here and aren't sure where you left off, go ahead and download `DeliveryDate-CompleteWithNote`.

How about adding a possible restaurant location you've scouted to the scene heading? To add this reference still, follow these steps:

1. Make sure the script editing window is active. (In your sample, this is the Screenplay window.)

2. Activate the Media tab in the right sidebar. (Don't forget you can display a hidden right sidebar, as discussed earlier in the chapter.)

3. Move your pointer and click at the end of the first scene heading location (RESTAURANT ENTRANCE).

4. Click on the Add Item (+) button in the Media window toolbar.

5. Browse to the image folder you created earlier, and open it.

6. Select the `Restaurant Exterior` image file, and open it.

Figure 3.12 shows the attached image, now displayed in the Media window, and a small media pushpin where you initially clicked in the text.

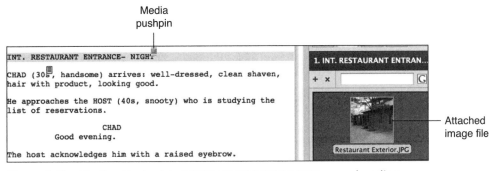

Figure 3.12 Media attached to RESTAURANT ENTRANCE scene heading.

Tip: Media pushpins can be dragged and dropped just like notes—so you can move them wherever you'd like in your script.

The sidebar image is just a thumbnail, of course. To display the full image in your system's default image viewer, double-click on the image. This opens the full-sized image in an image viewer (typically, the Photo Viewer in Windows, and Preview in Mac).

At this point you'll add a second reference still—for the restaurant bar that is a key location in the script. Navigate to scene 5, the first scene requiring the bar. (Don't forget that you can use the Scene Navigator to quickly double-click on the scene heading and display it in the script editing window.)

You'll follow the same four key steps (now that you're in the script editing window and the Media sidebar is activated):

1. Move your pointer and click at the end of the scene heading location (RESTAURANT BAR).

2. Click on the Add Item (+) button in the Media window toolbar.

3. Browse to the image folder you created earlier, and open it.

4. Select the Restaurant Bar image file, and open it.

Figure 3.13 shows the attached image and media pushpin.

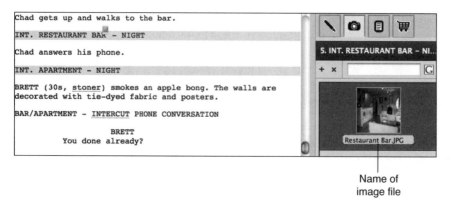

Name of
image file

Figure 3.13 Media attached to RESTAURANT BAR scene heading.

Tip: Just like with notes, you'll see in the sidebar only media attached to the current scene your pointer is placed in. To see the media attached to the first scene, double-click the first scene in the Scene Navigator. You can also see specific media by clicking once on the onscreen pushpin. (Be sure to return to scene 5 before proceeding further.)

You can continue to add media anywhere and everywhere in the script—whatever you might find useful in developing your project.

You can rename media in the sidebar. Click once on the media name in the sidebar. Try renaming the media as `Possible Restaurant Bar Location`. (This does not rename the image file in your image folder.)

Figure 3.14 shows the renamed media in the project file.

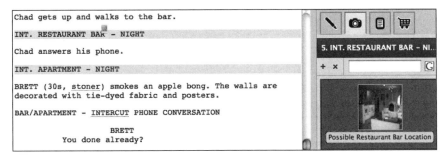

Figure 3.14   Renamed image in the sidebar.

You can, of course, delete media. Figure 3.15 shows the location of the Delete button (X) in the toolbar. Click it, and the image is removed from the project file. (This does not delete the original image in your image folder.)

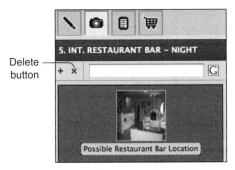

Figure 3.15   Deleting media by clicking on the Delete button in the toolbar.

Note: In the walk-throughs in this section, you have worked only with still images. However, you can just as easily attach audio or video files. Once you've attached them as media, double-clicking them launches the default media player for those files: for example, QuickTime for video on a Mac, or WinAmp for audio on a Windows PC.

Media Culled from Online Sources

Sometimes, you might want to include some generic reference media until you go out and scout locations or visit a prop house.

Celtx allows you to do a quick Google Image search to attach this media. Perhaps in scene 3 (the montage) you want to include a picture of a bottle of wine (perhaps to help with some early storyboarding).

Navigate to scene 3, click after the word "wine" in the scene, and in the Media sidebar, type `wine bottle` into the search text box. As Figure 3.16 demonstrates, click the Google Image Search (G) button next to it.

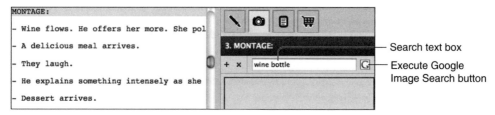

Figure 3.16   Use of Google Image Search in finding and attaching media.

A Google Image Search window opens in your browser. Visually select an appealing wine bottle, and then save the image to your local hard drive in an appropriately named folder. (Typically, this means bringing up a right-click or Ctrl-click browser context menu, choosing Save Image, and then completing the save operation.)

Tip: A good file management practice is to create a folder specific for your project media. In this instance, creating a folder called `Temporary Delivery Date Media` would be a good identifier of the kind of media collected in this folder.

Eventually, if you gathered a lot of media, you might need to create a `Delivery Date Media` parent folder and then have several subfolders including `Temporary Media`, `Location Stills`, `Actor Headshots`, and so on.

Back in Celtx, you can click the Add Item (+) button in the Media sidebar, and select the media file you just downloaded to your local drive.

Celtx displays an image of the media file in the Media sidebar, along with the media pushpin where you clicked earlier.

You can rename the media for your purposes within Celtx (for example, `wine bottle concept`), although the name of the original file on your local drive remains unchanged.

Figure 3.17 shows the capture and placement of the new reference media.

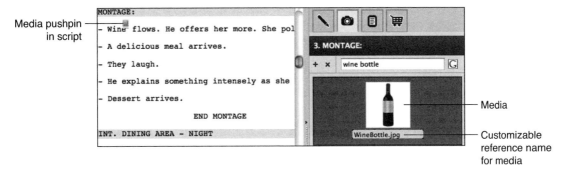

Figure 3.17   Wine bottle media added to project.

Who Owns the Media?

Although you may think that the media you find when using Google Image Search is free, the majority of media is legally considered to be intellectual property and is still owned by its creator. If distributed (outside of your production team) in any context by you, the media needs to be licensed or purchased. Some media is in the public domain (meaning that anyone can use it), and other media uses the Creative Commons license, which allows limited use of the media depending on the type of license granted.

In general, you should use Google Image "grabs" solely for temporary reference materials. Furthermore, you must be careful about not allowing an unlicensed image (whether secured through an Internet search, scanned photograph, or other method) in your final project. This is true, of course, for any kind of media: a music or an audio clip, a video insert, and so on.

For more information about Creative Commons licensing, visit http://creativecommons. org. Books like *Archival Storytelling: A Filmmaker's Guide to Finding, Using, and Licensing Third-Party Visuals and Music* by Sheila Curran Bernard and Kenn Rabin; *The Screenwriter's Legal Guide* by Stephen Breimer; and *The Pocket Lawyer for Filmmakers: A Legal Toolkit for Independent Producers* by Thomas Crowell provide further information on intellectual property and media licensing.

You can delete attached media at any time by clicking on the Delete button in the Media sidebar or the Delete button that appears if you float your pointer over the image. The delete operation can immediately be undone, if necessary.

The media you've attached is available in the script's Master Catalog, which Chapter 5 explores more fully.

Breakdown

Script breakdowns are so essential to media production that Chapter 5 discusses them in more detail.

Store

The Store tab provides links to information about the following:

- Celtx mobile apps (to be discussed in Chapter 13, "Celtx Script")

- Celtx Studios (to be discussed in Chapters 14, "Celtx Studios—Creation and Administration," and 15, "Celtx Studios—User Interaction")

- Low-cost Celtx add-ons (to be discussed in Chapter 16, "Celtx Add-Ons, Utilities, and Sketch Images")

Summary

This chapter covered the following:

- Using the Scene Navigator window in the left sidebar, allowing you to easily navigate either your scenes or your index cards.

- Building out your project by adding additional tabbed, editable windows—making it easy to add synopses or outlines, bookmarks, storyboards, sketches, calendars, and so on. (Subsequent chapters continue to explore this feature.)

- Using the Project Library in the left sidebar, navigating between different sections and catalogs.

- Annotating a script using the Notes window in the right sidebar. This includes attaching, moving, editing, and deleting notes.

- Attaching media to your script, using the Media window in the right sidebar. You're able to attach your own media (which may include still images, audio, or video), and do Google Image lookups for "temp" reference media.

The next chapter focuses on what happens when you have advanced your script to a stage where you can begin pre-production on the project. And Chapter 5 returns to the use of the right sidebar as you break down a script.

4 Creating and Editing Production Film Scripts

Chapter 2, "Getting Familiar with Celtx," looked at the basics of script composition, and Chapter 3, "Project Navigation, Library, Notes, and Media," examined how you can begin to navigate and annotate your script and include some reference media. All this work is typical in the initial creative process, while you're finding out if the project: a) is worthy of production, and b) can and should actually be funded (even if it's out of your own pocket).

But at a certain point (if you're lucky), your script will receive a "green light" from the funding source(s) and head for production. In some respects, you've already started a process known as pre-production, but now you move into pre-production in earnest. Pre-production includes the following, listed in no particular order:

- Location scouting
- Casting
- Initial set design, production design, and wardrobe design
- Scheduling
- Budgeting
- Storyboarding and pre-visualization

As the list suggests, the move into pre-production typically begins to involve a lot of people and a lot of interaction between them. Clear-cut communication is critical.

This chapter discusses Celtx's production revision features and how they help the cast and crew.

Note: The features discussed in this chapter apply to film scripts only, as other types of scripts (Stageplay, A/V) and projects (Comic Book, Novel) don't typically require as complex a workflow in the pre-production process.

Scene Numbering and Revision Flags in Pre-Production
In Chapters 2 and 3, you didn't worry about numbering scenes, for good reason: script composition often requires the reshuffling of scenes (one of the reasons that professionals like to use index cards when they're outlining narratives).

But the moment you enter pre-production on a film script and begin to involve other people in your production, scene numbers become quite useful. It helps when everyone knows that scene 3 is the one located in the railyard at night, requiring a prop gun and the two leading cast members dressed in survivalist gear.

Numbering scenes is essential.

But wait—now things get interesting. Film scripts change in the course of pre-production:

- The railyard might not be available, or a night shoot might be impossible due to budget cuts.

- The director may change her mind and decide that survivalist gear is the wrong type of wardrobe.

- An actor may have difficulty speaking a line of dialog, prompting a change to a new line.

- The prop gun may need to be explained by adding an earlier scene just before scene 3.

Each of these items requires a change in the film script and new pages being distributed to cast and crew so they have an up-to-date version of the script.

But how do you quickly let cast and crew know where the changes are on a page (so they aren't forced to fully read and compare two scripts)?

For the scene changes mentioned in the first three bullets, the industry long ago standardized placing an asterisk (*) or "star" at the right edge of any script line that might be changed. Figure 4.1 demonstrates this kind of revision mark on a printed script.

But the addition of a new scene discussed in the fourth bullet creates new complications. The simple solution would be to number the new scene as #3, renumber scene 3 as scene 4, renumber scene 4 as scene 5, and so on.

But now everyone's going to be confused when scene 3 is discussed. Is it the old scene 3, or the new scene 3?

A better solution is to retain the "lock" on the scene numbering, and instead, attach a letter to the new scene slipping in between scene 2 and scene 3. The new scene will be 2A. If two new scenes need to be placed between scenes 2 and 3, they become 2A and 2B.

Confusion about scene 3 never occurs, because scene 3 has remained scene 3.

See Figures 4.2 (the wrong approach to adding new scenes and scene numbers to a revised production script) and 4.3 (the right approach to adding new scenes and scene numbers to a revised production script) for slides illustrating this standard industry practice.

Location change—previously "restaurant."

Dialog change—previously "good evening."

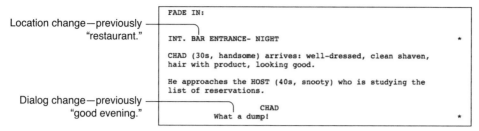

Figure 4.1 An illustration of changes made to dialog and location in a revised production script. The asterisk on the right edge is a revision flag, representing a change in the line.

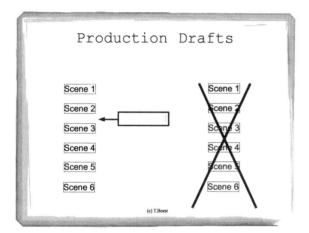

Figure 4.2 Although it seems logical, just renumbering all the scenes after the insertion of a new scene to a revised production script confuses everyone.

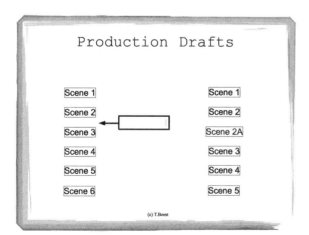

Figure 4.3 This slide shows the standard industry practice of inserting a new scene and then numbering it by using the preceding scene number and appending a letter to it. A new scene inserted between scene 2 and scene 3 becomes scene 2A.

Locking the Script

When a script is ready for distribution to cast and crew and commencement of pre-production, the media industry has a term for it: locking the script.

Caution: Locking a script for production is a big step, and professional screenwriters and script supervisors generally try to put off locking a script for as long as possible. (You'll see why soon.)

When you lock your script, you'll do the following:

- Number your scenes and then "lock" the assigned numbers. (That is, scene 3 will always be scene 3, no matter what changes may happen, including omission of the scene.)

- Assign the color white to the first production draft that is going out for distribution, meaning that all pages will be printed or photocopied on white paper.

For the walk-throughs in this chapter, you'll use a new version of the *Delivery Date* screenplay, which you can download from the book's Online Companion website: www.courseptr.com/downloads. The screenplay is titled DeliveryDate-ReadyToLock.

Once you've opened your practice project, activate the Typeset/PDF window.

Click the Format Options button. This dialog box was discussed in Chapter 2, but this chapter approaches it from the aspect of production. You'll notice that the dialog box has two tabs: General and Mores and Continueds. You should be on the General tab initially.

Figure 4.4 displays the Show Scene Numbers drop-down list box selected. Typically, professionals prefer that scene numbers be shown on both the left and right margins, making them even easier to visually access. Choose Both to activate this feature.

As discussed in Chapter 2, the General tab in the Format Options dialog box also allows you to do the following:

- Adjust the paper size if necessary

- Control the number of lines between scenes (1 is the commonly preferred setting, but some productions prefer 2)

- Trigger a page break between scenes (typically used if you're breaking out "sides" for auditions; some productions may prefer starting scenes on new pages)

- Show the title page, which you would typically want to do

If you switch to the Mores and Continueds tab, you find controls for handling dialog and scenes as they break across pages (see Figure 4.5). Celtx has already defined the exact layouts for these text cues, and you can feel safe checkmarking all the selections for a production script.

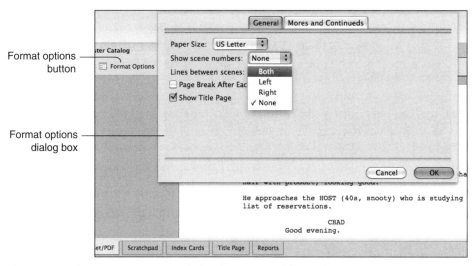

Format options button

Format options dialog box

Figure 4.4 The Format Options dialog box opened from the Typeset/PDF window, and the drop-down list box displayed for Show Scene Numbers (using the General tab).

Note: Some productions may want to reduce clutter on the page by declining to Show Character Continueds. Experiment with turning this setting on and off, and see if you have a preference regarding this feature.

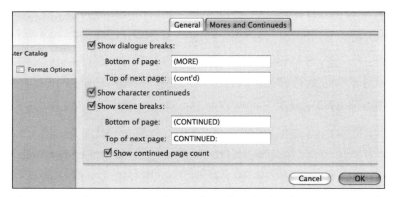

Figure 4.5 The Mores and Continueds tab in the Format Options dialog box, with all options checkmarked.

MOREs and CONTINUEDs

In production, cast and crew tend to focus on the current scene they're working with, rather than the totality of a screenplay. The use of MORE and CONTINUED is a text courtesy for cast and crew, so they can clearly follow lengthy dialog across a page break or know with certainty that a scene is spanning multiple pages.

If a scene continues across multiple pages, Celtx provides a page count for those continuations (as long as Show Continued Page Count is checked), making it easy for cast or crew to pull a specific scene out of the script with confidence it's complete.

Once you've finished making selections in the Format Options dialog box, click the OK button. Celtx renders a new version of your script. Figure 4.6 shows some of the results of your actions.

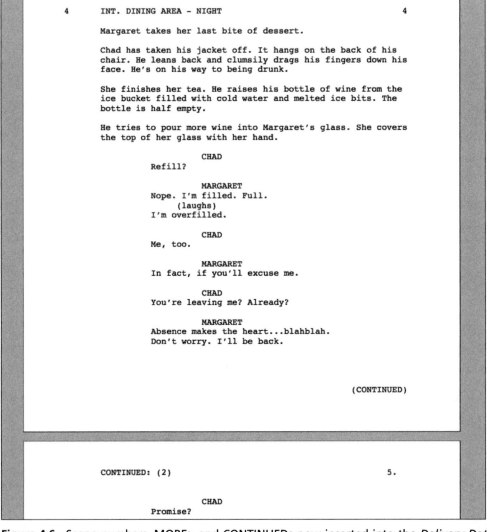

```
   4      INT. DINING AREA - NIGHT                            4

          Margaret takes her last bite of dessert.

          Chad has taken his jacket off. It hangs on the back of his
          chair. He leans back and clumsily drags his fingers down his
          face. He's on his way to being drunk.

          She finishes her tea. He raises his bottle of wine from the
          ice bucket filled with cold water and melted ice bits. The
          bottle is half empty.

          He tries to pour more wine into Margaret's glass. She covers
          the top of her glass with her hand.

                              CHAD
                    Refill?

                              MARGARET
                    Nope. I'm filled. Full.
                         (laughs)
                    I'm overfilled.

                              CHAD
                    Me, too.

                              MARGARET
                    In fact, if you'll excuse me.

                              CHAD
                    You're leaving me? Already?

                              MARGARET
                    Absence makes the heart...blahblah.
                    Don't worry. I'll be back.

                                              (CONTINUED)
```

```
          CONTINUED: (2)                                     5.

                              CHAD
                    Promise?
```

Figure 4.6 Scene numbers, MOREs, and CONTINUEDs now inserted into the *Delivery Date* script.

Note: The Format Options dialog box provides different options for different kinds of projects (A/V scripts, stageplay scripts, audio play scripts, and comic book scripts). This chapter's tutorial only looks at format options when using the screenplay template. See Appendix B, "Script Template Typeset/PDF Format Options," for a full description of each template's format options.

To lock the script, you need to make the Script window active. Once you've done that, pull down the Script menu and choose Revision Mode. Figure 4.7 displays the Revision Options dialog box that opens.

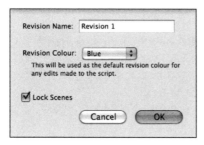

Figure 4.7   Revision Options dialog box opened from Script menu.

Revision Options covers three elements:

- The default name for the first set of revisions is `Revision 1`. You can change this to `1st revision`, `Revised Production Draft`, or any other phrase you would like, although the default phrase is perfectly suitable for productions. You may want to include the distribution date in the revision name: for example, `Revision 1—May 15, 2011`.

- As explained in the sidebar titled "Production Script Colors," blue is the industry standard color selected for the first set of revisions. As you move through sets of revisions, you can change to the next draft color.

- Lock Scenes is checked: the default operation for locking a script.

Caution: Unchecking Lock Scenes defeats the purpose of locking a script. Make sure you keep that item checked, if you're locking a script for production.

Click OK to close the dialog box, and be sure to save your project in its current state—but give it a new name: `DeliveryDateWhiteProductionDraft`. You may want to print out the entire script, to see how it looks with scene numbers, MOREs, and CONTINUEDs in place.

Now that you've locked your White Production Draft, you can begin making changes.

Production Script Colors and Sets of Changes

The earlier sidebar titled "Scene Numbering and Revision Flags in Pre-Production" discussed ways in which to flag revisions and let cast and crew know about changes in production drafts of the script.

But the most visual method of notification about changes is in the use of colored pages in production drafts.

When you lock a script, you begin with a "white" production draft or "white revision." But almost inevitably, particularly in a production with more than a few minutes' running time, production revisions become necessary.

You should never generate a production revision because of one or two typographical errors. Instead, a new set of changes should be meaningful in terms of changes in location, dialog, characters, props, scene blocking, scene actions, or added or omitted scenes.

Decades ago, the filmmaking industry more or less standardized a sequence of page colors for subsequent sets of changes (revisions):

- Blue

- Pink

- Yellow

- Green

- Goldenrod

- Salmon

- Cherry

- Buff

- Tan

- 2nd White

- 2nd Blue

- 2nd Pink

- and so on

As an example, say that changes are made to pages 1, 4, 8, and 12 in your white production draft. You would then print those revised pages on blue paper and distribute only the blue pages to cast and crew. You would also print a blue title page, which listed the Blue Draft, the date of its release, and sometimes, a list of the actual pages changed in that draft. Figure 4.8 shows a sample title page with two sets of changes—blue and pink—having been released.

Many productions don't bother using all the colors listed previously, especially because finding salmon- and cherry-colored paper is sometimes difficult! So it's common to see sequences of production revisions like this: white pages, blue pages, pink pages, yellow pages, green pages, 2nd white pages, 2nd blue pages, and so on.

It is common for big-budgeted feature films to cycle through two, three, or even more colored sets of revisions. Sometimes sets of changes are issued daily; more typically for productions without the luxury of months of shooting, blue and pink pages may be substantial, and then further sets of changes begin to dwindle in both scope and frequency (much to the relief of cast and crew).

A typical shooting script for episodic television or feature films is composed of a rainbow of colors.

Smaller productions and production teams may opt to continue printing revisions on white paper, while still labeling each set of changes with a color. For example, the name of the revision (which you can set with Revision Options in Celtx) might be `Blue Revision` or `Blue Draft`. That name is printed in the header of your revised pages, and the blue draft is still indicated on the title page.

Revising Locked Scripts

Figure 4.9 shows the new Revision toolbar in the script editing window, triggered when you clicked OK to ratify your Revision Options. You can now easily increment sets of changes, as necessary.

Adding New Scenes

It's time to commence the first set of changes. Navigate to the restaurant bar scene (scene 7) with the Scene Navigator. (See Chapter 3 for introduction of this feature.)

Figure 4.8 Sample script title page showing the release date for white, blue, and pink sets of revisions.

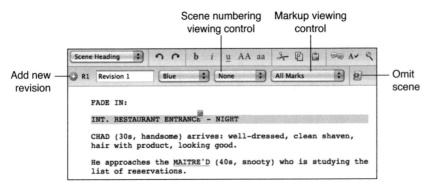

Figure 4.9 The Revision toolbar in the script editing window, making it easy to increment revisions and omit scenes.

In the revision, you've decided to have Chad momentarily exit the restaurant from the bar. At the end of the restaurant bar scene, modify the final action:

```
Chad walks away from the conversation and suddenly notices a back door out
to a rear parking lot.
```

Notice that the new text is highlighted in blue, a clear visual signal that this is part of the blue revision. If you would like, you can momentarily toggle to the Typeset/PDF window. An asterisk has been placed at the right of the revised action line.

Be sure you're back in the script editing window, insert a new line, and select Scene Heading as the element. Input the following:

```
ext. rear parking lot - night[ENTER]
```

The new scene heading is painted blue, and your Scene Navigator (in the left sidebar) now shows Scene 7A. Toggle to the Typeset/PDF window for a moment, and you see 7A bracketing the scene heading. (Be sure to toggle back to the script editor window to continue.)

Tip: Notice that as you begin typing the scene heading, Celtx tries to match it up with previous locations (that is, auto-complete the location). This helps you in quickly creating new scene headings when they are using already established locations, while maintaining consistency in identifying the locations you're using. This consistency will become even more important in Chapter 5, "Script Breakdowns and Catalogs."

By now you may have discovered that Celtx tries to auto-complete character names fronting dialog—further speeding up text input, and further assisting with maintaining consistency in the script.

You should be within an action element. Input the following:

```
Chad heads out to the parking lot, prepared to leave. But then he stops.
Looks back at the restaurant, guiltily.
```

Again, your text signals a revision with the blue highlighting.

Tip: Notice that the Index Card Navigator (which can be toggled to within the Scene Navigator) has cleared space for a card 7A. Naturally, you still have to fill out the content of the scene if you are continuing to maintain current index cards at this stage of production.

Figure 4.10 shows the totality of your revisions to date.

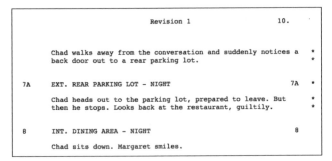

Figure 4.10 Addition of new scene 7A with new scene heading and action elements (seen in the Typeset/PDF window).

Note: You might think that your production will be in trouble if another new scene must later be added between scene 7 and scene 7A. But Celtx generates another unique scene number: A7. You then have 7, A7, and 7A in sequence. Celtx continues to generate unique scene numbers as necessary. (This style of numbering can be adjusted, as discussed later in this chapter.) However, if you find yourself frequently inserting new scenes inside previous new scenes, you likely locked the script too early.

Perhaps you realize that you're going to need an establishing shot of the restaurant to open your film. Here's how you can insert a new scene at the beginning of your script:

1. Scroll to the top of the script, and insert your pointer just after the colon in FADE IN.

2. Press the Enter or Return key.

3. Pull down the element drop-down box and select Scene Heading.

4. Input ext. restaurant—establishing—night.

Although you can add some action to this first scene, it isn't always necessary for an establishing shot. Figure 4.11 shows the results of your inserted scene. Notice that the Scene Navigator has now designated the new scene as scene 0A, because scene 1 already existed. You can, of course, drag the reference still of your restaurant exterior into scene 0A as well.

Automatic Changes to the Title Page

If you toggle to the Title Page editor, you notice that Revision 1 has been included on the title page. Now you can see why you may want to name the revision something else: Blue Draft, Blue Pages, or Blue Rev. (However, there's nothing wrong with Revision 1.)

Toggle back to the script editing window, and select Revision 1 in the Revision toolbar. Name the revision Blue Pages, and add today's date.

New scene inserted
(scene 0A)

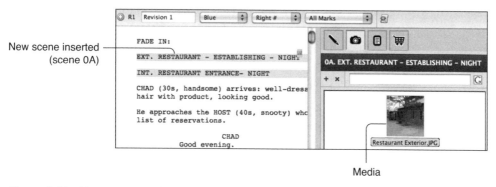

Media

Figure 4.11   New scene 0A inserted into script, and reference still dragged into new scene heading.

Figure 4.12 shows what happens when you toggle back to the Title Page editor. You see that the title page has automatically been updated.

Figure 4.12   Title Page editor with current revision notification.

Incrementing Revisions

Save the current project as DeliveryDate-BluePages, and make sure you're in the script editing window.

Click the green + button on the Revision toolbar. This brings up the Revision Options dialog box. Name this revision Pink Pages, and add today's (or tomorrow's) date. Click OK to close the dialog box.

The Revision toolbar reflects the current revision, and you're ready to practice making another set of changes.

Say you want to slightly modify the dialog on page 1 of the script. Scroll down to the dialog line "Thanks." You can add to this line:

Uhh, that's her, huh?

The new dialog is highlighted in pink. Figure 4.13 shows the revision in Typeset/PDF view, with its revision mark.

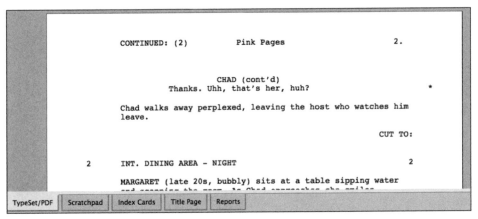

Figure 4.13 Added dialog in the pink revision pass, with revision mark.

Revision Viewing Controls
The Revision toolbar provides two different drop-down list boxes to affect onscreen display (you can find these list boxes in Figure 4.9):

■   A scene numbering viewing control list box allows you to display revision draft scene numbers in the script editing window on the left side, the right side, or both sides of the page of the page. You can choose not to display any numbers at all, if you prefer. (Note that this setting will not affect scene numbering on your printouts.) Figure 4.14 shows the list box choices: try them out to see what each choice does onscreen. A final selection in the list box—Fix—enables users to choose between a "Hollywood" style of revision scene numbering and a "Celtx" style of revision scene numbering. The Celtx style uses a 1.1, 1.2, 1.3 approach to scene

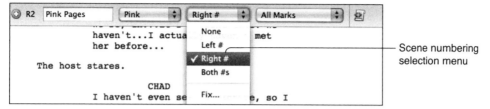

Figure 4.14   Revision toolbar with scene numbering viewing control list box.

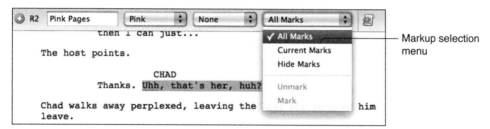

Figure 4.15   Revision toolbar with markup viewing control list box.

numbering, rather than the 1A, 1B, 1C approach to scene numbering. You can also customize your own approach to scene numbering and then save it as a preset. In most cases, the Hollywood style of revision scene numbering discussed in this chapter should serve you well. It is most recognizable to industry professionals.

- Figure 4.15 shows the markup viewing control list box, situated between the numbering control and the Omit Scene icon. Selecting Current Marks displays only the revision highlighting for the current (in this case pink) draft. Selecting Hide Marks hides all the revision highlighting (which may help in concentrating on the content, rather than seeing multiple colors marking which revisions went into which draft). If you select some of the revised material, you can choose to either Unmark or Mark it, allowing you to customize exactly how much markup you want to see while composing.

Omitting Scenes

Omitting scenes in Celtx is easy, and during production—due to the harsh realities of budget and schedule—you will likely be doing more deleting than adding.

To demonstrate the Omit Scene feature in the Revision toolbar, use the Scene Navigator to move to scene 7A while in the script editing view. Click anywhere within scene 7A (the rear parking lot).

Refer to Figure 4.9 for a reminder of the location of the Omit Scene button. Click Omit Scene, and the content of the scene is deleted. In addition, as Figure 4.16 shows, the word "OMIT" is placed in the script.

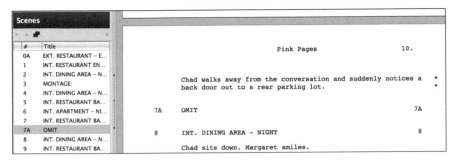

Figure 4.16   Scene 7A after being omitted.

Notice that scene 7A still exists in the Scene Navigator and the script: only its content has been omitted. If an actor had had lines in scene 7A, he would now know that those have been dropped, and that the scene would not be scheduled for shooting.

To practice scene omitting again, navigate to scene 3: the montage. Click the Omit Scene button to delete its content.

The Omit Scene button toggles to Restore Scene while the pointer is in the omitted scene element. Celtx maintains a revision history, and an omitted scene can be restored right away—or later in revisions—by clicking the Restore Scene button.

To practice this, click Restore Scene to bring back the montage (scene 3).

Save this version of the project as `DeliveryDate-PinkPages`.

Resetting Locked Scripts

In the course of production, you may discover that a script you thought was ready for locking really wasn't. Too many locations may need changing; too many scenes may need adding; or the client may decide to scrap the concept. You may be generating all new pages on each revision draft, and you may be winding up with a jumble of 1A, 1B, A1, and B1 scenes. The decision is made to "unlock" or "reset" the script.

With `DeliveryDate-PinkPages` open, pull down the Script menu and select Reset Revision Mode.

Figure 4.17 shows the triggered warning box: Reset Script Locking. This is a big step, so Celtx wants to make sure you know what you're doing.

You've been warned! Go ahead and select the Reset button.

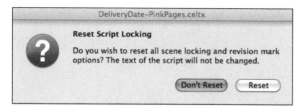

Figure 4.17 The Reset Script Locking warning box, triggered by the Script/Reset Revision Mode menu selection. (Note that this Script menu choice is only available when the script is in revision mode.)

In the Scene Navigator, all the scenes have been renumbered.

In the Typeset/PDF view, all revision marks have been removed, and in the Title Page view, reference to the revision draft has been deleted.

You can now continue to revise the script in a "pre-locked" state. When you are finally ready, you can lock the script and issue a new "white" production draft, commencing the revision cycle again.

Exporting to Final Draft and Movie Magic Screenwriter

Sometimes you may find that you've composed a script in Celtx, only to discover—as you head toward production—that the rest of the production team or company prefers using Final Draft or Movie Magic Screenwriter as part of the pre-production workflow.

To practice exporting a script that you can then import into Final Draft or Movie Magic Screenwriter, open `DeliveryDate-Complete`. (To obtain a fresh copy, go to the book's Online Companion website at www.courseptr.com/downloads and download the file from there.)

To export the script to a formatted text file, do the following:

1. Pull down the Script menu and select Export Script.

2. Create a name for the exported script (`DeliveryDate-Export` would make sense), choose a folder to send the exported script to, and select Save.

The script file has now been converted to a formatted text file that either Final Draft or Movie Magic Screenwriter can easily import.

Although a small amount of cleanup may sometimes be necessary for a lengthy imported script, you should be able to resume composition and revision in Final Draft or Movie Magic Screenwriter right away!

You can open the formatted text file in virtually any word processing program (Microsoft Word, OpenOffice Text) or in Google Docs, Zoho Writer, or Adobe Story.

Summary

This chapter covered the following:

- Locking the script and moving into revision mode

- Producing identifiable revision drafts by 1) using the industry convention of tagging them by color, and 2) using revision marks to indicate textual changes

- Creating new A and B scenes, allowing you to retain all your original "locked" scene numbers

- Using the Revision toolbar to control the amount of onscreen markup and scene numbering while editing

- Omitting scenes while retaining the deleted scenes' numbering and placement within the script

- Resetting revision mode in the event that the script was locked too early and must be overhauled before heading back into pre-production

The next chapter explores Celtx's script breakdown features, which can aid you whether you begin using them in the composition phase or the pre-production phase.

5 Script Breakdowns and Catalogs

Breaking down a script is the process of converting a script into catalogs and lists so assistant directors can start scheduling, production managers can start budgeting, location scouts can begin lining up locations, prop managers can start acquiring props, wardrobe departments can start assembling costumes for production, and so on.

Traditionally in film and television, assistant directors executed the breakdown, and all of it was done manually, using boards and magnets and strips of paper and markers. But now that ad-hoc and small production teams are ever more in vogue, almost anyone may have to break down a script.

In the past dozen years, software tools have been developed to automate much of the breakdown—but a handoff still has to occur where a marked-up script file is imported into the tool. Sometimes the import isn't 100% successful—and regardless of success, two or three software programs must be juggled to begin producing breakdowns.

Celtx is about breakdown as much as it's about scriptwriting. In this chapter, you'll begin to use Celtx's breakdown features to see how you can move further away from the old paper-and-markup methodology of breaking down scripts and create a more seamless workflow for ad-hoc and small shop production teams. In Chapter 7, "Reports," you'll see how to produce customized breakdown reports.

The process of breaking down scenes also gives you further practice in the use of the Project Library, which maintains catalogs and other elements for you.

Caution: This book demonstrates the breaking down of a script so you can explore Celtx's features. However, this is not meant to be a comprehensive tutorial about the general task of professionally breaking down a script, and sample breakdowns won't be 100% complete.

The Importance of Breakdowns

Breakdowns are equally important for every kind of project: stage, video, film, audio-play, and animation/CGI/machinima projects. Stage managers, Foley artists, and 3D modelers can use breakdowns in pre-production. Breakdowns can help in acquisition and inventory of props, audition scheduling, and virtual set building in CGI worlds—and this is just a small sampling of their uses.

You will find the script breakdown process to be repetitive and detail-oriented, but Chapter 7, "Reports," and Chapter 11, "Calendaring and Scheduling," show you the rewards reaped when a thorough breakdown is completed.

Marking Items for Breakdown

Open the project file DeliveryDate-Complete. (You may need to download a fresh copy of the project file from the book's Online Companion website: www.courseptr.com/downloads.)

Figure 5.1 shows the right sidebar after the Breakdown tab has been activated.

Adding Markup to the Script

A list of potential categories for script items is built in to Celtx. You'll start by marking up your characters to build a character list for the first scene.

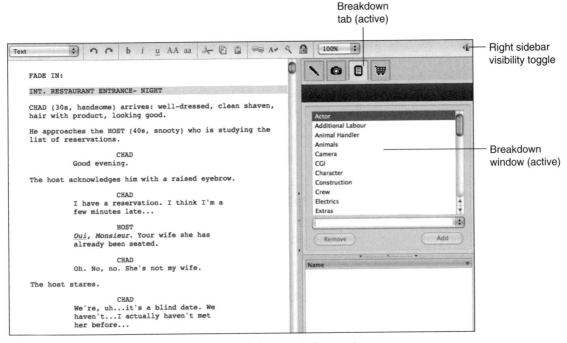

Figure 5.1 The right sidebar, with the Breakdown window active.

1. Highlight CHAD where he's introduced in the first scene.

2. In the Breakdown sidebar, notice that Chad's name has already been placed in the text box below the breakdown category list. Now you can select Character from the category list, and click the Add button.

Immediately, a one-item character list has been created in the lower part of the sidebar, which displays the active catalogs for the current scene your pointer is in. The marked-up item in the script now has a different font color.

To add the second character in the scene, highlight HOST where he first appears. Make sure Character is the category selected, and click Add.

The character list for this scene has expanded to 2 entries. Figure 5.2 shows what the character list looks like when expanded. (Double-click Character in the lower list to expand.)

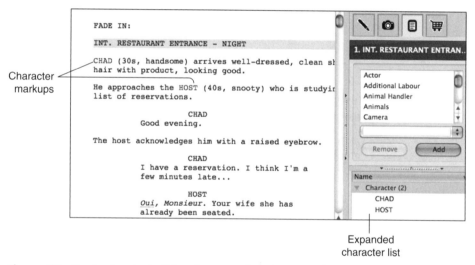

Figure 5.2 Beginning to build a character list: CHAD and HOST have been marked in the first scene, and the character list has been expanded with a double-click.

Note: The Project Library also reflects the total number of marked-up items in the Master Catalog. Later in the chapter, you learn how to use the Project Library in navigating catalogs.

Now you'll begin a second catalog, for props. Navigate to scene 3, the Montage. Several dinner props are needed for this sequence.

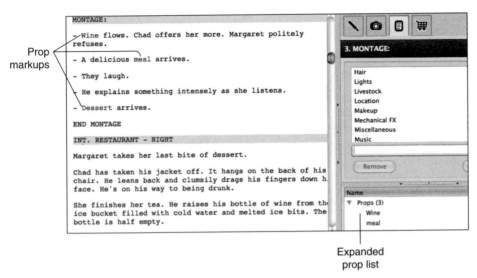

Prop markups

Expanded prop list

Figure 5.3 Beginning to build a prop list: Wine, Meal, and Dessert have been marked in the montage, and the prop list has been expanded with a double-click.

Highlight Wine, select Props from the breakdown category list, and click Add. Do the same for Meal and Dessert. Figure 5.3 shows the expanded prop list and marked-up props. The Master Catalog in the Project Library has expanded to five items.

Tip: Celtx color-codes types of markup, helping you to visually spot department items. For example, characters are red, effects are blue, practicals are purple, locations are yellow, and so on. If you mark up one word multiple times (as discussed later in the chapter), it inherits the latest markup in its color coding.

Save the project file with a new name, `DeliveryDate-PartialBreakdown`.

Note: Throughout this chapter, you'll be *selectively* marking up items in the script to demonstrate the breakdown process. Even with Celtx's time-saving features, full and complete breakdowns remain labor-intensive.

Tip: You can customize item categories. To do so, pull down the Tools menu, select Options, and select Categories. You can then define new categories, possibly for unusual departments or unique needs for a production. Most productions find every category they need already available in Celtx.

Removing Markup from the Script

Once in a while, you may mark up an item for breakdown, only to realize the selection is the wrong one or shouldn't be included.

Navigate to scene 4, highlight the phrase Melted Ice Bits, choose Props in the Breakdown category drop-down menu, and click Add in the Breakdown sidebar. The Master Catalog expands to six items.

You now realize that Melted Ice Bits is probably unnecessary as a procured production item. Highlight the same selection and click the Remove button in the Breakdown sidebar. This removes Melted Ice Bits as a breakdown item.

Caution: The Master Catalog still reflects six items in this example. To completely eradicate Melted Ice Bits, you need to locate the item in the Master Catalog and delete it. (Master Catalog interaction is described in the next section.) Sometimes, however, it's useful to retain a deleted item in the Master Catalog—because you never know when the deleted item may show up again in a revised scene.

The Master Catalog Database

Lists of characters, props, and the many other categories of items are extremely useful in pre-production, and Chapter 7 discusses generating breakdown and pre-production reports. But now you'll see how to detail these items in your Master Catalog.

Double-click the Master Catalog in the Project Library window to open it.

Tip: Double-clicking an entered item within an established list (for example, CHAD in the character list) also opens the Master Catalog and focuses on the double-clicked item.

Figure 5.4 shows the Master Catalog as it currently stands, with CHAD selected in the Name column.

Notice that your catalog is really a database of columns and rows. You can sort by item name or category, or other fields you haven't set up yet. For practice, click on the Category field to sort it alphabetically. (At this point, you have only characters and props.) As Figure 5.5 shows, clicking on Category again performs a reverse sort.

As Figure 5.6 shows, you can filter the catalog by any search criteria in the text box that is part of the Add/Remove toolbar in the Catalog window. For example, input `Character` in the filter to display only characters.

Tip: You probably noticed that the filter quickly recognized your criteria and narrowed the list to characters.

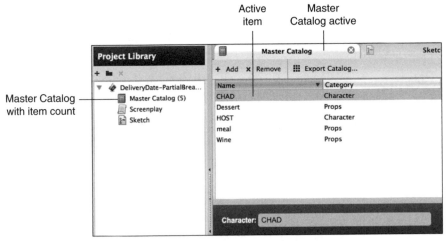

Figure 5.4   The Master Catalog with five items currently entered, and CHAD as the active item.

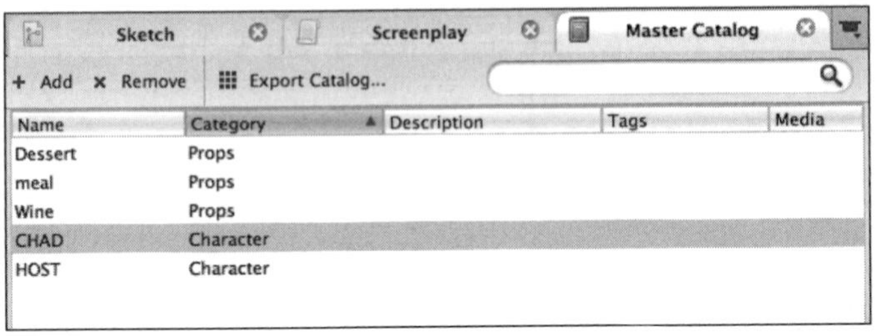

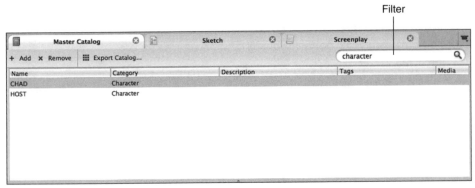

Figure 5.5   The Master Catalog reverse-sorted by Category.

Figure 5.6   The Master Catalog filtered for Character items.

To return to the complete view of Master Catalog items, delete the text in the filter box, and all five items should return to visibility.

Filling Out Forms in the Master Catalog

Double-clicking the CHAD item zooms into the catalog form for Chad. (Notice that you now have a CHAD tab added to your collection of tabbed windows.)

You can now detail the character of Chad in many different ways, including these:

- Building out a full description and character bio (including background, motivation, traits, and physical description)

- Designating the dramatic role (protagonist, antagonist, sidekick, and so on)

- Attaching potential headshots, concept sketches, or other related character media

- Connecting an actor from the actor list to the character, once cast

- Assigning a schedule ID

Detail sections are expandable and collapsible. For example, you may decide that the Motivation section isn't useful for a specific project, or you may not have time to detail Character Traits.

A detailed character bio, which this form helps build, can be useful for a casting director and may be useful for an actor and a director as well. Also, as you'll see later in this chapter, you can begin writing a script by filling out forms and detailing character bios, before you ever start writing scenes.

Figure 5.7 shows an in-progress build-up of a portion of Chad's onscreen form. Detailed Physical Description has been minimized to demonstrate that you can collapse or expand any section as you work through the form. See if you can duplicate the content displayed in the figure.

Now move to the Wine prop. Once it's selected in the Master Catalog, you see a somewhat different entry screen to build out. Details, procurement, and contact information are some of the data fields to use for a prop, along with the standard description and media fields. Figure 5.8 shows a build-out for the Wine prop. Again, see if you can duplicate the data in this form.

Note: If you created a `Temporary Delivery Date Media` folder back in Chapter 3, "Project Navigation, Library, Notes, and Media," you can add a still image of a wine bottle. Otherwise, go out and download a wine bottle image from Google Image Search, and see if you can add the media in this prop form.

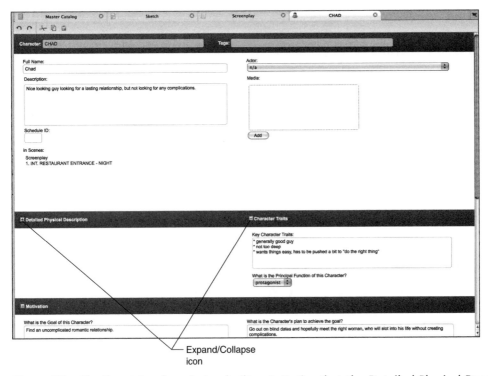

Figure 5.7   Chad's catalog form being built out. Notice that the Detailed Physical Description section has been minimized.

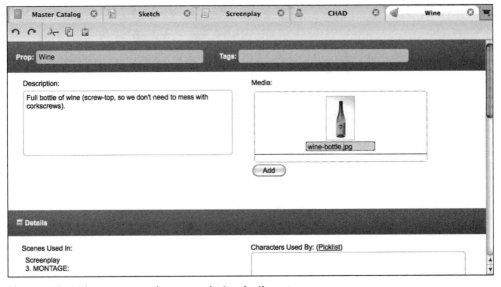

Figure 5.8   Wine prop catalog entry being built out.

Some categories are fairly generic in their data fields, whereas others require unique details: for example, the Wardrobe data screen provides a field for who's wearing the wardrobe piece. Appendix C, "Breakdown Item Data Fields," lists the default data fields for each category and its catalog form.

Tip: The Location data screen provides a useful feature: once a location's real address is entered into the form, an adjacent link immediately opens a browser window and maps the address using Google Maps.

Note: Each breakdown item can have tags entered in its data form. For example, you can tag props as `priority1`, `priority2`, and so on. You can also tag Wardrobe items as `contemporary` or `period`. You can enter multiple tags for any item.

Item tags provide another way for you to filter and sort items. Figure 5.9 isolates the Tags field in a catalog item form.

Figure 5.9   The default Tags field, which is found in all forms.

Creating Specific Catalogs Inside the Master Catalog

You can create specific catalogs inside the Master Catalog to expedite quick lookups.

For example, to add a Character Catalog, follow these steps:

1.   Click the Add button in the toolbar.

2.   The Select Item dialog box appears. Select the category on the left side of the dialog box—in this case, Catalog.

3.   In the right list box, scroll (if needed) and select Character as the catalog type.

4.   Click OK.

Figure 5.10 shows the Select Item dialog box, with Catalog and Character selected.

Figure 5.11 shows the new Character Catalog automatically created and listed in the Project Library. Specific catalogs simplify targeted lookups of a category, such as Wardrobe, CGI, or Extras (rather than having to filter the Master Catalog to study one category's items).

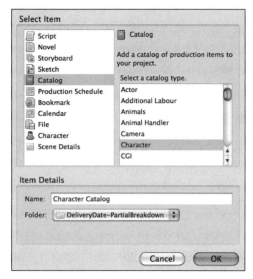

Figure 5.10   Select Item dialog box open, with potential catalogs listed on the left, and types of catalogs listed on the right.

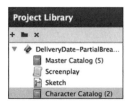

Figure 5.11   Project Library displaying new Character Catalog.

Project Library Shortcuts

You can create a shortcut to any catalog item in the Project Library. This can be helpful if you need to keep going directly to the item—perhaps to further fill out its form, or just because you need to frequently refer to data in the item form.

If you're in the Master Catalog, try dragging one of the character names into the Project Library and dropping the item icon onto the root folder. Figure 5.12 shows the results of dragging CHAD to the Project Library from the Master Catalog; a shortcut to his form now exists.

You can remove the shortcut at any time by triggering the shortcut's context menu and deleting the shortcut. The original catalog item remains intact.

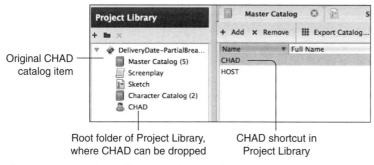

Original CHAD catalog item

Root folder of Project Library, where CHAD can be dropped

CHAD shortcut in Project Library

Figure 5.12 Project Library with new shortcut to the CHAD catalog item.

Fully Breaking Down a Script

Breaking down a script remains a detail-oriented process, even with the level of automation that Celtx provides (which is explored further in Chapter 7). Each scene needs to have items marked for the Master Catalog, so you can generate complete breakdown sheets and adequately schedule and budget your production.

Now you want to be more thorough in marking the character of Chad throughout the script. Chad is currently only marked in scene 1.

1. Return to the Screenplay using the Project Library (double-click on the Screenplay item), and navigate to scene 2 using the Scene Navigator.

2. Chad appears in the first action description in scene 2. Highlight his name.

3. Select the Character item in the Breakdown list box.

4. Now here's where things can get a little tricky. You can mark Chad as a character, but because you previously put CHAD (all uppercase) in the Master Catalog, you would wind up with two separate items and forms for the same character. Instead, click on the drop-down list box for the Character item (in this case, Chad), and as Figure 5.13 shows, you'll see CHAD and HOST already on the list.

5. Select CHAD to add his appearance to the character's breakdown form.

6. Click the Add button.

Continue marking Chad's first appearance in each scene. Figure 5.14 shows the character marked in scenes 3 and 4.

As you mark up the character through scenes, the scene appearances are cataloged and available on the character's catalog form. Figure 5.15 shows Chad's form (found in the Master Catalog) with his scene list updated.

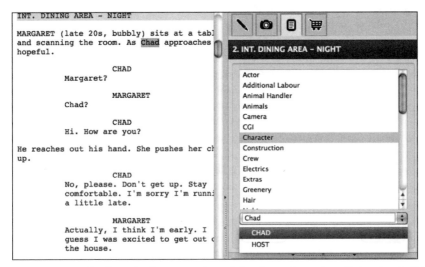

Figure 5.13   Chad marked in scene 2, and the drop-down box listing both CHAD and HOST as previously marked Characters in the Breakdown sidebar.

Chad's name in the script, highlighted
in red after breakdown tagging

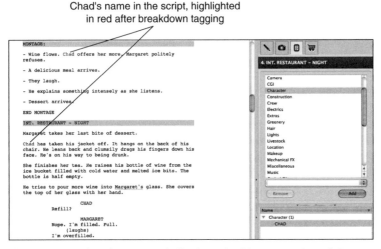

Figure 5.14   The character of Chad marked in scenes 3 and 4.

Tip: The same word in a scene can be marked multiple times, for different department items. For example, Chad could be marked for wardrobe and makeup the first time the word shows up in each scene.

Media professionals break down scripts in different ways. Some go through each scene and mark every breakdown element within the scene. Others may take a complete pass through the script marking characters, another pass marking props, and so on.

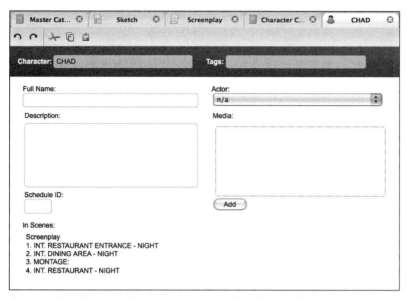

Figure 5.15   Chad marked in scenes 1–4. The Master Catalog has automatically updated the scene list in Chad's form.

Whichever way you break down a script, the outcome should be the same: capturing and cataloging all items that are necessary for effective pre-production. The better your breakdown, the smoother your pre-production and production.

A Complete Script Breakdown

Download the DeliveryDate-DemoBreakdown1 project file from the book's Online Companion website: www.courseptr.com/downloads. Then open the project.

This project file has more thoroughly marked up locations, wardrobe, props, makeup, and other department items.

Figure 5.16 shows the project file's Project Library with a number of catalogs established.

Figure 5.16   The Project Library for DeliveryDate-DemoBreakdown1.

Now open the Master Catalog to see the breakdown forms that have been compiled for pre-production.

You can perform several basic operations from a catalog item's context-sensitive menu. Figure 5.17 shows that right-clicking or Ctrl-clicking on an item allows you to Open, Duplicate, Rename, or Delete the selected item.

Figure 5.17   Context-sensitive menu for Master Catalog item.

Tip: Once in a while, particularly if you're copying and pasting many text blocks from a separate application (Word, Google Docs, whatever) into a Celtx project file, you may inadvertently create a catalog item you don't want or need. If you ever peruse the Master Catalog and spot an item that doesn't belong (for example, a mangled character name), bring up the item's context menu and select Remove. This only removes the item from the Master Catalog, not from the script text. If necessary, you can then search for the item in the Screenplay window and decide if it also needs removal.

Figure 5.18 shows an example of a prop form that has been opened up and fully built out.

Caution: Throughout this chapter, you've been breaking down a locked production script—the traditional starting point for script breakdowns. However, you can easily mark items during the course of script composition, long before the script is locked and in production revision mode.

However, most media professionals and screenwriters would advise against this approach. Early drafts of scripts typically change too frequently. Characters enter and exit scenes, props are changed, computer-generated imagery (CGI) may be added or subtracted, and so on. Although it may be useful to start some breakdown before the script is locked, you are likely to find that this will cost you at least as much time as it saves you.

Prop: Dessert   **Tags:** priority 1

Description:

chocolate cake; something to linger over

Media:

Add

□ Details

Scenes Used In:

Screenplay
3. MONTAGE:
4. INT. RESTAURANT - NIGHT

Characters Used By: (Picklist)

MARGARET, CHAD

Size:

big

Color:

chocolate

Era:

Figure 5.18   A fully filled-out catalog form in DeliveryDate-DemoBreakdown1.

In Chapter 6, "Reinventing Project Scripting I," you'll see how to use the Master Catalog to begin composition on a new script. This could accelerate the script breakdown when you go into pre-production.

Catalog Toolbar

Figure 5.19 shows the Catalog toolbar, which has buttons for several basic operations:

- **Add.** This adds further items to a specific catalog (like a Character Catalog or Prop Catalog), or triggers the Select Item dialog box in the Master Catalog for adding an item in any breakdown category.

- **Remove.** This triggers the Delete Item dialog box for the selected item with OK and Cancel choices.

- **Export Catalog.** This exports the catalog to a comma-separated-value (CSV) formatted file, which can then be read into almost any scheduling, spreadsheet, or database application.

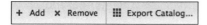

Figure 5.19   Catalog toolbar.

To practice exporting a catalog, make sure Master Catalog is the active tab. Then do this:

1. Click the Export Catalog button in the toolbar. (Figure 5.20 shows the Export List dialog box that is triggered.)

2. Browse and select the folder you would like the file to go into.

3. Change the file name if necessary.

4. Click Save.

Note: Although your walk-through involved the Master Catalog, Celtx exports any catalog that exists in your Project Library.

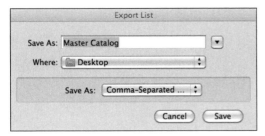

Figure 5.20   The Export List dialog box, triggered when the Export Catalog button is clicked.

You can now export the CSV-formatted file into Excel, Access, and many other programs for further manipulation.

Note: The Save As item in the Export List dialog box lists both comma-separated values and text files as the two exportable file formats. However, both selections generate CSV-formatted files: the first selection appends a .csv extension, whereas the second selection appends a .txt extension. The contents of both are identical.

Printing Forms and Catalogs

You can print individual catalog forms at any time by clicking on the Print button in the main toolbar.

Note: Although you can highlight multiple forms in the catalog, Celtx does not allow batch-printing of forms. The best approach to printing all data in the catalog is to export the catalog to a CSV-formatted file readable by Excel or OpenOffice, and then format and print the exported spreadsheet.

Summary

This chapter covered the following:

- Using the right sidebar to begin the process of script breakdown, which typically happens once you lock your script

- Marking up items in scenes, for compilation in the script's Master Catalog

- Removing item markup when necessary

- Accessing the Master Catalog, and sorting and filtering item categories

- Filling out item forms, to better gather and ratify information about everything from character motivation to prop procurement

- Establishing specific item catalogs for the Project Library

- Breaking down a complete script by marking items scene by scene

In Chapter 6, you learn how to compose a script using a different methodology than what you've seen in Chapters 2 through 5. And Chapter 7 looks at Celtx's Reports features, which allow you to generate breakdown sheets, script notes, audition sides, and other information.

6 Reinventing Project Scripting I

Chapters 2 through 5 walked through a traditional method of scripting a project and moving into pre-production:

- Chapter 2, "Getting Familiar with Celtx," covered Celtx's script editing features to get you started composing a script, outlining with index cards, readying a title page, and distributing the script via hard copy or a PDF.

- Chapter 3, "Project Navigation, Library, Notes, and Media," looked at some of the remaining screen real estate in Celtx to get a grasp on 1) the Scene Navigator and Project Library, and 2) annotation and media attachment features in the right sidebar.

- Chapter 4, "Creating and Editing Production Film Scripts," examined readying a script for pre-production: numbering scenes, locking script and scenes in moving into production revision mode, and adding/deleting scenes and material once you're in production mode.

- Chapter 5, "Script Breakdowns and Catalogs," showed how to break down a Celtx script, building up catalogs and lists that will be crucial when you distribute call sheets, schedules, and other pre-production documents.

Celtx opens new approaches to developing media projects. Not everyone, of course, writes or thinks in the same way. This brief chapter walks through a different way of writing a script, based on the features that have already been covered.

Building Out from Character

In the seminal book *The Art of Dramatic Writing*, Lajos Egri suggests that the writer build character "bone structures" before getting into the nitty-gritty of developing scene structure and linkage. The secret to a good plot, according to Egri, is having that plot grow naturally out of character behavior and the construction of a solid premise.

Character Bone Structure

The Art of Dramatic Writing proposes the use of three main categories for building a character's "bone structure":

- Physiology

- Sociology

- Psychology

The physiology of a character includes gender and ethnicity (when relevant), distinct features, physique, and height and weight.

The sociology of a character includes economic class, occupation, education, religion, family life, and political affiliation(s).

The psychology of a character includes goals, ambitions, frustrations, temperament, judgment, obsessions, attitude toward life, and introvert/extrovert orientation.

Flesh out all three of these categories, and you'll be much further on the path to creating fully realized characters.

You can use Celtx to construct a project using Egri's ideas. You can build out characters and other elements (if you choose to) first and then move to structuring and finally scripting.

To see this in action, begin a new project in Celtx. Use the film template (although you can really use any template to see this approach).

Perhaps you have the basic concept for *Delivery Date* and know who the key characters are. However, you don't know much about them yet and want to build a "bone structure" for each. Along the way, you have a few ideas for possible scenes.

In this approach, the Add icon is frequently used. Click Add, and in the Select Item menu, select Character. In the Item Detail text box, type in CHAD, and then click the OK button.

Chad has now been entered into the Master Catalog for the project, and a breakdown form is available to fill out.

Repeat the operation and add MARGARET as a character. After adding her to the catalog, save the project file as DeliveryDate-EarlyConcept.

Double-clicking on either character entry zooms into a catalog form and allows you to begin making notes about the character.

Figure 6.1 displays a character form for Chad, focusing on the character bone structure that Egri proposes.

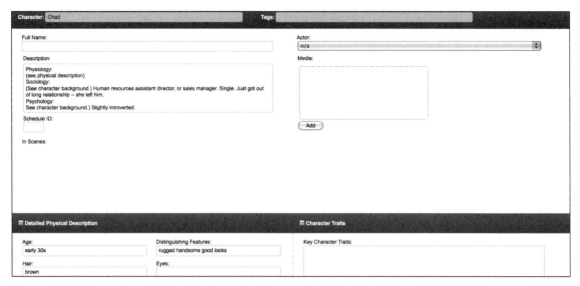

Figure 6.1 Data entered in Chad's character form, using *The Art of Dramatic Writing*'s concept of the bone structure as a template.

Figure 6.2 displays a character form for Margaret, focusing on the character bone structure that Egri proposes.

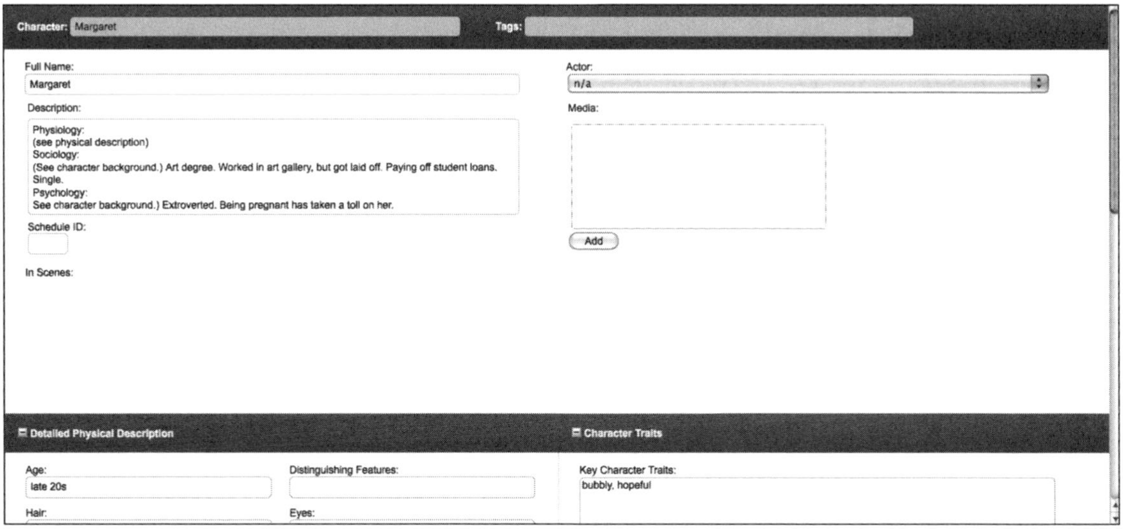

Figure 6.2 Data entered into Margaret's character form, using *The Art of Dramatic Writing*'s concept of the bone structure as a template.

You can, of course, use any template, paradigm, or methodology you want to begin building out your characters.

Using the archetypes identified in Christopher Vogler's *The Writer's Journey*, you might fill out the catalog forms as shown in Figures 6.3 and 6.4.

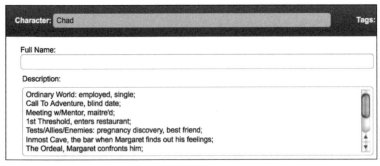

Figure 6.3   Data entered into Chad's character form, using a more archetypal approach.

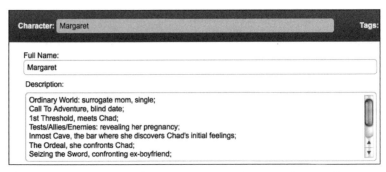

Figure 6.4   Data entered into Margaret's character form, using a more archetypal approach.

You may have some specific casting ideas (two friends or fellow students you really want to work with, or two actors you directed in a community theater play or staged reading). You can add that information into your project.

Click the Add icon in the main toolbar, and in the Select Item dialog box, select Catalog. Then select Actor as the catalog type, and click OK to close the dialog box.

An empty Actor Catalog now exists. A standard Catalog toolbar, offering Add, Remove, and Export Catalog buttons, and a search filter text box, is now available. Click the Add button, and type the name of the potential actor (in this case, Chad Brummet).

Chad Brummet enters the catalog, and as Figure 6.5 shows, you can now fill out basic information about the actor and attach a headshot to the form.

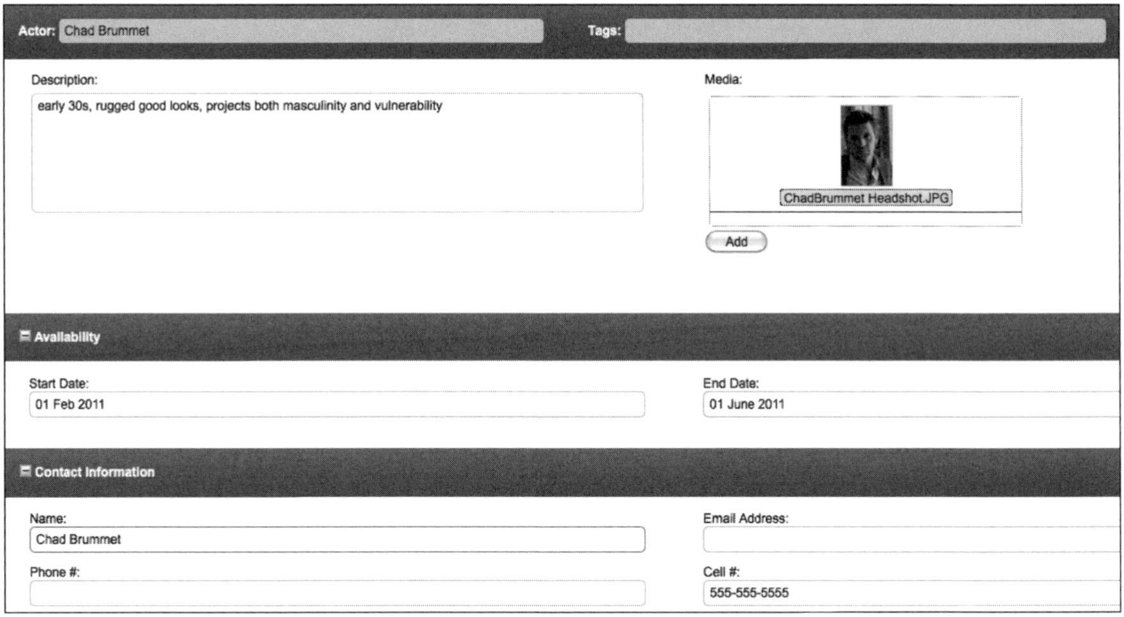

Figure 6.5   Sample actor form, with contact information and headshot.

Tip: You can change the name of catalogs in the Project Library at any time by right-clicking or Ctrl-clicking on the catalog's name and selecting Rename. For example, you can call the Actor Catalog a Potential Actor Catalog or Casting Call Catalog if you want.

You can continue to follow this process with other characters you begin conceptualizing (the best friend, the ex-boyfriend, and so on). You may find that some characters become unnecessary or don't support your core story. You may compile a small actor database: some actors you might audition, and some you won't.

The next section looks at how to use the Master Catalog to build up other aspects of your scripted narrative.

Imagining Scenes

You can begin to build a catalog of scene details, even though you may be a long way from structuring your complete story.

Click the Add icon, choose Scene Details in the Select Item list box, and type in Boy Meets Girl. Click OK to close the dialog box.

If you double-click on this item in the catalog, you'll zoom into a form where you can begin to map out key scene beats, the protagonist and antagonist in the scene, and so on. You may find this a more effective way to outline scenes because of the high level of detail in this form.

Figure 6.6 shows scene details filled out for a sample proposed scene.

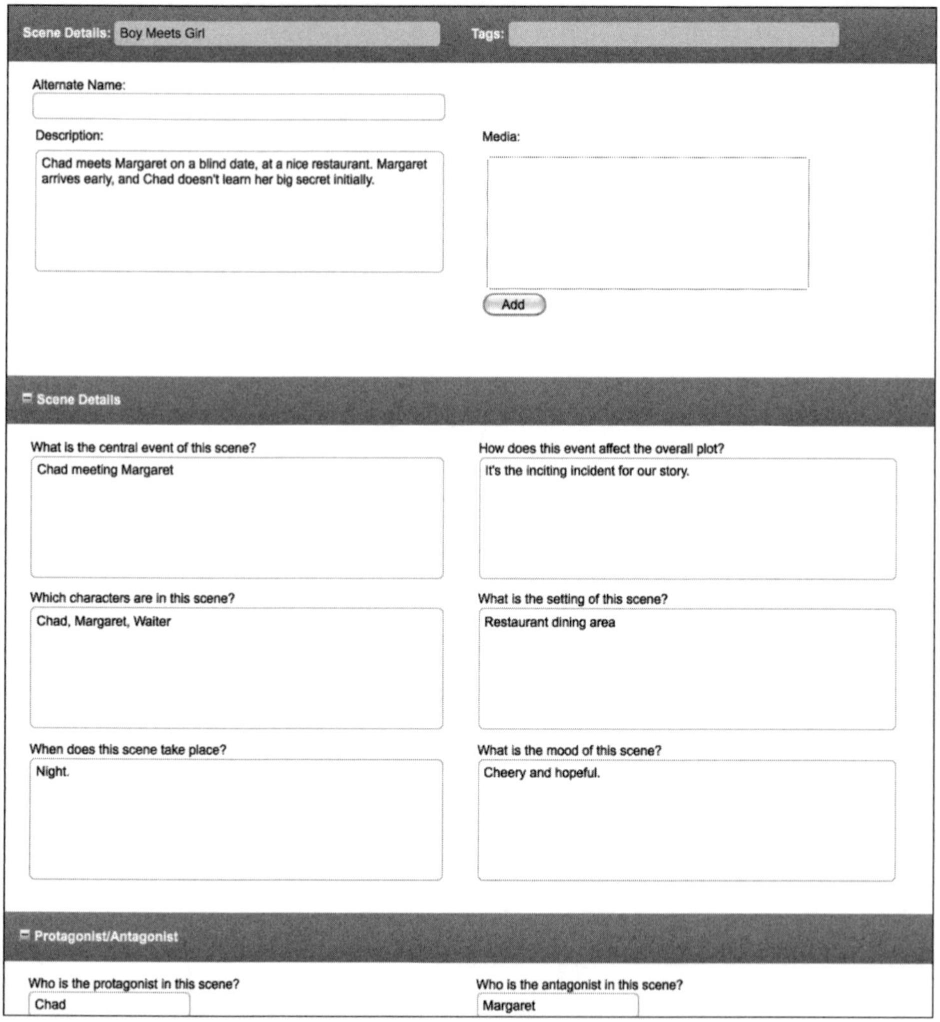

Figure 6.6 A possible scene with numerous details filled in.

Download the `DeliveryDate-SolidConcept` project file from the book's Online Companion website: www.courseptr.com/downloads. Then open the project to see a more built-out version of your script concept.

In Chapters 8, "Storyboards," and 9, "Sketches," you'll see how to add storyboards and sketches to further your concept.

Note: Although a film template was chosen for this walk-through, you could just as easily have chosen a comic book template or novel template to demonstrate this approach to writing. (You wouldn't have needed the Actor Catalog, of course.) You can easily apply concepts from *The Art of Dramatic Writing* and *The Writer's Journey* to any dramatic venue, from stageplay to comic book to novel.

Summary

This chapter has shown a different way to begin writing a script. The point is that Celtx offers you various approaches toward project development. You should experiment with different approaches and find the one that works best for you. (There is no "right" way to write and break down a script.) You may also discover that different approaches have their strengths for different kinds of projects.

In this chapter, you found that you could stay in the Master Catalog and begin to establish catalogs and catalog items for Characters, Actors, and Scene Details. Later on, you can begin to actually script scenes or comic book panels.

But as an alternate example, a video game designer may decide that starting with catalogs for Weapons, Vehicle, and Locations may be more effective (perhaps for kick-starting a concept sketch database). And this could ultimately lead to a project file containing numerous cut scenes to propel a video game narrative.

The next chapter discusses generating reports out of all the scriptwriting, annotating, and break-downs you've done in Chapters 2 through 5.

7 Reports

In Chapter 3, "Project Navigation, Library, Notes, and Media," you looked at how to annotate a script, and in Chapters 5, "Script Breakdowns and Catalogs," and 6, "Reinventing Project Scripting I," you broke down a script and filled out catalogs.

You're able to scroll through and study notes onscreen, and you're able to filter catalogs to concentrate on props or computer-generated imagery (CGI) or whatever you need. You can review your character forms and scene details and begin to draft scenes.

But the need to easily distribute your breakdowns, notes, and partial and complete scripts remains. Whether the distribution is on paper or via a PDF, the people you work with (or for) need the fruit of your labors. Following are some examples:

- A producer or cowriter needs to see script notes

- A location scout needs a list of desired locations

- Casting needs sides (scenes or partial scenes) to distribute to actors for auditions

- Cast and crew need breakdown sheets

This chapter focuses on Celtx's report features.

The Reports Window

Download the DeliveryDate-DemoBreakdown1 project file from the book's Online Companion website: www.courseptr.com/downloads. Then open the project. (You may have already downloaded this file while working in Chapter 5. But make sure you have an unedited version of the file.)

Make sure you're in the Screenplay sheet, and then click on the Reports tab to bring up the Reports window. Figure 7.1 displays the main Reports window when activated, with the right sidebar removed and the left sidebar substituting a Reports window where the Scene Navigator would be in Screenplay mode.

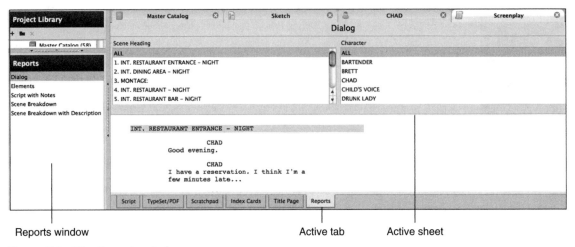

Reports window   Active tab   Active sheet

Figure 7.1 The Reports window.

The Reports panel on the left sidebar provides several categories of reports:

- **Dialog.** This is for distributing sides, or voice scripts or cue sheets for actors.

- **Elements.** This is for generating shot lists, character lists, and other kinds of lists.

- **Script with Notes.** This is for distributing notes with the script.

- **Scene Breakdown.** This is for breakdown sheets.

- **Scene Breakdown with Description.** This generates breakdown sheets that include descriptions for all breakdown items.

Adding Folders to the Project Library

As your Project Library gets built out, you may decide at a certain point that having multiple folders in the library helps with organization.

Perhaps you would like to place all catalogs in a separate catalog folder. In the Project Library panel, click on the Add Folder icon to open the Add Folder dialog box. Figure 7.2 shows the contents of the dialog box.

In the Name text box, type Catalogs. You can then indicate the location for the new folder. (In this case, only one location—the root folder—is possible.) Click OK to confirm.

You can now drag your catalog into the Catalogs folder.

As you head toward production, you may find it useful to have a Catalogs folder, a Storyboards folder, and a Scripts folder (if you have gone in a trans-media direction and have developed scripts for multiple platforms/venues). If necessary, you can even nest folders inside other folders.

Figure 7.2   The Add Folder dialog box (triggered by clicking the Add Folder icon), with a Catalogs folder about to be added.

Dialog Reports

These reports allow you to generate dialog-only printouts or PDFs. You may want to audition actors using a particular scene; you might want to give a heads up to the actor on the totality of his lines; you may be recording all the dialog separately from any live action (for narration, animation, voiceovers, or audio-only scripts); or you may be conducting an ADR session.

Perhaps you would like to produce an audition side for the Host character.

1.   In the Reports panel on the left sidebar, select Dialog.

2.   In the Scene Heading list box, select the first scene.

3.   In the Character list box, select HOST.

The Host has only one dialog line, so as Figure 7.3 shows, you have a short report that you can now print. (In this particular case, where the Host's cues are probably far more important than his dialog, you would probably want to use the entire scene as an audition side.)

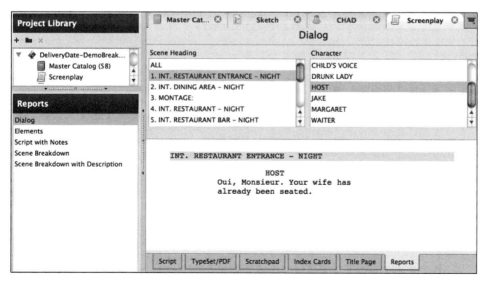

Figure 7.3   A dialog report for the Host: first scene only.

If you would like to assemble all the Host's dialog for a printout, you can select ALL in the Scene Heading list box. In selecting this, you get a list of all the scenes and all the dialog that the Host has. Because the Host speaks only in the first scene, this report is probably less useful to you than the first report you created.

Maybe you want to assemble all the dialog that both Chad and Margaret, the two central characters, have in the script. Assume that Dialog is already selected in the Reports panel.

1. In the Scene Heading list box, select ALL.

2. In the Character list box, select CHAD.

3. In the Character list box, select MARGARET with a Ctrl-click.

You now have a report containing the entirety of Chad and Margaret's dialog throughout the script. A couple of scenes lack dialog for the two, but they are still displayed. (Actually, it's a helpful reminder that the actors playing Chad and Margaret don't have to worry about dialog in those places.)

Tip: You can use the tagging technique employed for selecting actors to tag scenes. For example, you can tag scenes 1 and 3, or scenes 4, 5, 6, and 7—and then select one character or multiple characters for the dialog report.

Finally, if desired, you can print all the dialog for the entire script by selecting ALL in both the Scene Heading and Character list boxes. Figure 7.4 shows the complete script dialog report.

In summary, you can generate a report for any combination of scenes or actors.

Elements Reports

Elements reports allow you to put together any combination of script elements and any combination of scenes to generate customized scripts, scene lists, or shot lists.

Creating an Elements report may be a better way to create audition sides, because you can select all elements and then select one, two, or three scenes to print.

To practice creating an Elements report (again, the DeliveryDate-DemoBreakdown1 project file should be open and the Reports window should be active):

1. Select Elements in the Reports panel.

2. Select ALL in the Scene Heading list box.

3. Select Shot and Transition in the Element list box.

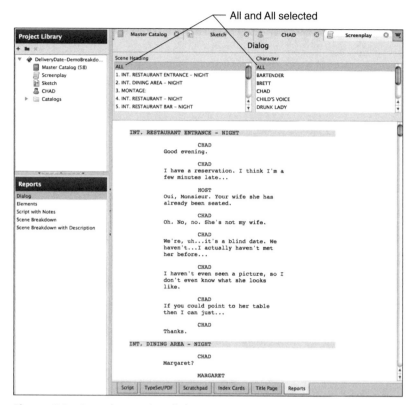

Figure 7.4   Complete script dialog report.

Figure 7.5 shows a simple scene list that includes transitions and other important shots in your script.

If you want to print a complete scene 1 and scene 4 to use as sides, take the following actions:

1. Select Elements in the Reports panel (if already selected, there is no need to reselect).

2. Select scenes 1 and 4 in the Scene Heading list box.

3. Select ALL in the Element list box.

You can customize these sides further, selecting all elements except transitions and parentheticals in the Element list box. In summary, you can customize a script report any way you want: printing only the actions, for example, or printing specific groups of scenes (perhaps for a staged reading excerpt).

Script with Notes Reports

This type of report nicely lays out all script notes with the script itself, something that can be useful during any stage of composition or production.

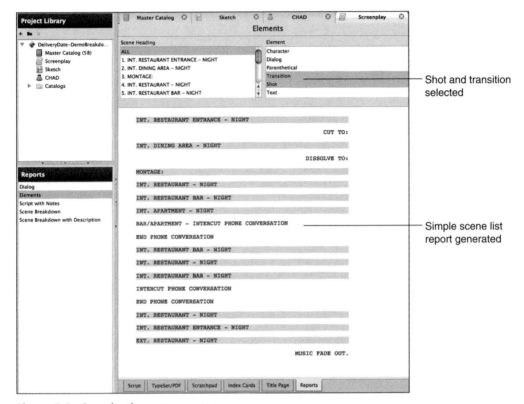

Shot and transition selected

Simple scene list report generated

Figure 7.5 Sample elements report.

To run this report, just select Script with Notes in the Reports panel. As always, you can then decide to print just a portion of the script by selecting specific pages while in the File, Print dialog box.

Figure 7.6 shows a Script with Notes report.

Scene Breakdown Reports

The generation of scene breakdowns is critical in pre-production. You can customize your breakdowns almost any way you want in Celtx.

To run a complete set of scene breakdowns (again, the DeliveryDate-DemoBreakdown1 project file should be open and the Reports window should be active):

1.   Select Scene Breakdown in the Reports panel.

2.   Select ALL in the Scene Heading list box.

3.   Select ALL in the Department list box.

4.   Select ALL in the Item list box.

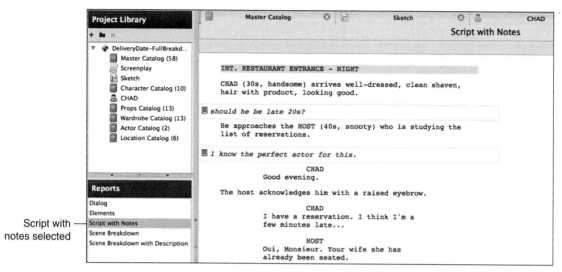

Figure 7.6 Script with Notes report.

Figure 7.7 shows the generation of a complete set of scene breakdowns.

To run a breakdown set just for props, do the following:

1. Select Scene Breakdown in the Reports panel.

2. Select ALL in the Scene Heading list box.

3. Select Props in the Department list box.

4. Select ALL in the Item list box.

If a particular vendor is handling one type of prop, you can customize breakdowns for that vendor. Perhaps wine is being handled by a local wine shop. Follow the same instructions as for the prop breakdowns, but select Wine in the Item list box.

Figure 7.8 shows just that kind of customized scene breakdown.

Your scene breakdowns can include media that's been attached to items. Check the Display Media box to toggle on the media for the wine prop. Unchecking the box removes the media for the current report.

In summary, you can run breakdowns for any combination of departments, and you can tag any combination of items. Typically, you run breakdowns for every department, and you run a complete set of scene breakdowns for an assistant director.

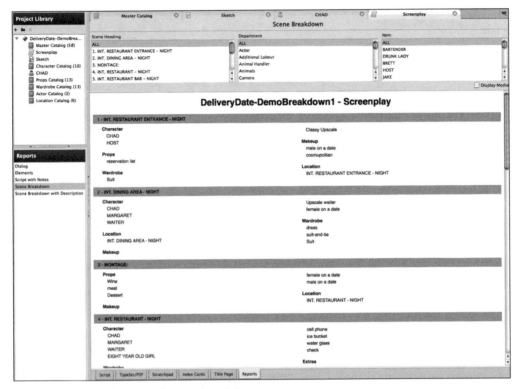

Figure 7.7   Complete set of scene breakdowns.

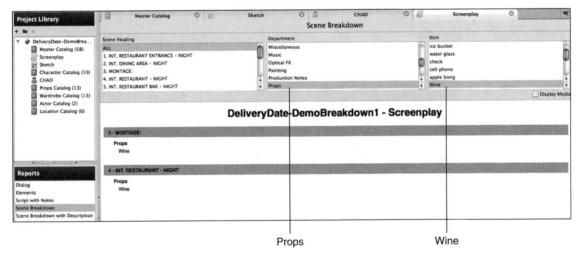

Figure 7.8   Scene breakdown for the Props department, focusing just on wine requirements.

Scene Breakdowns with Description Reports

The final type of report in the Reports panel is a variation on the Scene Breakdown report: Scene Breakdowns with Description includes an item's description in the breakdown.

To run a breakdown set with descriptions just for wardrobe, perform the following steps:

1.   Select Scene Breakdown in the Reports panel.

2.   Select ALL in the Scene Heading list box.

3.   Select Wardrobe in the Department list box.

4.   Select ALL in the Item list box.

Figure 7.9 shows a scene breakdown for wardrobe, which includes the wardrobe descriptions.

Once again, you can display media if desired. You can select as many or as few departments as necessary, and you can select all or some of the scenes for breakdowns.

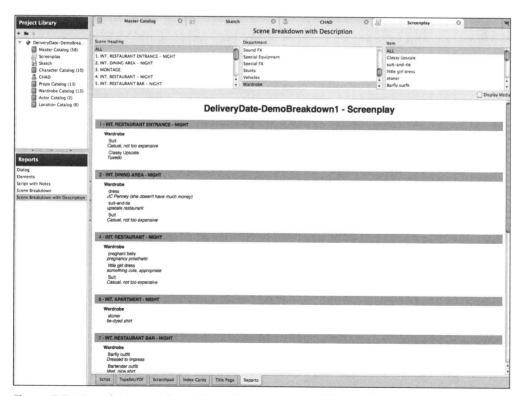

Figure 7.9   Complete scene breakdown for wardrobe, with descriptions.

Printing Reports

You can print all reports by clicking the Print button in the main toolbar.

Note: Currently, Celtx does not provide its own print-to-PDF feature for reports, although this feature may be available as one of your system's print options. Check with your system administrator if you're unsure about this.

Summary

This chapter looked at the following kinds of built-in reports that Celtx generates:

- **Dialog.** This is useful for applications including sides, voiceover sessions, animated character voice recording, actor cue sheets, ADR sessions, and any other dialog-focused needs.

- **Elements.** This is useful for applications including sides, customized partial scripts or partial scenes, shot lists, scene lists, and location lists.

- **Script with Notes.** This is useful for incorporating notes into a printed script for easy review and handwritten annotation.

- **Scene Breakdowns.** This is useful for generating any kind of customized scene breakdowns.

- **Scene Breakdown with Description.** This is useful when item descriptions are needed for customized scene breakdowns.

The next chapter begins examining some of Celtx's more unique features: the capability of adding sketches and storyboards to a project, and integrating this media with the script you've created.

8   Storyboards

*S*toryboarding is the process of using illustrations to pre-visualize shots, character blocking, lighting, set design, and camera placement and movement. Assembling the illustrations in sequence provides a rough feel for the emotional and narrative flow of a scene.

While storyboarding isn't required for the direction or shooting of a scene, many (if not most) directors and cinematographers find storyboards helpful for planning scenes and sequences. Clients and producers may require storyboards as one of the deliverables on a project and may desire review and input on these storyboards.

Storyboarding is appropriate for almost any kind of visual media project: stage plays, video and film shoots, animation and machinima, and even comic books. (The storyboards can be used as guides for design and completion of comic book panels.)

The illustrations can be crude, hand-drawn stickman-type sketches; sophisticated pen-and-ink drawings; or software-enabled renderings (using storyboarding, illustration or other image-creation tools). Artistic perfection is less important than a conveyance of characters and motion in two-dimensional space.

Celtx includes a sketch tool for use in storyboarding that is discussed in the next chapter.

Is Storyboarding a Necessity?

What is the role of storyboarding in creating a time-based media project, and how necessary is it? Matt Page, writer/director of the award-winning short film *Delivery Date* (which has been a model project in these tutorials), weighed in with his thoughts on these questions and on his own experiences storyboarding.

"I learned storyboarding in my high school media class, and I've been using it ever since. Storyboarding helps me plan what kind of equipment I need, how many camera moves I can get away with in one day, and what shots I can afford to get rid of if we're in a time crunch."

Matt itemizes the benefits of storyboarding:

- A realization of the visual style of the film.

- A way to communicate ideas to cast and crew. "For instance, some actors want to know how the shot we're doing fits into the puzzle. I shoot out of order most of the time. Showing the actor the storyboard helps them understand the ever-important 'before and after' of the shot we're doing so they know how to play it in a way that will make their performance continuous. As another example, oftentimes I think I'm being clear when explaining how I want a particular shot—but then when I see the monitor I find that it's not what I asked for. This isn't the DP's [director of photography's] fault. It's my difficulty in accurately describing the shot I see in my head. With storyboards I can show them the frame and draw arrows to indicate screen direction or a dolly move. Then I spend more time saying, 'Let's try slowing down on the push-in and then wait another second before you tilt down.' That's more efficient to me than rehearsing the scene and coming up with the shots on set."

Storyboarding is not about polished images. "The goal of each frame is to convey the lens size, the composition, how the camera moves (if at all), and what action occurs. I don't worry about drawing the right necklace on the female lead."

Matt points out, "There are many successful filmmakers who don't use storyboards." However, he cautions, "If you're not going to use them, at least have a detailed shot list—and pick a DP whose work you like so you'll be happy with the shots you get."

Ultimately, Celtx lets you decide what the best approach is to a project—and whether storyboarding can aid your production's on-set efficiency and final results.

Building a Storyboard

For this tutorial, download the `DeliveryDate-FullBreakdown` project file from the book's Online Companion website: www.courseptr.com/downloads. Then open the project.

Note: Once the project is open, notice that this version has added folders to the Project Library (a feature demonstrated in Chapter 7, "Reports") and consolidated some of the library items into these folders. The script has been locked for production (as discussed in Chapter 4, "Creating and Editing Production Film Scripts"), and an establishing scene has been added in the first set of revisions (*blue pages*).

You also need to download to your local drive several storyboard images from the Online Companion website: `DDShot1-1`, `DDShot2-1`, `DDShot2-2`, and `DDShot3-1`. Place these files in a new folder on your local drive called `DeliveryDate-Storyboards`.

To add a storyboard, click the Add icon in the toolbar. In the Select Item dialog box, choose Storyboard in the Select Item list box.

In the Item Details section of the dialog box, you can do the following:

- Change the name of the storyboard if desired (for example, `Preliminary Storyboard` or `Cut Scene PreViz`).

- Change the `Project Library` folder to place the storyboard in.

- Select the script that the storyboard is assigned to. In this case, select Screenplay.

Figure 8.1 shows a storyboard being added to the Project Library.

Becoming Familiar with the Storyboard Toolbar

With the storyboard added in the Project Library, you are now placed in the storyboard window. Figure 8.2 shows the Storyboard toolbar. The toolbar has four types of controls:

- An Add Sequence button, to build out the storyboard.

- A storyboard player.

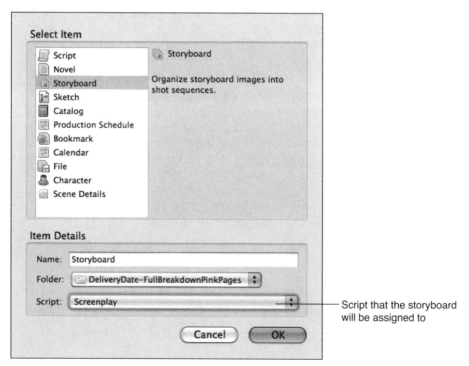

Figure 8.1   Storyboard being added to the Project Library.

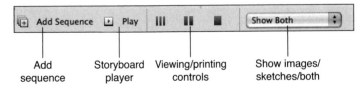

Figure 8.2 The Storyboard toolbar.

- Controls to view and print one, two, or three images across the screen or page.

- A drop-down menu allowing you to Show Images, Show Sketches, or Show Both in the onscreen display. (The Sketch tool is discussed in Chapter 9, "Sketches.") You're likely to have either sketches or images, although it's possible to be using both in a storyboard. When in doubt, it may be best to select Show Both from the menu.

Inserting and Adding Shots

With the storyboard added in the Project Library, you are now placed in the storyboard window; notice that the script's scenes have been picked up as sequences in your storyboard. The Sequences Navigator in the left sidebar allows you to easily navigate between sequences. (Double-clicking a sequence takes you to it.) You can even reorder sequences, although in this example with a script already composed and revised and a breakdown completed, that probably wouldn't be a good idea.

Note: The Sequences Navigator won't bother with A and B scene designations: it simply numbers sequentially. However, the scene headings are identical to those in the script.

You can now begin to add illustrations to create storyboard sequences. The Storyboard window presents your scene heading and frames for shot information and the attachment of the storyboard image.

You start with your establishing shot in scene 0A. (See Chapter 4, where you added an establishing shot prior to scene 1, after you were in revision mode.)

A drop-down menu in the storyboard editing window offers camera angle selections like Wide, Master, and Pan. Select Wide.

A text box provides space for notes, questions, or anything you'd like to tag the storyboard with. If you're still considering options, this is a good place to put them. Input:

`Establishing shot. Jib? Dolly? Boom?`

[Add Image] is a clickable prompt. Once it's selected, you can browse to `DDShot1-1` and open it.

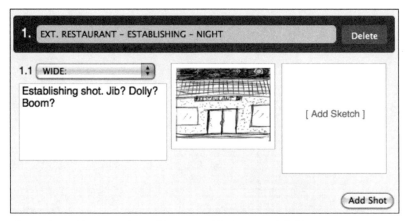

Figure 8.3   First storyboard image added to establishing scene.

Note: [Add Sketch] opens Celtx's Sketch tool, which the next chapter explores.

Figure 8.3 shows the start of the storyboard build. Note that the shot has been numbered 1.1.

Tip: Figure 8.3 depicts the one-shot editing window layout (as opposed to the two-shot or three-shot layout). Use the view/print controls in the Storyboard toolbar to cycle through the different layouts and see their differences.

Because there are no more shots in scene 0A/sequence 1, you can scroll down to sequence 2 and repeat the process:

1. For the type of camera angle, select Two-Shot.

2. In the notes text box, input Chad enters, looking good.

3. Click on [Add Image] and browse to DDShot2-1. Open the file.

You now have shot 2.1, but this scene requires several shots. As Figure 8.4 shows, you can click on the Add Shot button to stay within the scene and move to the next shot.

When you've clicked Add Shot, you see that shot 2.2 is ready for information and image. You can repeat the process you've been using for the downloaded images DDShot2-2 and DDShot3-1 (which goes in the next scene, in the dining area). Figure 8.5 shows the two shots assigned to the Chad/host sequence, with camera angle designations and brief notes, displayed in the two-shot across layout. (Go ahead and change to that layout now.)

Figure 8.4   Adding shots within storyboard sequences.

Figure 8.5   Sequence 2 showing two shots, using the two-shot across layout.

Moving Shots and Using the Sequences Navigator

The storyboard window offers standard drag-and-drop manipulation for shots that have been inserted. For practice, try dragging shot 2.1 and seeing if you can insert it after shot 2.2. Then see if you can reverse the reorganization.

Dragging and dropping shots allows you to experiment with the ordering of shots in your scenes. You may find new ways of conveying suspense or creating humor by changing your shot orders; this may trigger additional production script revisions.

The Sequences Navigator offers the possibility of reshuffling sequences or shots with Move Down/Move Up buttons.

Note: You can also drag and drop sequences in the navigator, just like you can drag and drop scenes and index cards in their respective navigators.

Figure 8.6 shows the Move Down and Move Up buttons. Try moving the establishing restaurant shot into a later sequence and then moving it back to the top of the film. The navigator also allows you to move shots around within a single sequence.

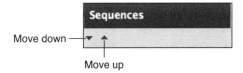

Figure 8.6   The Sequences Navigator's Move Down and Move Up buttons.

Once you've finished this practice, save the project file as `DeliveryDate-FullBreakdown& Partial Storyboard` on your local drive.

Adding Sequences

Sometimes, it may be necessary to add one or more additional visual sequences that haven't been scripted. (You may do the scripting later, or you may bypass it if this is a last-minute addition to production.)

Figure 8.7 shows the Add Sequence button in the Storyboard toolbar. Clicking the Add Sequence button places an additional sequence at the end of the current sequence order. You can then move the sequence to any location in the Storyboard using the Sequences Navigator's Move Down/Move Up buttons. You can rename the sequence by triggering the context menu of the item.

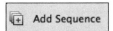

Figure 8.7   The Add Sequence button in the Storyboard toolbar.

Deleting Shots

You can delete shots easily. For practice, add one more shot to the dining area sequence. This should create shot 3.2. Notice that once you click in the shot frame, a Delete button (X) is available. You can also delete just the image, while retaining the shot frame, indicated camera angle, and notes. Figure 8.8 shows the new shot frame, along with the Delete buttons. (Chapter 9 discusses sketches.)

Go ahead and delete the empty shot frame.

Tip: The two-shot and three-shot layouts enable separate Delete controls for frame and image; the one-shot layout only has a Delete control for the entire frame.

You can easily scroll from sequence to sequence and add shots and storyboard images as necessary, further building your script's storyboard.

You can expand the Sequences Navigator to display every shot. Click on the arrow just to the left of numbers 1 and 2. Your shot notes now function as a "title" for the shot. Figure 8.9 shows all the shots displayed in the Sequences Navigator.

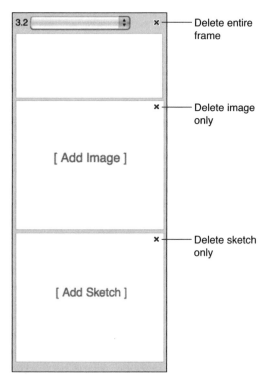

Figure 8.8 New shot frame and Delete buttons.

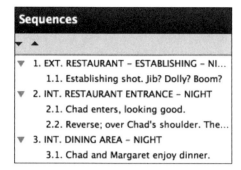

Figure 8.9   Shots expanded in the Sequences Navigator.

Playing Back the Storyboard

Figure 8.2 shows the location of the storyboard player in the toolbar. To use it, click the Play button.

As Figure 8.10 shows, a new storyboard image viewer window (separate from the Celtx project file window) opens. A Control toolbar opens at the bottom of the window, along with a Shot Playback Delay toolbar.

The default delay between images is 2 seconds. Clicking the + button increments the delay; clicking the − button decreases the delay. You may prefer a 4- or 5-second delay: try changing the delay just to see how that works.

Click the Play button in the Control toolbar to see the storyboard play in slideshow style, with the delay between images that you just set.

Although the sample here is brief, you can already see how useful this feature is: with a completed storyboard, you can literally play back a simple animatic—a pre-visualization of your film.

The Control toolbar allows you to rewind to the first shot or fast forward to the last shot. Forward and reverse controls are also available, like almost any music or video playback system.

When you are finished playing back the storyboard, you can close the window and return to your Celtx project file.

Storyboard Image Sizes and Aspect Ratio

Images are compressed as necessary to fit into Celtx's storyboard panels. As a general rule of thumb, your storyboard images should be small: JPEGs or PNGs are ideal image formats.

When played back in the image viewer, the images are stretched anamorphically if necessary and presented in a 4:3 aspect ratio, with a white border placed around a 160×120 pixel frame.

Control toolbar

Play button

Shot Playback
Delay toolbar

Figure 8.10   The storyboard playback window.

Printing the Storyboard

To print your storyboard, follow these steps:

1. Make sure the storyboard is the active window.

2. Select your preferred layout on the toolbar (one-, two- or three-shots).

3. Click on Print in the main toolbar, or pull down the File menu and choose Print.

4. Your printer driver and setup may offer the option of printing to a PDF (for electronic distribution); if you're on a Mac, you probably also have the option of creating a Preview (which defaults to PDF format). Otherwise, you can print a hard copy of the storyboard.

Figure 8.11 shows the results of printing to PDF or hard copy: scenes, shot numbers, shot notes, and images are laid out for reference or annotation.

Figure 8.11 Sample page from storyboard printout/PDF.

Viewing a Fully Storyboarded Script

Download the DeliveryDate-FullBreakdown&Storyboard project file from the book's Online Companion website: www.courseptr.com/downloads. Then open the project and select the storyboard window from the Project Library.

Click the Play button from the storyboard window to open the playback window. Click the Play control to see a full playback of the storyboard for the script.

Summary

This chapter looked at the following:

- Building a storyboard by designating shots within sequences defined by the script's scenes

- Adding shots within sequences

- Moving shots between sequences and changing the order of sequences in the overall narrative

- Playing back shot sequences in a continuous pre-visualization of the shooting script

- Printing the storyboard

The next chapter looks at how Celtx's Sketch tool can contribute to storyboarding.

9 Sketches

For most productions, storyboarding doesn't need to get fancy or sophisticated. Any basic rendering of the shot should be all that you need. But your stickman images may still be less than satisfactory if you're a perfectionist—and scanning images for digital conversion can be time consuming. Yet, you may not want to master another software program just for creating basic storyboards.

Alternatively, you may have storyboard images, yet sometimes need to create a sketch to convey a last-minute scene that was added, or a Plan B for a particular shot.

Or, you may elect to map out floor plans of your shots, either as companions to an existing storyboard or as the sole storyboard for your project.

Celtx provides a Sketch tool for creating basic storyboard images. This chapter explores use of the tool.

There are two primary approaches to using Celtx's Sketch tool, although you can also combine these two approaches into a third approach:

- Creating standalone sketches that can be placed into one or more folders within the Project Library. (You don't need to place sketches into folders, but more than a few sketches likely dictates further organization in the Project Library.)

- Creating sketches that are gathered into the storyboard either as accompaniment to uploaded images or as the primary type of image for the storyboard.

- Creating some standalone sketches, as well as sketches within the storyboard.

Creating Standalone Sketches in the Project Library

Download the `DeliveryDate-FullBreakdown&Storyboard` project file from the book's Online Companion website: www.courseptr.com/downloads. Then open the file. (If you just completed Chapter 8, "Storyboards," you may already have this file on your local drive.)

You've probably already noticed that every Celtx project file, when created, includes a `Sketch` item already in the Project Library. Double-clicking the `Sketch` item opens the Sketch window, along with a Palettes sidebar on the right side.

"Sketch" is a pretty generic name—not too helpful if you really start creating sketches. You can rename the Sketch item and any other item in the Project Library by right-clicking or Ctrl-clicking on the item and choosing Rename from the context menu.

For practice, name this Intro Host; then click on the OK button to confirm the name change. Notice that the window tab name updates at the same time the Project Library item updates.

Figure 9.1 shows the Intro Host window and the default Palettes sidebar.

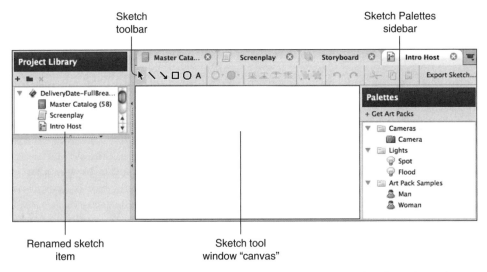

Figure 9.1   Renamed Sketch item in Project Library panel, the Sketch tool window "canvas," and the Palettes sidebar.

Building a Sketch

The default Palettes sidebar, which comes with the basic Celtx download, provides a limited set of 2D objects to begin sketching floor plans of shots:

- Camera

- Spot Light

- Flood Light

- Man

- Woman

It's not much, but it still allows you to draw up a basic floor plan for shots involving actors.

Note: Celtx provides for a vast expansion of these objects, with the addition of low-cost art packs. Chapter 17, "The Celtx Community," discusses these art packs, along with other low-cost add-ons that extend Celtx's capabilities.

It's possible that your team's or institution's Celtx installation already includes additional art packs. This chapter just uses the default palette's objects; see Chapter 17 for more ideas on how to use an expanded array of objects.

Aside from placing and manipulating objects on your canvas, you can draw basic shapes and add text to your sketches.

You can drag objects onto the canvas and then rotate and resize them. Try dragging Man onto the canvas. Figure 9.2 shows the object placed, as well as rotate and resize handles on the object.

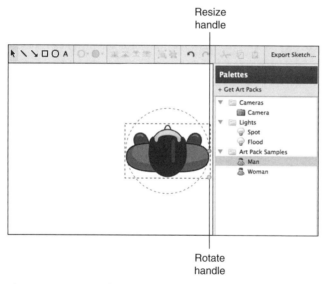

Figure 9.2   Man object placed on the Sketch canvas, with handles for rotating and resizing.

You'll create a top-down view of the first moment you see the host in the story (fortunately, a pretty simple shot).

The shot is an over-the-shoulder one from Chad's point of view as the host hovers over the podium. Experiment with the rotate and resize handles to see how they work, and drag a second Man object onto the canvas. Figure 9.3 shows a second male character placed within the scene.

At this point, you'll add a camera and a spot light. By now you know the steps for placing objects in the sketch:

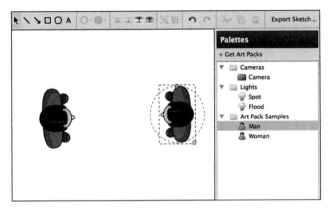

Figure 9.3 Two male characters placed within the shot.

1. Drag the desired object onto the sketch canvas.

2. Resize and rotate the object as needed.

Figure 9.4 shows the complete shot sketched out, with two male characters, a camera, and two spot lights positioned.

Figure 9.4 Camera and spot lights added to over-the-shoulder shot.

Note: It's probably a good idea to save the project file at this point, while you continue exploring the Sketch tool.

Using the Sketch Toolbar

The Sketch toolbar offers a number of typical drawing functions (moving from left to right on the toolbar):

- Drawing tools for lines, arrows, circles, rectangles, and text boxes
- Fill and stroke color selectors for shapes

- Upper/lower plane selectors, allowing the user to control which object will be on top and which will be on bottom when two objects overlap

- Group and ungroup tools

- Undo, cut, copy, and paste editing tools

Figure 9.5 examines the Sketch toolbar and breaks out its tool sets.

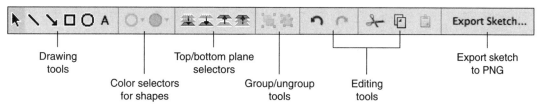

Figure 9.5 The Sketch toolbar.

Grouping and Overlapping

Once you have multiple objects placed on the canvas, you can group objects and move several objects as a unit. Grouping the two male characters involves three steps:

1. Click a male character to select the object.

2. Shift-click a second male character. (The object clicking order—left to right or up then down—doesn't make a difference.)

3. Click on the Group button. (Look for the text tip to pop up, if you're unsure which button this is.)

Figure 9.6 shows the two characters now grouped together (a single highlight box surrounds them).

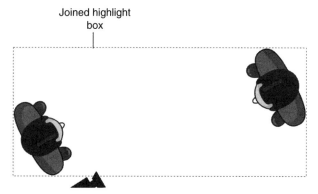

Figure 9.6 Two characters grouped.

Now try moving the characters around the canvas. Notice that they move in tandem.

Once you've moved the grouped objects, try using the Undo button on the toolbar to return them to the original position.

Caution: You may discover with your mouse or touchpad that you can "draw" a box around a group of objects to temporarily group them and move them in tandem. However, this temporary grouping disappears when you do additional editing in the sketch. To permanently group objects together, be sure to use the Group button on the Sketch toolbar.

You can group as many objects as you want—there's no limit.

Now try moving the group so that the left character has the camera overlapping his shoulder. Chances are, the character is on top of the camera. To correct this:

1. Select the object to shift its top or bottom placement. (In this case, click on the camera to adjust the 2D plane it lies on.)

2. Click the Raise button in the toolbar.

Figure 9.7 shows the results when you click the Raise button. The camera is now on the upper plane, hugging the character's shoulder.

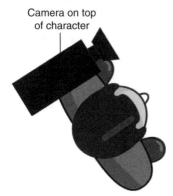

Camera on top
of character

Figure 9.7 Camera object raised to upper plane in sketch.

The four plane selectors follow:

- **Lower to Bottom.** If you have multiple overlapping objects, this lowers the selected object(s) to the bottom of the stack.

- **Lower.** This lowers the selected object(s) one layer.

- **Raise.** This raises the selected object(s) one layer.

- **Raise to Top.** If you have multiple overlapping objects, this raises the selected object(s) to the top of the stack.

If you decide later on to ungroup an object set, the steps are simple:

1. Select the grouped set. (You see the dotted highlight box around the group; in this case, it should be the two male characters.)

2. Click the Ungroup button in the toolbar.

Drawing Tools

See if you can return the shot sketch to roughly the way it looked in Figure 9.4.

Labeling your characters and making any necessary shot notes is generally useful, especially for anyone else you're sharing this sketch with.

To label the left character (Chad), do the following:

1. Click on the text box button (the A).

2. Click on the canvas where you want the text label (anywhere near Chad is fine).

3. An Edit Text dialog box pops up. Here you can input text, add italic or boldfacing (or both), and change the font and font size. Input Chad and change the font size to 20 points.

4. Click the OK button to finish inserting the text label on the canvas.

Figure 9.8 shows the Edit Text dialog box in use.

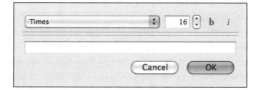

Figure 9.8   Edit Text dialog box, triggered when the text box button is selected and the user has clicked on the desired text box location.

Notice that the text box button remains selected, making it easy to add additional text boxes.

See if you can add a second text box that contains the text Host.

Tip: Grouping the character with the character's name label is a good idea. If you have to reposition the character, the name label will then move in tandem.

Figure 9.9 shows the sketched shot with both characters labeled.

Figure 9.9 Both characters labeled in the sketch.

You can add some simple camera notations with another text box. Create a third text box and input Shot: Clean Single on Host.

Figure 9.10 shows our sketched shot with both characters—and the camera shot—labeled.

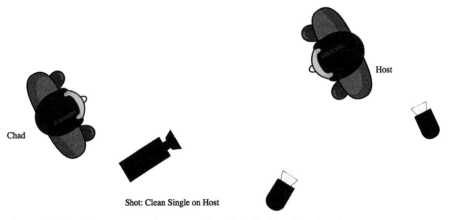

Figure 9.10 Characters and camera shot labeled in the sketch.

If necessary, you can move the text boxes for better placement. Make sure you're back in selection mode (the first button clicked on the toolbar); then click on a text box. You can now drag the text box wherever you want.

Tip: Double-clicking a selected text box opens the Edit Text dialog box so that you can edit the text box.

If you want, you can now place circles or rectangles around the text boxes. Click the Rectangle tool to activate it, and draw a rectangle (by clicking and dragging) around the Chad text box.

The rectangle overlays the text, but as already demonstrated in the chapter, you can select the rectangle and then click the Lower toolbar button to tuck it beneath the text. You can proceed to use the Stroke Colour and Fill Colour buttons to further customize the text box.

Adding a New Standalone Sketch to the Project Library

Adding a new sketch to the Project Library is just like adding any item:

1. Click on the Add button.

2. From the Add Item dialog box, select Sketch from the list box on the left.

3. In the Name text box, change the generic `Sketch` name to `Host POV`.

4. Click the OK button.

Figure 9.11 shows a complete sketch for the reverse shot, shooting over the shoulder of the Host character to focus on Chad.

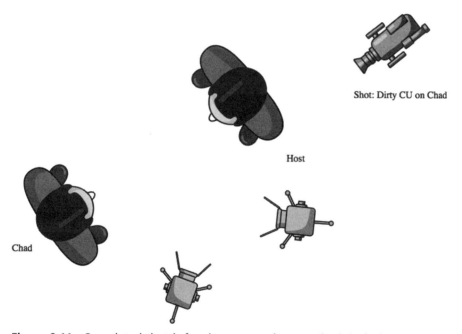

Shot: Dirty CU on Chad

Host

Chad

Figure 9.11 Completed sketch for the reverse shot on Chad, including text labels. The *CU* in one text label represents a close-up.

Try to create a similar-looking sketch by using the techniques discussed in this chapter.

Managing Standalone Sketches in the Project Library

You should now have two sketches in the Project Library: `Intro Host` and `Host POV`.

Unique sketch names definitely help navigation, but if you use the Project Library to create many sketches, the library quickly becomes cluttered.

Creating a folder to hold all the sketches is useful.

As discussed in the sidebar titled "Adding Folders to the Project Library" in Chapter 7, "Reports," you can click on the Add Folder icon inside the Project Library sidebar to open the Add Folder dialog box. In the Name text box, input Sketches.

Figure 9.12 shows the new Sketches folder in the Project Library.

Figure 9.12   New Sketches folder in the Project Library.

You can drag the two sketches (Intro Host and Host POV) into the Sketches folder. As this action illustrates, organizing your materials helps you quickly find items when you need them. When you've finished moving the sketches into the Sketches folder, be sure to save the project file.

Tip: You can add folders inside of other folders, making it possible to nest folders. As an example, you can create sketch folders for each of your scenes. Celtx encourages a consistent information hierarchy; the bigger your project, the more you are rewarded for organization.

Creating Sketches Within the Storyboard

You may prefer to consolidate sketches in a single storyboard. For this tutorial, continue using the DeliveryDate-Breakdown&Storyboard project file. (If it becomes necessary, download a fresh copy of the project file from the Online Companion website found at www.courseptr. com/downloads.)

Activate the Storyboard window and scroll down to Scene 5, where storyboard images for shots 5.1 through 5.4 reside. (Alternatively, you can double-click on Scene 5 in the Sequences Navigator.)

Add sketch

Figure 9.13   The [Add Sketch] button in the Storyboard window.

Figure 9.13 shows the shot 5.1 frame with the [Add Sketch] button. Click the button to open a sketch window.

Notice that the window is automatically titled shot 5.1. (The tab shows the name.) Building a sketch here is, of course, identical to the process discussed in the previous section.

Figure 9.14 shows a completed sketch of a top-down view of shot 5.1. See if you can create a similar-looking sketch, using the basic objects provided in the Sketch tool and the techniques discussed earlier in this chapter.

Note: For a more detailed top-down view of shot 5.1 using Celtx's add-on artpacks, see Chapter 16, "Celtx Add-Ons, Utilities, and Sketch Images."

Once you've finished your sketch, move back to the Storyboard window and navigate to scene 5 again so you can build a sketch for shot 5.2.

Figure 9.15 shows a completed sketch of a top-down view of shot 5.2, along with tabs for the two sketches. If your sketch looks similar to the figure, you've mastered using the Sketch tool.

Save your project file. To display your sketches in the storyboard, select Show Sketches in the drop-down list box in the Storyboard toolbar. Figure 9.16 displays the Show Sketches selection, along with the view of a scene 5 sketch.

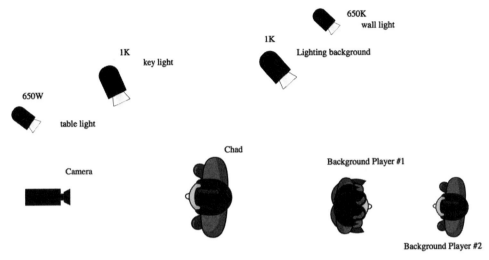

Figure 9.14 A top-down view of shot 5.1, designed using the Sketch tool.

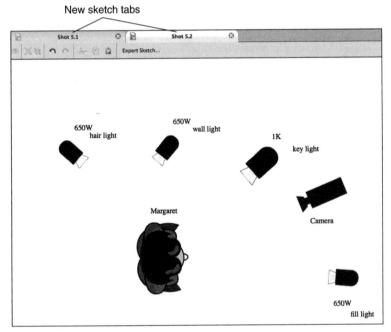

Figure 9.15 Top-down view of shot 5.2, and tabs for the new sketches.

Show Sketches

| Show Images |
| Show Sketches |
| Show Both |

— Drop-down list box for controlling storyboard displays

Figure 9.16 Show Sketches selected in the Storyboard toolbar.

Caution: Closing sketch windows before saving the project file may result in losing the sketch window. As Figure 9.17 shows, Celtx triggers a Save Document dialog box when you attempt to close an unsaved sketch in the storyboard, confirming your intention to delete the sketch.

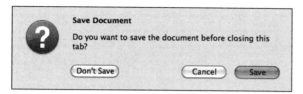

Figure 9.17   Closing an unsaved storyboard triggers the Save Document dialog box.

The drop-down list box in the Storyboard toolbar provides three display options:

- Show Images
- Show Sketches
- Show Both

Experiment with all three selections to see how you can control the storyboard display.

Note: Through version 2.9, Celtx does not play back sketches in a simple animatic, like it can with storyboard images. (See Chapter 8.)

Exporting and Printing Sketches

Sooner or later, it becomes useful to share the sketch, import it into another image viewer or image manipulation program, or import it into a PowerPoint presentation or Word document.

Earlier in this chapter, Figure 9.5 showed the location of the Export Sketch button in the Sketch toolbar. With a sketch window open, click Export Sketch to trigger the dialog box.

Figure 9.18 shows the Export Sketch dialog box, which allows you to uniquely name the sketch, decide which folder it should go into, and identify that the sketch will be exported into a PNG format—a universal format for viewing, editing, and printing images.

To directly print a sketch from the Celtx project file, simply click on the Print icon in the toolbar. If you plan to print sketches, you may want to input more identifying text inside text boxes placed on the Sketch canvas.

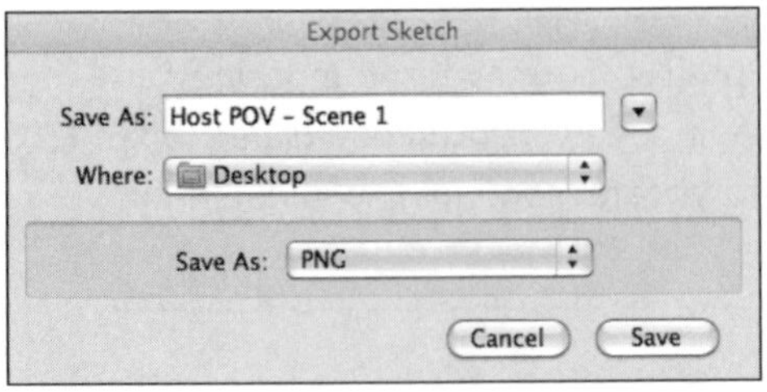

Figure 9.18 Export Sketch dialog box, triggered from the Sketch toolbar.

Sketch printouts are generated in one of two ways:

- From the sketch editing window, you can print standalone sketches, one sketch at a time.

- From the storyboard window, you can select to a) show sketches, or b) show both sketches and (storyboard) images. You can then generate a printout similar to the sample shown in Figure 8.11 in Chapter 8.

Standalone Sketches Versus Storyboard Sketches

You can continue to add sketches for some or all of your shots within the storyboard. You can also continue to add standalone sketches—either to provide top-down views of your shots or for other purposes.

Whether to build standalone sketches in the Project Library, or sketches contained in the storyboard, is really your decision. Storyboard sketches are best used as specific aids for storyboarding (providing convenient floor plans for shots and blocking). Standalone sketches can also be used this way, but they may be even better used for additional floor plan or side view designs. (See Chapter 16 for a discussion of additional sketch art packs that vastly expand the capabilities of the Sketch tool.)

Sketches Versus Images

Celtx's Sketch tool is a simple aid for floor plan designs and other designs (if additional sketch images are acquired, as discussed in Chapter 16). For some projects, simple floor plan sketches may be all you need for helping to pre-visualize your production.

Furthermore, the additional Celtx sketch images make it possible to easily storyboard comic books, without the need for creating images by hand or on a computer.

Storyboard images created using other illustration programs or by hand (and then digitized) clearly give you a much broader scope of visuals. For many projects, this may be a preferred method of pre-visualization.

You may also find that using both images and sketches helps your project. The choice is yours, and the only way to find out your preferences is to try out both the storyboarding and sketching features in Celtx.

Summary

This chapter looked at the following:

- Building standalone sketches using the basic object palette provided by Celtx

- Using the Sketch toolbar to further manipulate objects and customize content

- Renaming sketches and creating a sketch folder for storing standalone sketches

- Adding sketches within the storyboard, either serving as adjuncts to other storyboard images or serving as the primary storyboard image creator

- Displaying sketches only within the storyboard

- Printing sketches

- Using Celtx's Sketch tool as either an addition or an alternative to attaching storyboard images

Chapter 8, "Storyboards," and Chapter 9, "Sketches," have explored Celtx's pre-visualization features. Chapter 10, "Reinventing Project Scripting II," looks at how to build a script thinking in visuals first, as many comic book artists and animation artists do (from the classic days of Disney 2D animation to state-of-the-art Pixar animation).

10 Reinventing Project Scripting II

Chapters 8, "Storyboards," and 9, "Sketches," looked at Celtx's storyboard and sketch tools as part of a pre-production workflow triggered when a script was locked and breakdowns had begun (or even concluded). Traditionally, especially in live action films, this was when storyboarding commenced.

Historically, however, animated films and cartoon shows frequently started with storyboarding. And now that production teams may be formed rapidly and expected to develop projects within days, storyboarding may begin simultaneously with—or may even precede—scripting. In addition, some media creators may be far more comfortable "outlining" a script by starting with storyboards.

Recognizing that the definitions of and approaches to scriptwriting have continued to expand, the Writers Guild of America has been actively organizing animation creators and video editors when they have been clearly structuring the narrative and creating the story for animated films, "reality" television, video games, and other "new media" formats. Screenwriting has, indeed, changed.

This chapter demonstrates a much more visually oriented approach toward scripting.

Storyboarding Scripts

So what if you're a graphic artist first, and you decide to build your story through storyboards?

This tutorial borrows from *Deja Vu*, an award-winning animated short made by filmmaker Sean Hannon, to illustrate a storyboard-first approach to scripting.

Download these files from the book's Online Companion website (www.courseptr.com/downloads): `dejavu-storyboard_01`, `dejavu-storyboard_02`, `dejavu-storyboard_03`, `dejavu-storyboard_04`, `dejavu-storyboard_05`, `dejavu-storyboard_06`, and `dejavu-storyboard_07`. For organizational purposes, place them in a folder called `DejaVu Storyboards`.

Chapter 8 walks you through the storyboarding process from the vantage point of a script in pre-production or nearing pre-production, but you'll go step by step here as you imagine building a storyboard that becomes the springboard for a script.

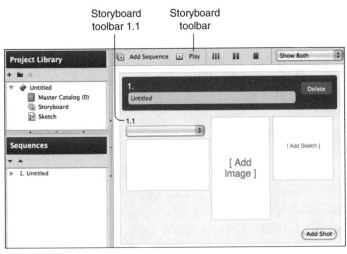

Storyboard
toolbar 1.1

Storyboard
toolbar

Figure 10.1   New project file opened when Storyboard project template has been selected from the Welcome to Celtx screen.

Start up Celtx, and in the Welcome to Celtx screen, select Storyboard from the Project Templates list box. Figure 10.1 shows the results: a new project file with the Storyboard window front and center, and Sequence 1 and Storyboard 1.1 ready to be filled out.

Sequence 1 has been started but is untitled. You can start to fill the sequence with some storyboards, following these steps:

1. Click the Add Image button in the first storyboard panel.

2. Browse to the `DejaVu Storyboards` folder you set up earlier.

3. Select `DejaVu-storyboard_01`.

4. Open the image file.

Figure 10.2 shows the first storyboard image inserted into the first sequence.

This is the title sequence, and it will be a single shot. Now click on the Add Sequence button in the Storyboard toolbar. (See Figure 10.1 if you're not sure where the toolbar is.)

As Figure 10.3 shows, you now have a second sequence added.

To add storyboard image 2.1, do the following:

1. Click the Add Image button in storyboard 2.1.

2. Browse to the `DejaVu Storyboards` folder you set up earlier.

3. Select `DejaVu-storyboard_02`.

4. Open the image file.

Figure 10.2 Storyboard image inserted into the storyboard. (The editing window is currently in a one-across layout.)

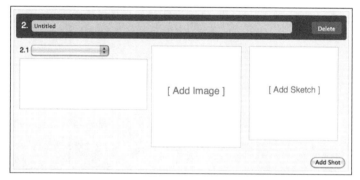

Figure 10.3 Sequence 2 added to the storyboard.

Sequence 2 has a number of storyboards. See if you can follow the same approach in inserting images 3 through 7. As Figure 10.4 shows, you should end with sequence image 2.6.

Save your work in progress. You can call it `DejaVu-FirstStoryboards`.

Now you'll go back and begin scripting these images.

Scroll back up to Sequence 1. Name this sequence `Title`.

Then click on the drop-down list box and choose Extreme Wide Shot.

In the text box below that, input the following:

`Title Shot - Deja Vu`

Figure 10.5 shows the first sequence with name and notes entered.

Storyboards in Sequence 2 also need names and notes. See if you can enter the following information for these storyboards. (Don't forget to save your work occasionally.)

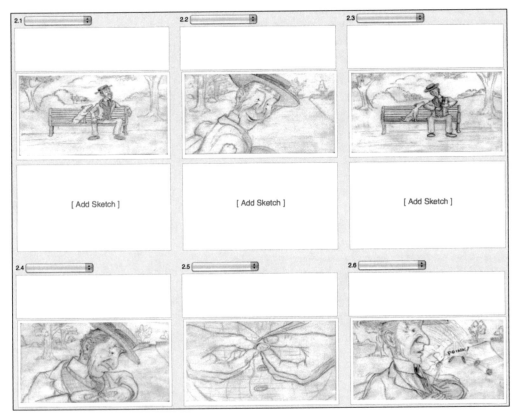

Figure 10.4   Storyboard Sequence 2: six images, using the three-across layout. Shot 2.6 is a close-up, as a button pops up and strikes the protagonist's nose.

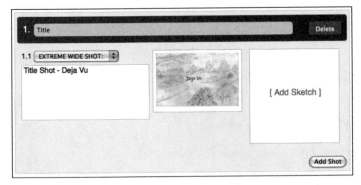

Figure 10.5   Sequence 1 named and brief notes entered.

- Title for Sequence 2: MacAlistair And Chester In Central Park.

- Storyboard 2.1: Shot, WIDE; Notes, An elderly man, MACALISTAIR, sits on a park bench. His dog, CHESTER, paws at his elbow.

- Storyboard 2.2: Shot, OVER THE SHOULDER; Notes, Chester gets his master's attention.

- Storyboard 2.3: Shot, TWO SHOT; Notes, MacAlistair tells Chester he gets it, and he's ready to go home.

- Storyboard 2.4: Shot, MEDIUM CLOSE-UP; Notes, MacAlistair starts buttoning the vest, but it's not so easy.

- Storyboard 2.5: Shot, CLOSE-UP; Notes, MacAlistair is having a lot of trouble with the button.

- Storyboard 2.6: Shot, MEDIUM SHOT; Notes, The button suddenly pops up, hits MacAlistair on the nose, and ricochets to the ground.

Figure 10.6 shows Storyboard 2.6 with image and basic script information.

As Chapter 8 discussed, you can begin to use the Sequences Navigator in the left sidebar to expand and collapse sequence images (see Figures 8.6 and 8.9). Move Up and Move Down buttons allow you to move around individual images, reordering the story sequencing.

The Storyboard toolbar (refer to Figure 10.1) provides a Play button, allowing you to run a simple pre-visualization animatic of the images. See Chapter 8 for a fuller discussion of this feature.

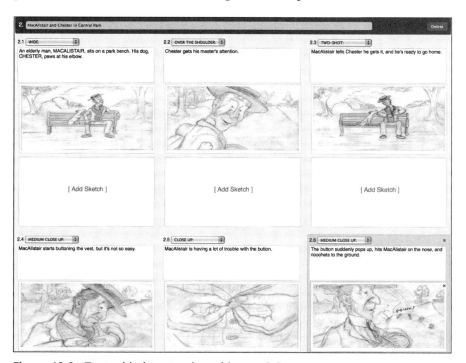

Figure 10.6 Text added to storyboard image 2.6.

Figure 10.7   The storyboard playback tool in operation, currently paused at the second shot.

Figure 10.7 shows the animatic being run for *Deja Vu*.

If you want, you can download a more built-out storyboard for *Deja Vu* from the book's Online Companion website (www.courseptr.com/downloads): dejavu-bigger_storyboard. This can offer you an opportunity to experiment with storyboarding features and even allow you to start building an index card outline or write opening scenes for the script. (Two sample index cards are included in the file.)

Continuing to Build via Visualization

You can continue building the project through storyboards first, and then moving back to some initial note-taking that can ultimately evolve into a production script (whether for a screenplay, a stageplay, or even a comic book). You can add in sketches as well. (See Chapters 9; 13, "Celtx Script"; and 17, "The Celtx Community.")

Is this a better way to develop a time-based media project? For some creators, it might be. If you think in pictures first, try this approach; you may find it frees you to concentrate on the project as you see it, rather than concentrating your efforts on dialog and stage directions.

In this chapter's example, you had the good fortune of having sequential storyboards to begin building your narrative. Clearly, you might have storyboards for partial sequences and sequence concepts. You might storyboard some sequences, script out other sequences, and then fill in the gaps as necessary. You may be in a collaboration where one person scripts and the other person storyboards, and each works at a preferred pace tackling different sequences.

There is no right way or wrong way to build a project. The goal is to build a project as creatively, rapidly, and effectively as possible. You may think better in pictures, or you may think better in traditional scripted scenes. As Yoda famously said, there is no trying—there is only doing.

Summary

This chapter looked at a nontraditional, more art-centered approach to building a project. You can decide to script a narrative through storyboards or sketches first. You may be partnering with other collaborators with different skill sets: so as one person scripts, another person storyboards.

Traditionally, software applications have had a tendency to dictate user approach to projects; Celtx's goal is to enable the user to find his own best approach to media pre-production.

The next chapter looks at the detail-oriented process of production calendaring and scheduling and how Celtx can integrate this into the pre-production workflow.

11 Calendaring and Scheduling

Production is all about keeping on schedule. Fall behind, and your costs start ballooning. Do that frequently, and you won't be able to keep personnel beyond their scheduled days, meaning you'll have to start cutting corners and omitting scenes.

Traditionally, an assistant director created calendars, schedules, and call sheets by hand after a script was laboriously broken down. More recently, software applications have been designed to handle production scheduling, but this has meant using one application to script, another to tag the script, another to storyboard, and still another to break down the script and schedule production.

Celtx's primary goal is to better integrate the entire pre-production workflow. This includes providing calendaring and scheduling features and the ability to produce and distribute call sheets—an on-set necessity. This chapter explores these essential pre-production features.

Calendaring

Celtx has a built-in calendar tool for tracking events and tasks. For this tutorial, download the `DeliveryDate-FullBreakdown&Storyboard` project file from the book's Online Companion website: www.courseptr.com/downloads. Then open the project.

Caution: It's a good idea to save your project file after making various edits and additions as you'll do in the chapter. You can also set the auto-save feature by pulling down the Tools menu and choosing Options. (See Appendix D, "Menu Bars and Icon Toolbar," for a full discussion of all menu options.)

To add a new calendar in the project file, follow these steps:

1. Click the Add button in the toolbar.

2. The Add Item dialog box appears. Select Calendar on the left side of the dialog box.

3. If necessary, you can change the name of the calendar in the Name text box, but for now, keep it as `Calendar`.

4. Click OK.

Figure 11.1 shows the new calendar that has been created. Notice that it has been added to the Project Library.

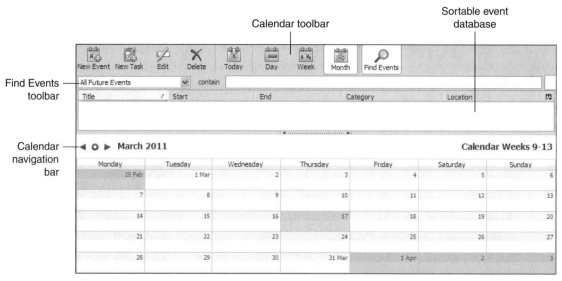

Figure 11.1   New calendar added to project file.

A project calendar might be particularly useful in the initial development and pre-production phases, although you can maintain it throughout production. You can use the calendar for anything from keeping track of project collaborators' anniversaries and birthdays to scheduling client meetings and casting sessions.

In addition, you can use a calendar as a project management tool, tracking tasks and their status and progress toward completion.

Celtx's calendar separates events and tasks. The following sections look at each of these.

Events

Events can be one-time appointments or time commitments, or they can be repeating meetings, anniversaries, and so on.

Setting Up Events

Your production team might schedule a weekly phone meeting to discuss progress. To enter a new event, click the New Event button in the toolbar.

Figure 11.2 shows the New Event dialog box, with event data entered. You'll fill out the following data fields:

- **Title.** In the text box, input Weekly Pre-Prod Phone Meeting.

- **Location.** In the text box, input over the phone.

- **Category.** Select Projects from the drop-down list box.

- **All Day Event check box.** Leave this unchecked.

- **Start.** Select April 5, 2011 from the pop-up calendar, triggered when you pull down the Date list box; select 1:00 p.m. from the Time list box. (Notice that the time is set using a 24-hour clock, so 13:00 indicates 1 p.m. You can select 5-minute increments.)

- **End.** Select April 5, 2011 from the pop-up calendar, triggered when you pull down the Date list box; select 1:45 p.m. from the Time list box. (Again, this uses a 24-hour clock.)

- **Repeat.** Select Weekly from the drop-down list box.

- **Reminder.** Select 15 Minutes Before from the drop-down list box.

- **Description.** Input the following: Weekly team member updates and task assigning.

Figure 11.2   New Event dialog box, with data fields filled in.

Click on the Save and Close button. Figure 11.3 shows the calendar with the weekly meeting now entered.

Now you'll set up a second calendar event. You can double-click on a desired date to set up a new event. Use the navigation bar if necessary to scroll to April 2011.

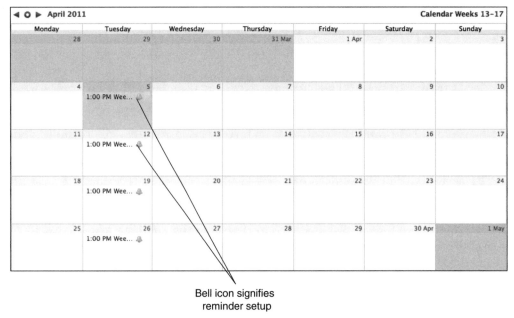

Bell icon signifies
reminder setup

Figure 11.3   Weekly meeting (with reminder) calendared.

Tip: The navigation bar contains Forward and Backward buttons, as well as a Today button situated between them.

Double-click on April 6, 2011. Figure 11.4 shows a New Event dialog box filled out with a one-time event.

To see what happens when you close the dialog box without trying to save, click the Close button in the title bar. As Figure 11.5 shows, the safety net of a Save Event dialog box is triggered, checking to see if you want to save, not save, or cancel the action. Select Save. The calendar now has both a weekly event and a one-time event entered.

Calendar Views

The toolbar includes daily, weekly, and monthly view buttons (like almost any desktop or mobile calendar application). Try out each of the views to see how they look. Figure 11.6 shows a weekly view of the April 4–10, 2011 calendar.

Editing Events

Perhaps you would like to change the Husband's birthday! entry to a dinner appointment with the spouse:

Figure 11.4 One-time birthday event entered.

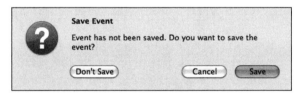

Figure 11.5 Save Event dialog box, triggered when you close an event dialog box without previously saving your additions or changes.

1. Select the calendar entry to edit—in this case, Husband's birthday! (the entry should be highlighted after the selection).

2. Click the Edit button in the toolbar.

3. Make the necessary changes in the Edit Event dialog box. (In this case, uncheck All Day Event; set the Start time to 6:00 p.m.; and set the End time to 8:00 p.m.)

4. Click the Save and Close button in the dialog box.

Follow these steps to edit any calendar entry.

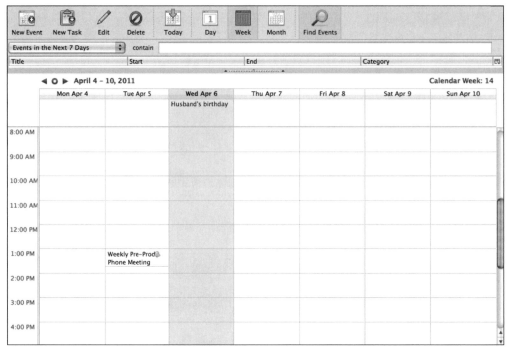

Figure 11.6 Typical weekly calendar view.

Tip: Double-clicking the calendar entry also triggers the Edit Event dialog box.

Finding Events

Figure 11.7 shows what happens when you click on the Find Events button in the toolbar. (This is typically already activated when you start a new calendar.) A sortable columnar list of calendared events is displayed between the toolbar and the calendar.

The headings selector allows you to control which column headings to display. Click on the selector to display the headings. Checked headings will display. Then try checking Location to add that heading to the list.

You can search for specific types of events using the Find Events toolbar above the column headings. The drop-down list box on the left allows you to narrow the list of events to today's events, the next week's events, the next two weeks' events, the next 31 days' events, or the current month's events.

Caution: The drop-down list box setting search range criteria is always based on the system's current calendar date. If today is October 19, 2011, the next 31 days' events will span the range from October 20 to November 19.

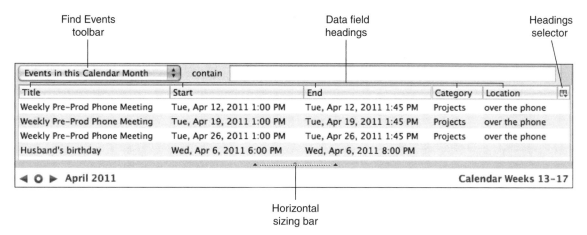

Figure 11.7   Find Events button selected in the toolbar; sortable list of events displayed.

The Search box allows you to type in any phrase, such as phone meeting, to restrict your listing. Figure 11.8 shows the results of this search, based on a 31-day lookup.

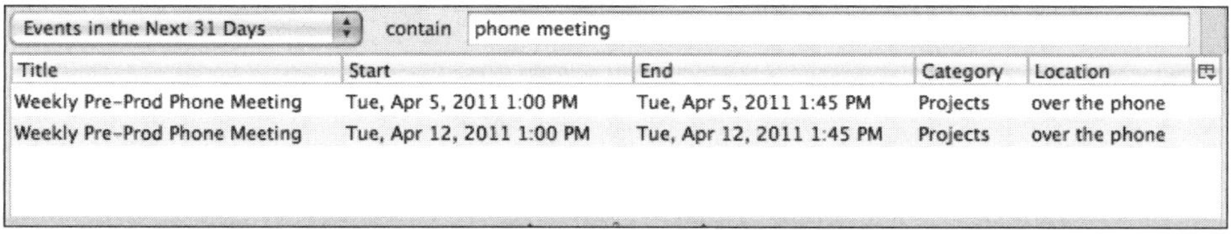

Figure 11.8   All phone meeting entries searched for and listed.

Note: A horizontal sizing bar separates the Find Events window from the calendar. (See Figure 11.7 for its location.) You can click on the sizing bar to collapse the window at any time, or you can resize the window if you'd like. (If you've collapsed the window, click the sizing bar to reopen the window.)

Clicking Find Events toggles off the columnar display.

Deleting Events

For this walk-through, make sure you're currently in the monthly view and that you're displaying April 2011, where we've entered two events.

Follow these steps to delete an event:

1. Select the calendar entry to delete—in this case, any of the Weekly Pre-Prod Phone Meeting entries. (The entry should be highlighted after the selection.)

2. Click the Delete button in the toolbar.

3. Because this event is a weekly one, a Delete Repeating Event dialog box pops up. As Figure 11.9 shows, you have a choice of deleting a singular instance of this event or deleting all instances of this event. Click on the Delete Just This Occurrence button.

Weekly Pre-Prod Phone Meeting
is a repeating event

Delete just this occurrence

Delete all occurrences

Cancel

Figure 11.9   The Delete Repeating Event dialog box.

Tip: If the entry was a one-time event, clicking the Delete button immediately deletes the event.

Tasks

Task assignments turn the calendar into a basic project management tool. You can track task progress, adjust the duration of tasks, and check them off when completed.

Setting Up Tasks

For project management purposes, you can set up tasks that you can track in the calendar. To set up a task, click the New Task button in the Calendar toolbar. (See Figure 11.1 for the toolbar location.)

Figure 11.10 shows the New Task dialog box, with task data entered. This dialog box works much like the New Event dialog box. Fill out the following data fields:

■ **Title.** In the text box, input Scout Locations.

■ **Location.** In the text box, input various.

■ **Category.** Select Projects from the drop-down list box.

■ **Start.** Select April 7, 2011 from the pop-up calendar, triggered when you pull down the Date list box; select 9:00 a.m. from the Time list box. (Notice that the time is set using a 24-hour clock, and you can select 5-minute increments.)

■ **Due Date.** Select April 21, 2011 from the pop-up calendar, triggered when you pull down the Date list box; select 9:00 a.m. from the Time list box.

- **Status.** Select In Process from the drop-down list box. You'll see that you can also designate the task as Needs Action, Completed On (where you'll then specify a completion date) and Cancelled.

- **% Complete.** Input 0; you can set this anywhere from 0 to 100.

- **Repeat.** Keep Does Not Repeat as the setting.

- **Reminder.** Keep No Reminder as the setting.

- **Description.** Input the following: `Scout possible shooting locations`.

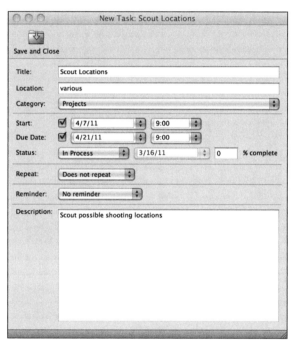

Figure 11.10   New Task dialog box, with data fields filled in.

Click the Save and Close button. Figure 11.11 shows the new task placed in a sortable task list in the left sidebar, underneath the Project Library.

For further practice, set up a second task. Figure 11.12 shows a New Task dialog box setting up a prop acquisition expedition.

Once you've filled out the data fields as Figure 11.12 shows, click the Save and Close button to place the new task in the task list in the left sidebar. (As with the New Event dialog box, you can click the dialog box's Close button instead, and a Save Task dialog box double-checks your intent—a nice little safety feature!)

Sortable   Heading
column headings   selector

Figure 11.11   New task entered in a task list displayed in the left sidebar.

Figure 11.12   New Task dialog box with task data entered for prop acquisition.

Viewing and Sorting the Task List

The task list has sortable data field headings, such as Done, Priority, and Title. You can add, change, or reduce the headings you want to display. Adding another data field's heading involves two steps:

1. Click the heading selector. (See Figure 11.11 for its location.)

2. Check the desired heading. (In this case, check Due.)

The Due Date heading should now be added to the displayed columns. Click on the Due Date column heading to sort the currently listed tasks by due date. Clicking the second time on Due Date reverse-orders tasks by their due date.

Figure 11.13 shows the heading selector menu pulled down, with Done, Due, and Title currently checked.

Figure 11.13   Heading selector menu, with Done, Due, and Title selected.

Tip: You can click and drag the vertical sizing bar to enlarge the task list layout. This is especially helpful if you decide to display a number of data fields that you can sort by.

Editing Tasks

Editing a task is as simple as double-clicking the task in the task list. This opens the Edit Task dialog box (which is identical in content to the New Task dialog box displayed in Figure 11.10), where you can update the status, percentage of completion, and other fields.

You can cancel a task in the Status field and still keep it on the task list. (For example, you might cancel the acquisition of a shooting permit that you now realize you won't need.) This will retain a record of time spent on a task, even if the task is cancelled later.

Completing Tasks

Figure 11.14 indicates the best way to indicate task completion. Checking off the task in the Done column removes the task from the to-do list.

Done
check box

Figure 11.14 The Done column check box, used when a task is completed.

For practice, mark the Scout Locations task as done. The task disappears from the to-do list. But to take pride in your work and review any completed tasks, mark the Show Completed Tasks check box. Figure 11.15 shows the check box marked, and the Scout Locations task with a strike-through to indicate completion.

Show completed
tasks check box marked

Strike-through for
completed tasks

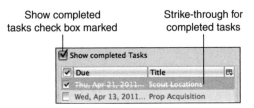

Figure 11.15 Showing completed tasks in the task list.

If you inadvertently mark a task as complete, simply uncheck the Done box next to the task. This removes the strike-through and returns the task to the active to-do list.

Deleting Tasks

Sometimes you may set up a task and realize later on that it never belonged in your to-do list. Eliminating a task is simple:

1. Select the task you want to delete in the calendar. (For our walk-through, select the Purchase Props task.)

2. Click on the Delete button in the Calendar toolbar. (Alternatively, you can press Delete on the keyboard.)

Maintaining Multiple Calendars

Like any item in the Project Library, you can rename the calendar (or duplicate or delete it) via its right-click or command-click context menu. (See Chapter 3, "Project Navigation, Library, Notes, and Media," for a full discussion of how to use the Project Library.) You can name the calendar Project Management Calendar or Mary's Calendar—whatever is useful.

You can also maintain multiple calendars in the same project file. As an example, you can have a Wardrobe Calendar, a Project Management Calendar, and a Team Calendar. This makes the most sense with larger productions; for smaller productions, one calendar is probably sufficient.

Note: As of version 2.9, you cannot print Celtx calendars. However, you can share them with other users through Celtx Studios, which is discussed in Chapters 14, "Celtx Studios: Creation and Administration," and 15, "Celtx Studios: User Interaction."

Scheduling

If necessary, download the `DeliveryDate-FullBreakdown&Storyboard` project file from the book's Online Companion website at www.courseptr.com/downloads.

You can add a production schedule in the same general way you added a calendar early in this chapter:

1. Click the Add button in the toolbar.

2. The Add Item dialog box appears. Select Production Schedule on the left side of the dialog box.

3. If necessary, you can change the name of the production schedule in the Name text box, but for now, keep it as Production Schedule.

4. Pull down the Script drop-down list box and select Screenplay. (Because project files can have several scripts contained in a single project, you need to specifically select the script you're creating a production schedule for.)

5. Click OK.

Figure 11.16 shows the new production schedule that has been created. Notice that the production schedule has been added to the Project Library.

The Production Schedule window contains the following:

■   A scrollable scene database to assist with scheduling

■   A sizing bar to collapse or expand the database as necessary

■   A production calendar

■   Subtabs for Production Schedule and Reports

Production Scheduling

Production scheduling includes the determination of scene lengths (*eighths*) and script days, along with the setting of start and end dates for shooting.

Figuring Production Scene Lengths

Traditionally, scenes are measured using eighths of a page. For example, a scene may span 2 4/8 pages (that is, 2 1/2 pages) or 1 5/8 pages.

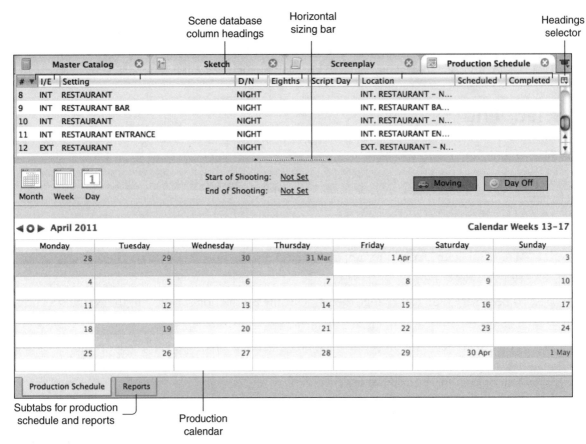

Figure 11.16 New production schedule added to project file.

Letter-sized pages contain 54 printed lines (6 lines per inch, with a one-inch top and bottom margin). A4 paper, used in Europe and many other countries outside of North America, can contain 57 printed lines due to its longer length.

Fifty-four (or 57) divided by 8 is roughly 7—so 7 lines will constitute 1/8 of a page.

In practice, some rounding is inevitable, but with a little practice measuring scenes, you'll soon be able to decide whether a scene runs 2 3/8 or 2 4/8 pages with confidence.

The Scene Database

The top part of the production schedule contains a columnar scene database. The default column display is for all fields in a scene record:

- Scene number
- Interior or exterior

- Setting

- Day or night

- Scene length (eighths)

- Script day (that is, the shooting day)

- Location (full screen heading, including interior/exterior, setting, and day/night)

- Scheduled (date)

- Completed (date)

As is typical with a columnar data display, columns are sortable by clicking on the headings. You can try this later in the chapter, in "Sorting the Scene Database."

Figure 11.17 shows the headings selector menu, brought down when you click on the Field Selector button to the right of the column headings. Here you can control the selection of fields displayed by checking or unchecking field names. For example, you can skip displaying the Completed column until production is underway.

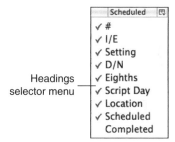

Figure 11.17   Headings selector menu showing selected and available fields to display in the columnar database. Note that Completed is unchecked.

Note: The scene database is collapsible and resizable using the horizontal sizing bar (see Figure 11.16). Sometimes you may want to concentrate solely on the production schedule; other times the display of both scenes and calendar will be useful.

The Scene Data Form

Figure 11.18 shows the Edit Scene dialog box, opened when you double-click on any of the scene records in the database.

All the dialog box fields were listed in the previous section. Only three of the fields are actually editable here: Description, Eighths, and Script Day. The top three fields in the dialog box are

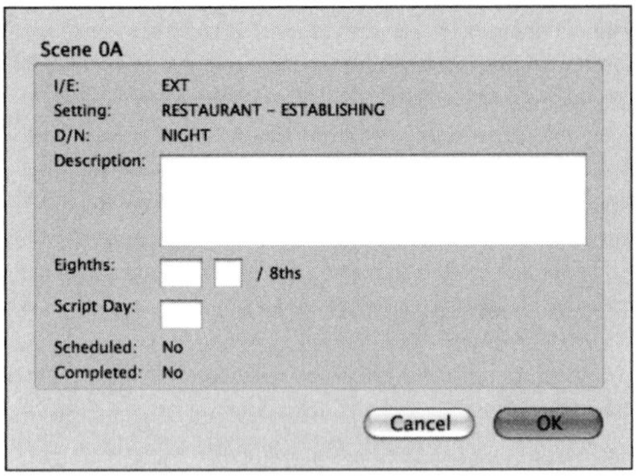

Figure 11.18   Edit Scene dialog box, triggered by double-clicking a record in the scene database.

established in the scene heading, and the last two fields adjust when the record interacts with the production calendar (to be described later).

As usual, you can either OK or Cancel any changes. Go ahead and keep this dialog box open as you move forward.

Scheduling Scenes

You'll work with the scene database first, assigning descriptions and lengths to scenes. If you've continued from earlier, you should have the establishing exterior restaurant scene open. If not, go ahead and open it (by double-clicking) from the scene database. You'll begin supplying additional information for the scene, as described here:

1.   As you shall see shortly, brief scene descriptions will be useful when you print schedules. In the Description text box, input Establishing restaurant.

2.   This scene is merely an eighth of a page. Enter 1 in the Eighths box. You can either leave the Whole Number Box blank or enter 0.

3.   You can assign a shooting day (Script Day) immediately—or figure out your schedule using the production calendar. For now, leave the Script Day field blank.

4.   Click OK to update the record.

Try this with the next record (INT. RESTAURANT ENTRANCE). Input Chad enters restaurant in the Description text box. Enter 1 and 1 in the Whole Number and Eighth fields. Skip the Script Day field and click OK for the changes.

This process would continue if you worked through an entire script. But in the interest of convenience, go ahead and download the DeliveryDate-EditedSceneRecords project file from the book's Online Companion website at www.courseptr.com/downloads. Then open the project.

Sorting the Scene Database

You can visually sort the database by clicking on the column headings. For example, you can sort scenes by their length by clicking on the Eighths heading. The first click sorts the scenes from shortest to longest length (low to high), whereas a second click reverses the sort so you can examine the longest scenes at the top of the database list.

Figure 11.19 shows a low-to-high sorting of scenes by their lengths.

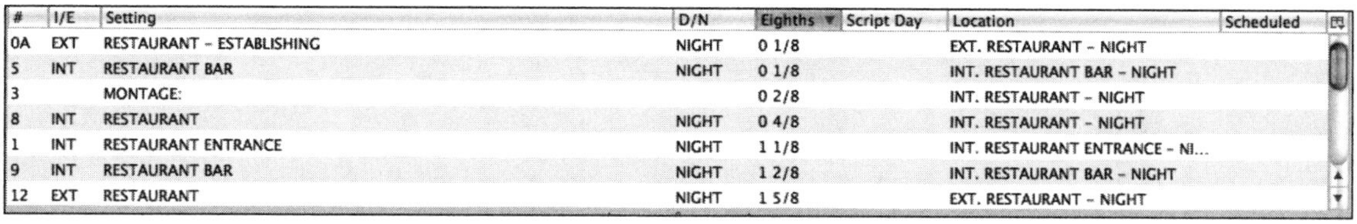

#	I/E	Setting	D/N	Eighths ▼	Script Day	Location	Scheduled	
0A	EXT	RESTAURANT – ESTABLISHING	NIGHT	0 1/8		EXT. RESTAURANT – NIGHT		
5	INT	RESTAURANT BAR	NIGHT	0 1/8		INT. RESTAURANT BAR – NIGHT		
3		MONTAGE:		0 2/8		INT. RESTAURANT – NIGHT		
8	INT	RESTAURANT	NIGHT	0 4/8		INT. RESTAURANT – NIGHT		
1	INT	RESTAURANT ENTRANCE	NIGHT	1 1/8		INT. RESTAURANT ENTRANCE – NI...		
9	INT	RESTAURANT BAR	NIGHT	1 2/8		INT. RESTAURANT BAR – NIGHT		
12	EXT	RESTAURANT	NIGHT	1 5/8		EXT. RESTAURANT – NIGHT		

Figure 11.19 Scenes sorted by length, from shortest to longest.

Re-sorting the scenes by scene number simply requires a click of the # heading.

Setting Shooting Dates

The area above the production calendar provides for bracketing the start and end of your shooting schedule and setting up off days and moving days (when necessary). You can also choose to view the calendar by month, week, and day.

To set the first day of shooting, click the link next to the Start of Shooting prompt. (It should read Not Set.)

Figure 11.20 shows the Shoot Days dialog box triggered when you click on either the Start of Shooting or End of Shooting prompt.

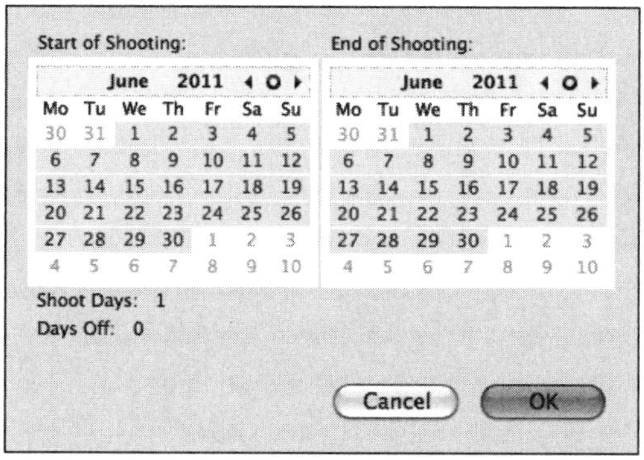

Figure 11.20 Shoot Days dialog box for setting the start and end of shooting.

The two calendars (for start and end) are standard scrollable calendars. For the Delivery Date shooting schedule, do the following:

1.   Select June 1, 2011 for the start of shooting.

2.   Select June 5, 2011 for the end of shooting.

Note: Notice that as soon as you select a start date, the end date calendar automatically jumps to the start month if necessary.

The Production Schedule display now shows the start and end dates, notated in year-month-day format.

The production calendar remains on the current date (or whatever last date you advanced it to), but using the calendar's Back and Forward buttons, you can move to June 2011 to see the start and end calendarings displayed. Figure 11.21 shows June 2011 with start and end dates marked.

One month back, go to today, one month forward calendar navigation buttons

Figure 11.21   Start and end dates marked for shooting.

Tip: If you're using a netbook or other small-screen device, you may have trouble fully seeing date markups on the calendar. Be sure to collapse the scene database if you need to expand your calendar view.

With the start and end of shooting set, you can now mark any off days or moving days in your schedule. For this example, assume that June 3 has been reserved for a different project, and you need to make this a nonshooting day for cast and crew.

Two buttons, for Moving and Day Off, are designated. Drag the Day Off button onto the June 3 calendar space. Figure 11.22 shows the results of this action: you'll see that Day Off is now marked for the date.

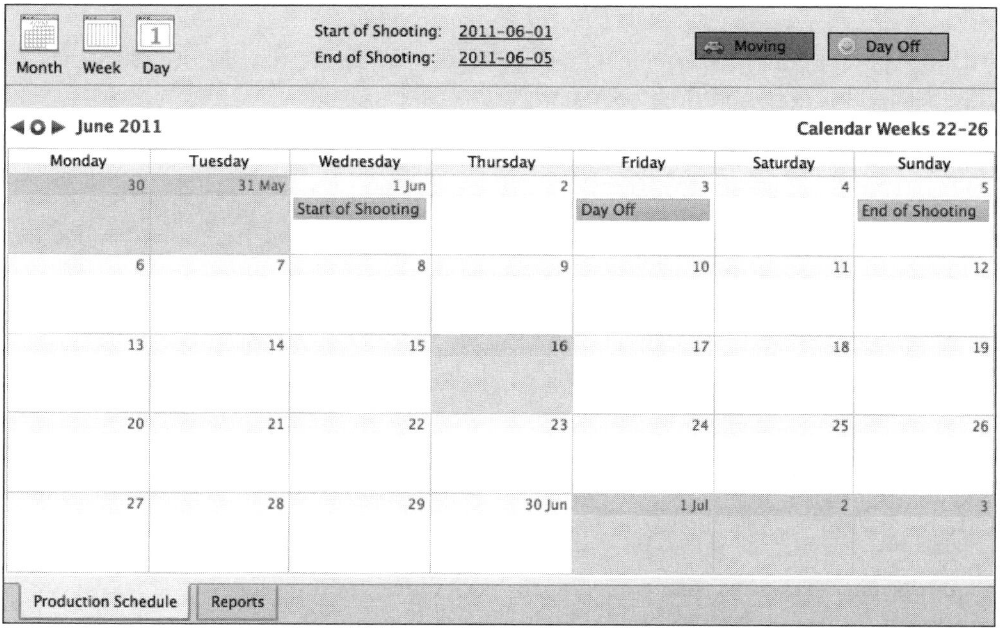

Figure 11.22   June 3 marked as Day Off—after dragging the button onto the date.

Although this production doesn't require a move, others may—and dragging the Moving button onto the date marks it for that task.

Tip: The default time set for Moving is 8:00 a.m. to 10:00 a.m. Double-clicking the Moving mark-up opens a dialog box where you can adjust the start and end time of the move and add a description and comments to it.

Scheduling Days

To begin attaching scenes to shooting days, you need to display both the scene database (although you can resize it as necessary) and the production calendar.

Try to assemble a first day of shooting. There are several key goals for scheduling:

- Maximize the number of pages shot per day.

- Minimize the moves between locations.

- Consolidate all the scenes in a particular location. (This helps achieve the first two goals.)

Fortunately, *Delivery Date* requires few locations.

Scheduling a scene for a day simply requires that you drag the scene onto the desired date. Try dragging scene 1 onto June 1, 2011. Figure 11.23 shows the results of that operation.

Note: If necessary, re-sort your scene database by scene number. That makes it easier to locate scenes for this drag-and-drop operation.

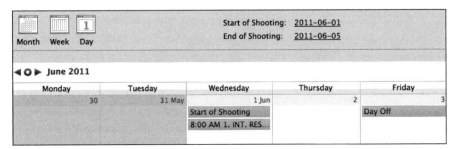

Figure 11.23   Scene 1 assigned to Shoot Day 1 on June 1—after dragging the button onto the date.

Notice that a checkmark has now been placed in the Scheduled column, making it easy to evaluate which scenes have been scheduled and which haven't been. (The column can be sorted to separate scheduled and nonscheduled scenes.)

Try assigning Scenes 2, 3, and 8 to the first shoot day, using the same drag-and-drop technique. That will give you 3 6/8 pages to shoot—probably a full day. Scene 3—the montage—is a little misleading in its length, because it requires multiple shots and setups.

Figure 11.24 shows all four scenes assigned to the day.

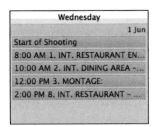

Figure 11.24   A full shoot day scheduled in production calendar.

Again, you may need to collapse the scene database to better see the scenes assigned to the day. In addition, you can switch the calendar view to a weekly or daily view. Go ahead and click the Day button to see June 1's scheduled scenes.

Celtx automatically assigns two-hour blocks for your scenes starting at 8:00 a.m., but you can adjust these if necessary. Figure 11.25 shows the Edit Event dialog box, which opens when you double-click on the Montage scene (or any scene).

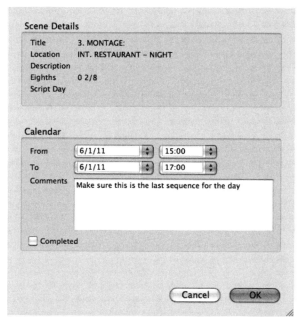

Figure 11.25   The Edit Event dialog box, triggered when assigned production calendar scenes are double-clicked.

This dialog box picks up fields previously entered in the scene's data form: Title, Location, Description, Eighths, and Script Day.

You can interact with the following calendar fields:

- From (scene start date and time)
- To (scene end date and time)
- Comments (a text box for notes about scene production)
- Completed (a yes/no check box)

If you have the Montage Edit Event dialog box open, do the following:

1.   Go ahead and adjust the end time for the scene. You can see how you can also adjust the date for the scene (but if a script day has already been selected, you need to go back and adjust that).

2. In the Comments text box, input `Make sure this is the last sequence for the day.`

3. Click OK to save the changes and close the dialog box.

Figure 11.26 shows the Edit Event dialog box with the Montage scene commented and time-adjusted.

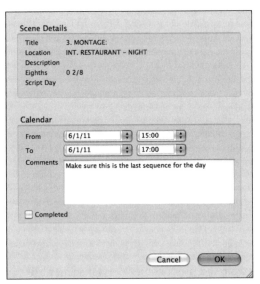

Figure 11.26   The Edit Event dialog box with data fields filled out.

Balancing scenes and locations isn't easy, and some trial and error—particularly when you're new to scheduling—is inevitable.

Having adjusted the Montage scene's start and end times, you need to adjust scene 8's start and end times as well.

Your crew is going to hate you if you neglect to schedule a lunch break. Figure 11.27 displays Script Day 1 in the daily view—and you'll see that an hour has been spared for lunch.

To enter the lunch break, just double-click on the empty hour (12 noon–1 p.m.). A New Event dialog box opens, and you can enter the necessary details and times, as Figure 11.28 shows. Click OK to confirm the entry.

When you're confident that you have your scenes assigned to the right days, you can double-click on scenes in the scene database and begin entering script days. In this example, you could open each of the four scenes assigned to June 1 and input 1 into the Script Day field.

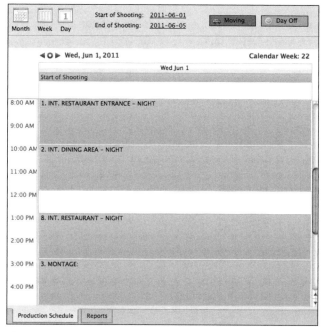

Figure 11.27   Script Day 1 with four scenes assigned for shooting, seen in the daily view.

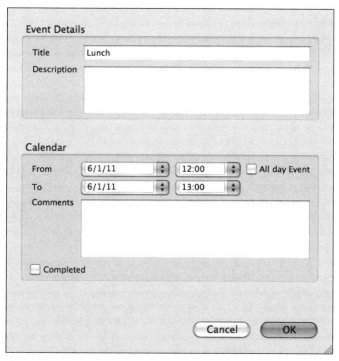

Figure 11.28   Lunch break scheduled in a New Event dialog box.

Note: There is no right or wrong order in the entering of script days and the assignment of scenes to calendar days. You might assign a few script days right away, do all your dragging and dropping, and then finish the rest of the script day entries.

Once again, the typical process would be to continue dragging scenes onto calendar days, adjusting times when necessary, and commenting the scenes. But in the interest of convenience, go ahead and download the `DeliveryDate-FullyCalendared` project file from the book's Online Companion website at www.courseptr.com/downloads. Then open the project.

Scheduling New Events in the Production Calendar

For certain productions, it may be useful to include nonshooting events. For example, you might want to include the wrap party in the production schedule.

In this case, perhaps you would like to schedule the wrap party for June 6:

1. Open the production schedule in the `DeliveryDate-FullyCalendared` project file.

2. Advance to June 6, 2011 in the calendar.

3. Double-click on the calendar date. (You can be in the monthly, weekly, or daily view.) This opens the New Event dialog box.

4. Input `Wrap Party` in the Title text box.

5. Set the time for 8:00 p.m. to 11:55 p.m.

6. Add any comments or a description as you'd like.

7. Click OK to save the data.

Figure 11.29 shows the New Event dialog box with wrap party data entered into it.

Marking Scenes as Completed

To tag a scene as completed, simply double-click on a scene in the calendar to open the Edit Event dialog box (see Figures 11.25 and 11.26), and mark the Completed check box. Then click OK to close the dialog box.

The scene now has a checkmark in the Completed column of the scene database.

If you haven't already, be sure to save the current project file. Now that you have all this scheduling data, you can begin distributing schedules and call sheets to cast and crew.

The Value of Call Sheets and Production Schedules

According to producer Peter McCarthy (whose credits include *Sid and Nancy* and *Repo Man*), "Call sheets are the marching orders that keep everyone on the same page, from

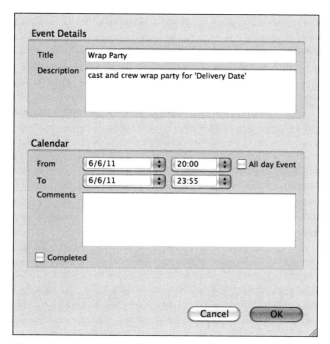

Figure 11.29   The New Event dialog box is triggered when you double-click on a calendar date. Data for a wrap party has been entered in this example.

weary keys who've been on a show for months, to nervous day players." He compares call sheets to a set's daily newspaper, and as the day moves on, to a "score card that lets the crew know if they're making the day."

McCarthy finds every kind of production report to be useful:

- "Daily Schedules help you to learn every minute detail of the script, and the more one knows, the more one can responsibly delegate and be a source of true information."

- "Weekly schedules form the building blocks of a shoot and help one plot the long haul."

- "One-line schedules let you play, juxtaposing scenes to discover the most efficient, creative way to maximize your resources and talent."

McCarthy observes, "Smart, prudent, efficient scheduling takes craft," and even then, "Production schedules change, big time."

Celtx generates all these production reports, increasing the odds that you'll be prepared on set, no matter what happens.

Production Reports

Media production long ago standardized on a set of schedules, call sheets, and other reports for distribution to cast and crew. To explore these, make sure you have the `DeliveryDate-FullyCalendared` project file open (download it if you need to from the Online Companion website) and the Production Schedule window open.

Figure 11.30 spotlights the Reports subtab. Click on it to open the window.

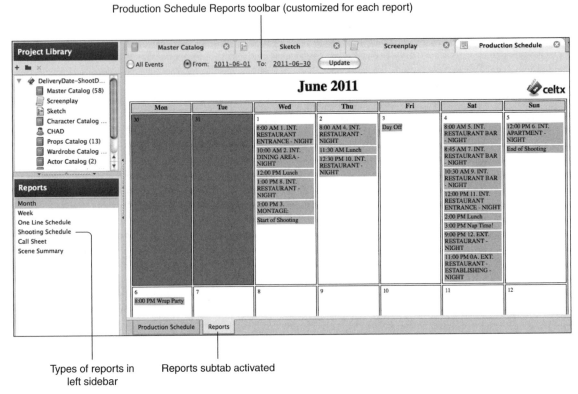

Figure 11.30 The Reports subtab, with a monthly schedule report displayed.

Celtx provides the following production schedule reports, all of which are visible in the Reports window of the left sidebar:

- `Month`

- `Week`

- `One Line Schedule`

- `Shooting Schedule`

- Call Sheet

- Scene Summary

Producing the report requires that you select the type of report you'd like in the left sidebar.

Month
This report selection prints a monthly view of the production calendar. (See Figure 11.30.) Figure 11.31 shows the Month Report toolbar, which allows the following:

- The inclusion of All Events, or a specific timeline of events (checked on or off)

- Date links, which allow editing of the start or end date

- The Update button to execute changes

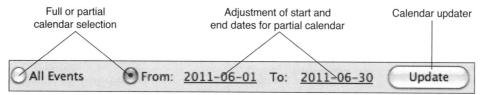

Figure 11.31   The Month Report toolbar, with 1) radio buttons to indicate all events or a time-demarcated set of events; 2) links to adjust the start and end dates; and 3) an Update button to refresh the calendar.

Week
This report selection prints a weekly view of the production calendar (as shown in Figure 11.32). Notice that the toolbar is identical to the Month Report toolbar shown in Figure 11.31.

One Line Schedule
This report selection prints an industry-standard one-line schedule, providing an at-a-glance columnar overview of shoot days and scenes scheduled for each day. Figure 11.33 displays the fields in the report:

- Scene (number)

- IE (interior or exterior scene?)

- Scene Description (picked up from the scene heading)

- D/N (day or night scene?)

- 1/8ths (length of scene in page eighths)

- Cast (in scene)

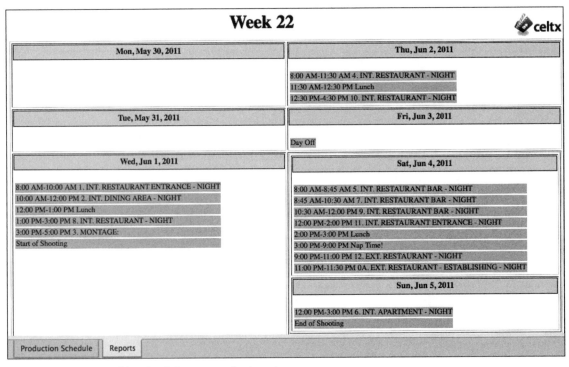

Figure 11.32   A weekly schedule report displayed.

One Line Schedule - DeliveryDate-ShootDays&SceneDescs   ⬧ celtx

Scene	I/E	Scene Description	D/N	1/8ths	Cast
		Day 1 - 6/1/11			
1	INT	RESTAURANT ENTRANCE Chad arrives looking for his blind date	NIGHT	1 1/8	
2	INT	DINING AREA Chad and Margaret first get to know each other	NIGHT	1 7/8	
8	INT	RESTAURANT Chad returns to Margaret; he's got a plan to skedaddle -- he gets one more call	NIGHT	0 4/8	
3		MONTAGE: Montage of eating and drinking scenes as dinner progresses and Chad and Margaret get more comfortable with each other		0 2/8	
		Day 2 - 6/2/11			
4	INT	RESTAURANT Chad discovers Margaret is pregnant and freaks out; he texts his buddy for a phone call bailout while Margaret is in the bathroom; she returns and his call comes in	NIGHT	2 7/8	
10	INT	RESTAURANT Margaret chews out Chad; then her ex- walks in, but Chad says he will escort her out	NIGHT	2 1/8	
		Day Off - 6/3/11			

Production Schedule   Reports

Figure 11.33   A one-line schedule report displayed.

Notice again that the toolbar is essentially identical to toolbars seen for the previous report selections, allowing you to view and print a full schedule or narrow in on a range of days.

Shooting Schedule

This report selection, shown in Figure 11.34, provides a more detailed look at each shoot day, listing all cast and crew elements that have been part of the script breakdown.

Notice again that the Shooting Schedule toolbar is essentially identical to the toolbar shown in Figure 11.31, allowing you to view and print a full schedule or narrow in on a range of days.

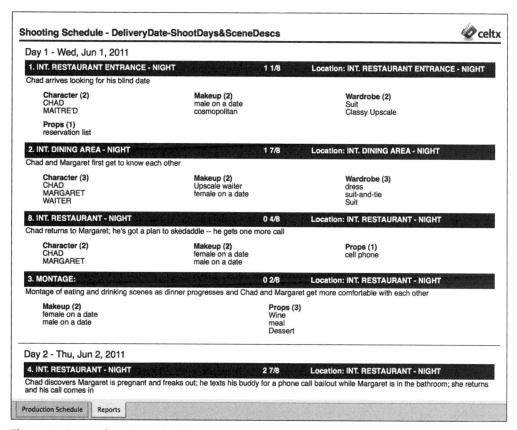

Figure 11.34 A shooting schedule report displayed.

Call Sheet

This report selection prints an industry-standard daily call sheet, listing the day's scenes, along with cast, extras, and crew. In addition, the call sheet provides a start time for the day (a crew call), contact information, additional location information (for example: to "park in the dirt parking lot"), and even the day's weather forecast.

Call sheets are generated daily, as call times. Weather and location information often change on a daily basis—and the production manager inputs and edits these changeable data fields as necessary.

Figure 11.35 shows the call sheet header, with editable text boxes filled out for the following:

- Crew Call

- Production Company

- Production Team

- Contact Information

- Production/Location Information

- Weather

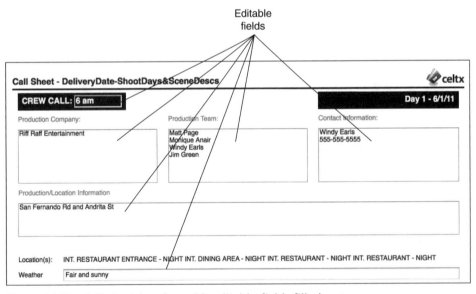

Figure 11.35 Call sheet header, with editable fields filled out.

Figure 11.36 displays the body of the call sheet, listing the day's scenes, scheduled shoot times, and personnel (cast, extras, and crew) for the day.

Scene	I/E	Scene Description	D/N	1/8ths	Cast
1	INT	RESTAURANT ENTRANCE Chad arrives looking for his blind date	NIGHT	1 1/8	
2	INT	DINING AREA Chad and Margaret first get to know each other	NIGHT	1 7/8	
8	INT	RESTAURANT Chad returns to Margaret; he's got a plan to skedaddle -- he gets one more call	NIGHT	0 4/8	
3		MONTAGE: Montage of eating and drinking scenes as dinner progresses and Chad and Margaret get more comfortable with each other		0 2/8	

ID	Character	Cast	Scenes and Times
	CHAD	Chad Brummet	1 (08:00), 2 (10:00), 8 (13:00)
	HOST	Liam Lockhart	1 (08:00)
	MARGARET	Juliet Lopez	2 (10:00), 8 (13:00)
	WAITER		2 (10:00)

Extras			Scenes and Times

Crew			Scenes and Times

Figure 11.36   Typical call sheet information in the body of the report, indicating the day's scenes and personnel.

The Call Sheet toolbar allows you to do the following:

- Select the shoot day for the call sheet

- Update the call sheet if you've done further script breakdown or edited the script since the last call sheet generation

Figure 11.37 displays the Date Picker dialog box, triggered when you select the shoot day link in the toolbar.

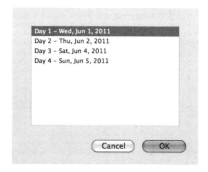

Figure 11.37   Date Picker dialog box, triggered when the shoot day toolbar link is selected.

To select your call sheet's shoot day, just click on the desired day and select OK.

Scene Summary

This report selection, shown in Figure 11.38, lists unscheduled, scheduled, and completed scenes. This summary is useful to run daily during production, to have an easy-to-read reference that tracks production progress.

Scene Summary - DeliveryDate-ShootDays&SceneDescs   celtx

Unscheduled Scenes			
Scheduled Scenes			
0A	EXT	RESTAURANT - ESTABLISHING establishes restaurant at night	NIGHT
3		MONTAGE: Montage of eating and drinking scenes as dinner progresses and Chad and Margaret get more comfortable with each other	
4	INT	RESTAURANT Chad discovers Margaret is pregnant and freaks out; he texts his buddy for a phone call bailout while Margaret is in the bathroom; she returns and his call comes in	NIGHT
5	INT	RESTAURANT BAR Chad answers his phone, safely in the bar	NIGHT
6	INT	APARTMENT Brett talks to Chad on the phone	NIGHT
7	INT	RESTAURANT BAR Chad interacts with bar patrons; it's not going well	NIGHT
8	INT	RESTAURANT Chad returns to Margaret; he's got a plan to skedaddle -- he gets one more call	NIGHT
9	INT	RESTAURANT BAR Chad takes the call, but Margaret looks for him and overhears how he really feels talking to Brett	NIGHT
10	INT	RESTAURANT Margaret chews out Chad; then her ex- walks in, but Chad says he will escort her out	NIGHT
11	INT	RESTAURANT ENTRANCE Chad and Margaret run right into Margaret's ex-, but Chad comes to the rescue and gets Margaret through the ordeal	NIGHT
12	EXT	RESTAURANT Chad has learned a lesson, and it looks like there may be a future for the twosome	NIGHT
Completed Scenes			
1	INT	RESTAURANT ENTRANCE Chad arrives looking for his blind date	NIGHT
2	INT	DINING AREA Chad and Margaret first get to know each other	NIGHT

Figure 11.38 Scene summary report displaying unscheduled, scheduled, and completed scenes. In this example, scenes 1 and 2 have been marked as complete.

The Update button in the toolbar provides a report update if you've gone into the production schedule to edit scene status, shoot day scheduling, and other schedule items.

Summary
This chapter covered the following:

- Building and editing calendars for general use in tracking tasks, events, and other scheduled items necessary in pre-production.

- Building a production calendar to schedule shoot days, moving days, and off days. Scheduling shoot days includes assigning script lengths to scenes and then assigning those scenes to specific days.

- Running a variety of production reports based on the production schedule, including monthly and weekly views of the production schedule, industry-standard one-line and shooting schedules, call sheets, and scene summaries (to track completion progress).

The next chapter briefly explores Celtx's built-in sample projects so you can see the tools and features they illustrate.

12 Exploring Celtx's Built-In Sample Projects

eltx provides several built-in sample projects (one for each script template) to help you learn the totality of the program's features. This chapter briefly looks at each of the sample projects to highlight key demonstration points.

You can gain access to sample projects any time you start Celtx. If you've never used Celtx before, sample projects are visible in the Sample Projects list box in the right half of the Welcome to Celtx dialog box. If you've used Celtx before, the Recent Projects list box contains a text link to Samples.

In either instance, you can select the preferred sample from the list box, and Celtx opens the project file.

Celtx provides six sample projects:

- *Wonderful Wizard of Oz* (which demonstrates use of the Screenplay template)

- *A Day at the Races* (which demonstrates use of the A/V Script template)

- *War of the Worlds* (which demonstrates use of the Audio Play template)

- *Importance of Being Earnest* (which demonstrates use of the Stageplay template)

- *The Mechanical Shakespeare* (which demonstrates use of the Comic Book template)

- *Alice's Adventures in Wonderland* (which demonstrates use of the Novel template)

Wonderful Wizard of Oz: Screenplay Template

The *Wonderful Wizard of Oz* sample project is built around a brief excerpt from the screenplay of MGM's *The Wizard of Oz*. The sample project includes these demonstrations:

- Index cards (feature discussed in this book's Chapter 3, "Project Navigation, Library, Notes, and Media")

- Script breakdown (features discussed in this book's Chapter 5, "Script Breakdowns and Catalogs")

- Script notes (feature discussed in this book's Chapter 3)

- Conversion to stageplay (feature discussed in this book's Chapter 2, "Getting Familiar with Celtx")

- Text document (an excerpt from the original novel) inclusion (feature discussed in this book's Chapter 3)

- Media attachment (feature discussed in this book's Chapter 3)

- Bookmarks inclusion (feature discussed in this book's Chapter 3)

- Storyboarding (features discussed in this book's Chapter 8, "Storyboards")

- Production schedule (features discussed in this book's Chapter 11, "Calendaring and Scheduling")

- Use of catalogs and the Project Library to manage the preceding items (features discussed in this book's Chapter 3)

Figure 12.1 shows the sample project file from the vantage point of the script editing window. It illustrates the Project Library, Scene Navigator, and Notes windows.

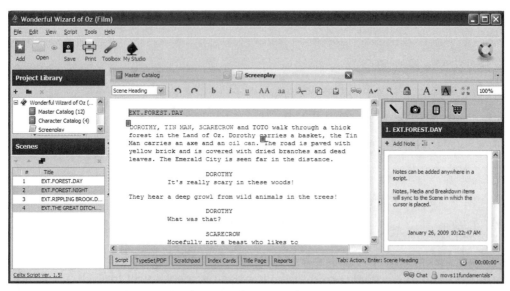

Figure 12.1 *Wonderful Wizard of Oz* sample project file, with the script editing window active and left and right sidebars displayed.

Figure 12.2 shows the Master Catalog, with various categories (actor, character, sound, props) populated.

You can save out the project file to a new name and experiment with adding, deleting, and editing items.

Figure 12.2 *Wonderful Wizard of Oz* Master Catalog containing numerous items in various categories.

A Day at the Races: A/V Script Template

The *A Day at the Races* sample project is built around an informational documentary script. The sample project includes these demonstrations:

- Script breakdown (features discussed in this book's Chapter 5)

- Script notes (feature discussed in this book's Chapter 3)

- Inclusion of research notes and PDFs (feature discussed in this book's Chapter 3)

- Media attachment (feature discussed in this book's Chapter 3)

- Storyboarding (features discussed in this book's Chapter 8)

- Index card demonstration (feature discussed in this book's Chapter 3)

- Use of catalogs and the Project Library to manage the preceding items (features discussed in this book's Chapter 3)

Figure 12.3 shows the sample project file from the vantage point of the script editing window and illustrates the Project Library, Scene Navigator, and Notes windows.

Figure 12.4 shows the storyboard.

You can save out the project file to a new name and experiment with adding, deleting, and editing items.

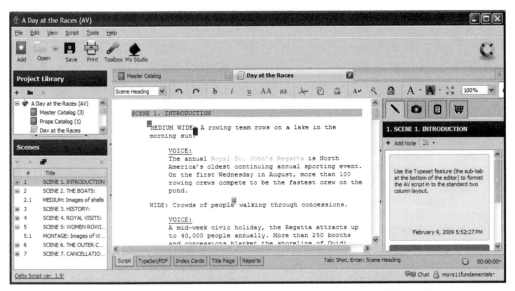

Figure 12.3 *A Day at the Races* sample project file, with the script editing window active and left and right sidebars displayed.

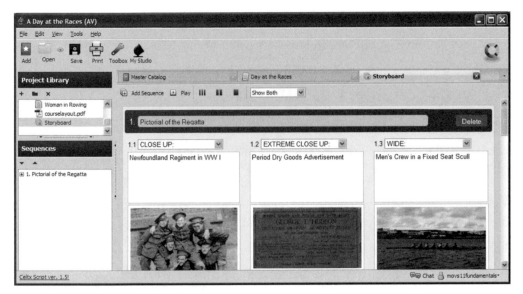

Figure 12.4 *A Day at the Races* storyboard.

War of the Worlds: Audio Play Template

The *War of the Worlds* sample project is built around Orson Welles's famous radio theater broadcast. The sample project includes these demonstrations:

- Script breakdown (features discussed in this book's Chapter 5)

- Script notes (feature discussed in this book's Chapter 3)

- Inclusion of research notes and links (feature discussed in this book's Chapter 3)

- MP3 media attachment (feature discussed in this book's Chapter 3)

- Index card demonstration (feature discussed in this book's Chapter 3)

- Use of catalogs and the Project Library to manage the preceding items (features discussed in this book's Chapter 3)

Figure 12.5 shows the sample project file from the vantage point of the script editing window and illustrates the Project Library, Scene Navigator, and Notes windows.

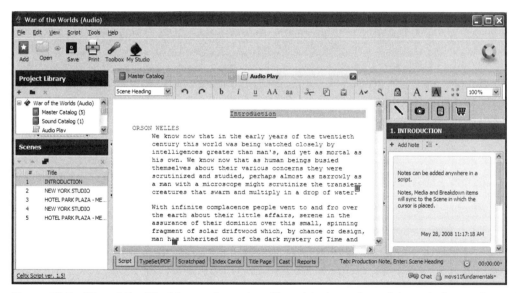

Figure 12.5   *War of the Worlds* sample project file, with the script editing window active and left and right sidebars displayed.

Figure 12.6 shows the cast list editor in the Audio Play window.

You can save out the project file to a new name and experiment with adding, deleting, and editing items.

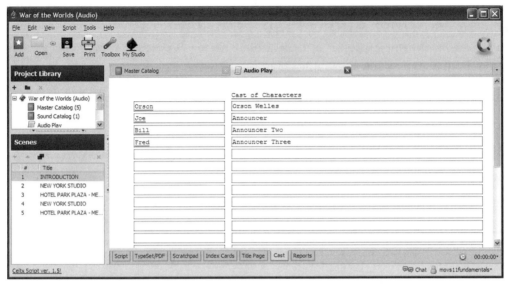

Figure 12.6   *War of the Worlds* cast editor.

Importance of Being Earnest: Stageplay Template

The *Importance of Being Earnest* sample project is built around a brief excerpt from the famous Oscar Wilde play, first produced in 1895. The sample project includes these demonstrations:

- Script breakdown (features discussed in this book's Chapter 5)

- Script notes (feature discussed in this book's Chapter 3)

- Text document (a synopsis and playwright bio) inclusion (feature discussed in this book's Chapter 3)

- Media attachment (feature discussed in this book's Chapter 3)

- Reference image collecting, using the storyboard (feature discussed in this book's Chapter 8)

- Production schedule (features discussed in this book's Chapter 11)

- Use of catalogs and the Project Library to manage the preceding items (features discussed in this book's Chapter 3)

Figure 12.7 shows the sample project file from the vantage point of the script editing window and illustrates the Project Library, Scene Navigator, and Notes windows.

Figure 12.8 shows the Master Catalog, with various categories (actor, character, props, set, location) populated.

You can save out the project file to a new name and experiment with adding, deleting, and editing items.

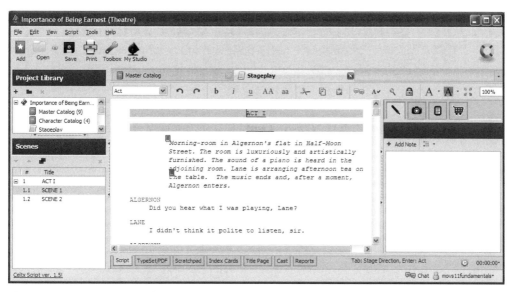

Figure 12.7 *Importance of Being Earnest* sample project file, with the script editing window active and left and right sidebars displayed.

Figure 12.8 *Importance of Being Earnest* Master Catalog containing numerous items in various categories.

The Mechanical Shakespeare: Comic Book Template

The sample project *The Mechanical Shakespeare* is built around a demonstration of a comic book project authored by Wallace Anthony Ryan. The template includes the following:

- Script breakdown (features discussed in this book's Chapter 5)

- Script notes (feature discussed in this book's Chapter 3)

- Text document (a synopsis and playwright bio) inclusion (feature discussed in this book's Chapter 3)

- Page Navigator (feature discussed in this book's Chapter 3)

- Media attachment, including finished comic book art (feature discussed in this book's Chapter 3)

- Research image collecting, using the storyboard (feature discussed in this book's Chapter 8)

- Index card demonstration (feature discussed in this book's Chapter 3)

- Use of catalogs and the Project Library to manage the preceding items (features discussed in this book's Chapter 3)

Figure 12.9 shows the sample project file from the vantage point of the script editing window and illustrates the Project Library, Page Navigator, and Notes windows.

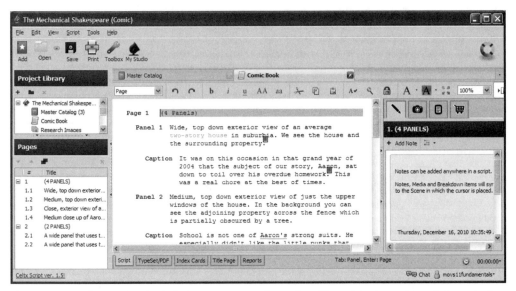

Figure 12.9 *The Mechanical Shakespeare* sample project file, with the script editing window active and left and right sidebars displayed.

Figure 12.10 shows research images collected in a storyboard.

Figure 12.10   *The Mechanical Shakespeare* research image collection (using the storyboard as a repository and play-back/slideshow tool).

You can save out the project file to a new name and experiment with adding, deleting, and editing items.

Alice's Adventures in Wonderland: Novel Template

The *Alice's Adventures in Wonderland* sample project is built around Lewis Carroll's beloved 1865 novel of the same name. The template includes the following:

- The full text of the novel, divided into chapters, which also demonstrates the Chapter Navigator (feature discussed in this book's Chapter 3)

- Media attachment (feature discussed in this book's Chapter 3)

- A text note (feature discussed in this book's Chapter 3)

- Index card demonstration (feature discussed in this book's Chapter 3)

- Use of catalogs and the Project Library to manage the preceding items (features discussed in this book's Chapter 3)

Figure 12.11 shows the sample project file from the vantage point of the script editing window and illustrates the Project Library and Chapter Navigator in the left sidebar and the right sidebar with Notes activated.

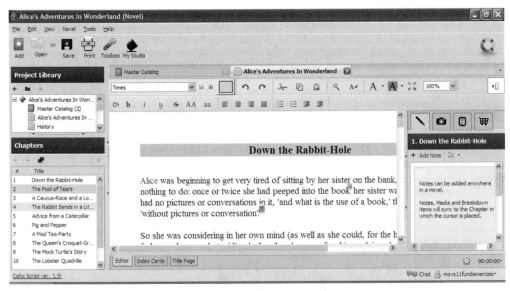

Figure 12.11 *Alice's Adventures in Wonderland* sample project file, with the text editing window active, a chapter heading, and left and right sidebars displayed.

Just like with scripts, you can use Celtx's breakdown features to fully break down your novel and export the catalog to a spreadsheet or other comma-separated value (CSV)-savvy program.

To experiment with the novel template (which could also be used for short stories, academic papers, articles, and other text documents), you can save out the project file to a new name and experiment with adding, deleting, and editing items.

Summary

This chapter briefly reviewed the sample project files that are included with Celtx:

- *Wonderful Wizard of Oz* (which demonstrates use of the Screenplay template)

- *A Day at the Races* (which demonstrates use of the A/V Script template)

- *War of the Worlds* (which demonstrates use of the Audio Play template)

- *Importance of Being Earnest* (which demonstrates use of the Stageplay template)

- *The Mechanical Shakespeare* (which demonstrates use of the Comic Book template)

- *Alice's Adventures in Wonderland* (which demonstrates use of the Novel template)

The next chapter looks at Celtx Script, an app that enables working with Celtx projects on iPhones, iPod Touches, and iPads—and syncing of projects between desktop/laptop systems and mobile devices.

13 Celtx Script

Scripting has evolved from use of the typewriter, to use of the desktop computer, to use of the laptop computer. However, in an ever-more mobile world where production teams and companies are ad-hoc and virtual—and where scripts may need to be composed in almost any location—the ability to use mobile devices like iPhones, iPod Touches, and iPads for composing, editing, and viewing scripts is extremely helpful.

Celtx has the Celtx Script app for these mobile devices. (And as this book went to press, Celtx was already working on an Android app.) Celtx Script is available in iTunes's app store, and for a minimal fee, the app further expands Celtx's value as a scripting tool.

This chapter explores Celtx Script's features and capabilities.

What Celtx Script Does and Doesn't Do

Celtx Script focuses on script editing. The storyboarding, breakdown, and production features available in the desktop/laptop application of Celtx are not available in the mobile Script app. (However, all breakdown and storyboarding is preserved as you sync across devices.) Celtx Script won't replace Celtx for the entirety of pre-production workflow, but it will enable the composition, editing, and reviewing of scripts on-the-go and in any location.

Note: From here on, this book will refer to the desktop/laptop Celtx application simply as *desktop Celtx*.

Acquiring Celtx Script

Celtx Script is only available in the iTunes app store (until the Android app is released later in 2011). The easiest way to find the app is to hop onto the Celtx website (http://celtx.com) in your browser and select Mobile in the set of navigation tabs.

Figure 13.1 shows the Celtx Mobile webpage.

If you're in iTunes, you can also search for Celtx in the app store. Figure 13.2 shows the Celtx Script information page in the iTunes app store.

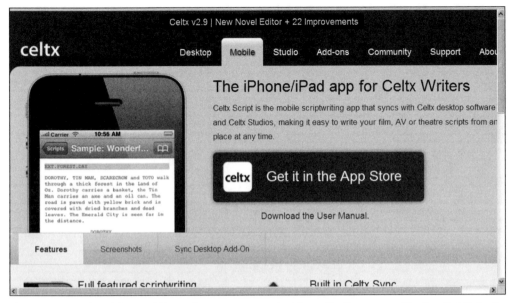

Figure 13.1 The Celtx Mobile webpage, accessed at http://celtx.com, with the Get It button for navigating directly to the app.

Figure 13.2 The Celtx Script information page on iTunes.

Purchasing Celtx Script is like purchasing any other iTunes product or app: it requires an iTunes account.

Note: The app is universal. You can use it on your iPad, iPhone, or iPod Touch—and users are entitled to free upgrades as they're released.

Once you've purchased and downloaded Celtx Script, you can sync your mobile device to your desktop or laptop system and add the app to your device.

Note: For general information on syncing mobile devices and using mobile device apps, visit Apple's website or consult one of the many excellent books on mobile computing, such as Course Technology's *Take Your iPad to Work*.

Opening and Using the App

Once Celtx Script is on your device, open the app. Figure 13.3 displays the home screen: the Scripts page.

Note: Throughout this chapter, screen shots will be taken from an iPod Touch. All user interactions are identical across the spectrum of Apple's mobile devices. The iPad provides much larger screen real estate for Celtx Script, and consequently you may find minor variances in look and feel as you execute tasks on it.

From the Scripts page, you'll be able to do the following:

- Select a script for viewing or editing

- Begin a new script

- Delete a script

- Select a script to duplicate or email

- Sync a script with desktop Celtx and with Celtx Studios

- Access the Celtx Script Owner's Guide

A sample project file film script, *Wonderful Wizard of Oz* (also a desktop Celtx sample, as discussed in Chapter 12, "Exploring Celtx's Built-In Sample Projects"), is included to help you get comfortable with the Script app.

Help/Owner's manual button — Edit button

Sync — Add new script

Figure 13.3 Celtx Script Index page, displaying the sample project file *Wonderful Wizard of Oz*. Toolbars are placed at the top and bottom of the screen.

Note: It's instructive to compare the complete *Oz* sample project file in desktop Celtx to the script supplied in the Script app. When scripts are synced between devices, you'll find that storyboards, production schedules, catalogs, and more are left behind on the desktop.

You can change the script on your mobile device and sync the script back to desktop Celtx. No changes will be made to Project Library items in the project file; changes will be made only to the script.

Celtx Script Settings

Your mobile device's Settings app controls several features in Celtx Script:

- **Remember Login.** You can instruct Celtx Script to remember that you're logged into the sync server, or compel you to re-enter login data each time you try to sync. (The latter may be preferable if you use a Google or Facebook account for syncs of personal work, while also using a Celtx Studio account in the classroom or at work. Syncing issues are usually the result of conflicting account logins.)

- **Font Size.** You can modify the default font size of 18 points, reducing it (to fit more text into the screen) or raising it for better onscreen visibility.

Viewing/Editing Scripts

To open a script for viewing or editing, simply tap on the script listing on the Scripts page. Figure 13.4 shows the open *Oz* script, which you can then scroll through (either horizontally or vertically) to begin reading.

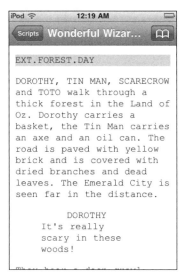

Figure 13.4 *Wonderful Wizard of Oz* sample script, opened in Celtx Script.

Tapping into the script brings up an onscreen keyboard and element toolbar.

Tip: Celtx Script works in either portrait or landscape mode. Try both and see which you prefer.

Keyboard Editing

To practice keyboard editing in Celtx Script, try adding the word Enchanted before Forest in the scene heading.

You can make any additions or deletions to the text within any of the script elements.

The app provides these other standard text-editing features:

- **Select/Select All.** Selector accessed if you tap and "hold" (press) within text. You can choose to select a single word or an entire textual element (a dialog block or scene heading, for example).

- **Cut/Copy.** Once you've selected text, this tiny button menu pops up, and you can choose what to do with the selected text.

- **Paste.** Once text has been cut or copied, a tap-and-hold in a different area of text brings up this button, along with the opportunity to Select or Select All.

For practice, try selecting Dorothy's second line ("What was that?"). Figure 13.5 shows the button menu displayed when you tap-and-hold within the line.

Figure 13.5 Select/Select All menu triggered when selecting Dorothy's line "What was that?"

Choosing Select All highlights the entire dialog line and triggers the Cut/Copy menu. Choose Copy.

Now tap and hold at the end of Dorothy's first line: "It's really scary in these woods!" You should trigger the Select/Select All/Paste menu. Choose Paste. This should insert a copy of the line "What was that?"

For further editing practice, tap after the question mark, and use the backspace key on the screen keyboard to delete "What was that?"

Editing within Celtx Script takes a little practice and patience (particularly on the iPhone/iPod Touch small screen), but you'll increasingly become comfortable adding, deleting, cutting, copying, and pasting text within the editing window.

When you're finished editing, tapping the OK button in the toolbar dismisses both the keyboard and the toolbar. However, now you'll take a closer look at the toolbar. (If you've dismissed it, a tap in the text brings it back up.)

Element Toolbar

Figures 13.6 through 13.10 display the Element toolbar for each script template. As the figures demonstrate, the buttons in this toolbar will adjust to the template you're using.

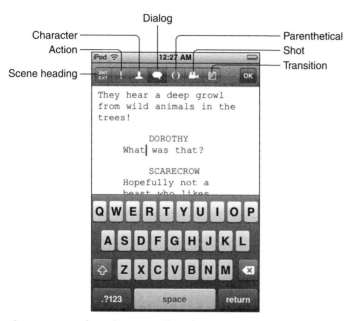

Figure 13.6   The editing toolbar for the Screenplay template.

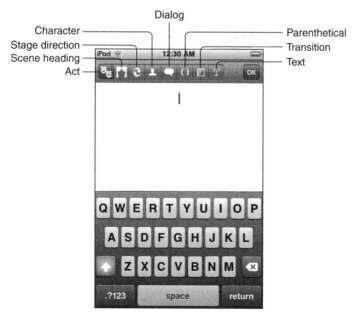

Figure 13.7   The Editing toolbar for the Stageplay template.

Figure 13.8   The Editing toolbar for the A/V template.

Figure 13.9   The Editing toolbar for the Comic Book template.

When you're editing a script, selecting a button in the Element toolbar changes the element where the pointer is currently placed in the script text. When you're composing a script (to be discussed shortly), selecting the button establishes the element for the text you're about to input.

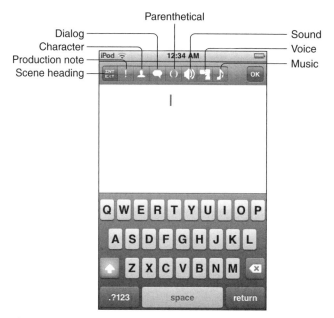

Figure 13.10   The Editing toolbar for the Audio Play template.

To practice this, tap into Dorothy's first line: "It's really scary in these woods!" Select the Parenthetical element button in the toolbar, and you'll find that the text has been formatted as a parenthetical. Tap the Action Element button in the toolbar to restore the text to dialog.

Tip: Input an open parenthesis at the beginning of dialog, and you'll immediately be working inside a parenthetical element.

As mentioned earlier, tapping the OK button in the toolbar dismisses the keyboard and toolbar to better enable full-screen viewing of the script.

Navigating the Script

Figure 13.11 displays the title bar with buttons bracketing the script title.

Tapping the Scene Index button displays the scene list for the current script. Figure 13.12 displays the scene list for the sample *Oz* script.

Note: The iPad screen also displays the scene you're currently in.

Tapping a scene takes you directly into the scene. It's a handy way to navigate, particularly in longer scripts.

Never thought you could compose a new screenplay on a handheld device? Keep reading.

Current script title

Scripts index
button

Scene Index

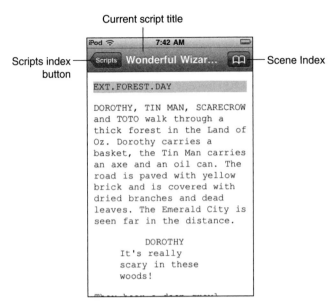

Figure 13.11 The title bar while in viewing/editing mode.

Figure 13.12 The Scene Index for Oz.

Creating New Scripts

Navigate to the home screen, the Script Index. (See Figure 13.11 for placement of the Script Index button in the title bar.)

Figure 13.3 identifies the buttons on the Scripts page. Tap the + to begin authoring a new script. Figure 13.13 shows the Select Script Type screen, with buttons for Screenplay, Audio Visual (A/V), Stageplay, Comic Book, and Audio Play template choices.

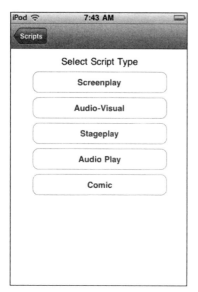

Figure 13.13   The Select Script Type screen, with buttons to select available templates.

For this walk-through, tap Stageplay.

Title Page Creation

As Figure 13.14 shows, selecting any template triggers the title page editor, with text boxes for Script Name and Author(s).

Call your new script *Practice Play*. Enter your name in the Author(s) text box.

The title page editor includes a Celtx Sync toggle. Click the toggle to sync this script to the desktop, when you choose to do so.

Once you've entered the information, tap Done in the top toolbar. (Cancel aborts the script creation.)

You are returned to the home screen, and you see your new *Practice Play* included in the script list.

To begin composing the play, tap the script name.

Composing the New Script

In this template, the editor starts with an Act element. You can input the act and continue with a scene heading and initial stage direction (as discussed in the section titled "Keyboard Editing").

Figure 13.14   Title page editor with text boxes and Celtx Sync toggle.

Figure 13.15 shows the beginning of a new play script. See if you can duplicate its contents.

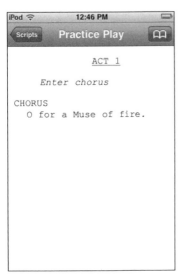

Figure 13.15   Sample of initial script composition, using the Stageplay template.

Tip: Any time you're composing or editing in the Script app, changes are automatically saved. Saving is built into the app and doesn't need triggering or selecting.

Syncing Scripts Between Mobile Devices and Desktop/ Laptop Devices

Clearly, the value of Celtx Script becomes enhanced when scripts can be passed back and forth between handheld devices and the desktop/laptop devices typically used for intensive script composition and editing.

To enable this, you first need to install a free plug-in for use with the desktop version of Celtx.

Installing the Sync Add-On

To download the Sync add-on, head to Celtx.com, click on the Mobile tab, and scroll down to find the Sync Add-On for the Desktop section of the webpage. Locate the Download button and download the free add-on.

Once you've downloaded the add-on, you're prompted to restart Celtx to finish the add-on installation. Once Celtx reopens, you are ready to begin syncing from mobile device to desktop, or the reverse.

Syncing from the Mobile Device to the Desktop

From the Scripts page, tap Sync. A sign-in screen then asks for a Celtx account user name and password, or a Facebook or Google account sign-in. Pick the sign-in of your choice, and once you've entered the necessary information, the Celtx server is contacted, and scripts designated to sync are transmitted.

Caution: All mobile syncing requires Internet access for your mobile device. If sync isn't working, check that you have an active Internet connection.

Opening Synced Scripts on the Desktop

To open a synced script from the mobile device, start your desktop Celtx. Then begin a new script. For the walk-through here, choose the Theatre (Stageplay) template.

Note: Celtx automatically places an Act 1 heading and a Scene 1 heading. You can delete these for this exercise.

As Figure 13.16 shows, pull down the Script menu and select the menu item Import Script.

Importing can then be done either to text or to your mobile device. Choose From iPhone/iPad.

The iPhone/iPad Script Sync login screen appears (if you haven't previously logged into the sync server). Fill in the necessary information, and sign in.

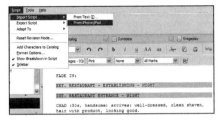

Figure 13.16 Script menu pulled down and Import Script selected. Two import choices reside on the submenu.

Caution: Be sure the login you use is the same one you've been using with Celtx Script, and with your Celtx studio if you're using this platform. Unless the logins match, syncing between sources won't work.

As Figure 13.17 shows, the iPhone/iPad Script Sync dialog box now lists synced scripts that you can import. In this example, you have only one script, *Practice Play*, to import. Select the script and click on the Import button.

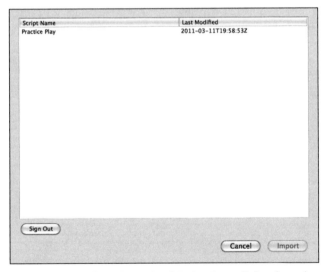

Figure 13.17 The iPhone/iPad Script Sync dialog box showing scripts currently designated for syncing.

Your short script appears in the screenplay editor, and you can continue to edit and add to the script—and then sync the script back to your mobile device.

Syncing from the Desktop to the Mobile Device

For this walk-through, download the DeliveryDate-FullBreakdown&Storyboard project file from the book's Online Companion website at www.courseptr.com/downloads. (This project file was used in Chapter 11, "Calendaring and Scheduling." You may already have the project file on your local drive.)

Open the project and make sure the Screenplay tab is activated. As Figure 13.18 shows, pull down the Script menu and select the menu item Export Script.

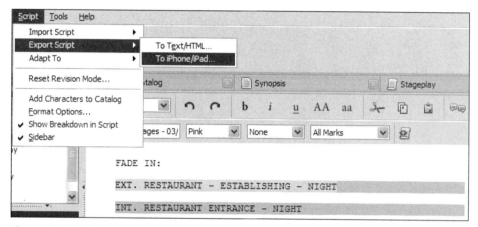

Figure 13.18   Script menu pulled down and Export Script selected. Two export choices reside on the submenu.

Exporting can then be done either to text or to your mobile device. Choose To iPhone/iPad, which triggers the iPhone/iPad Script Sync dialog box shown in Figure 13.17.

The script title displays in the text box at the bottom of the dialog box. You can modify the name if necessary. Then choose the Export button to sync the file.

Open Celtx Script on your mobile device. Select Sync from the Scripts home screen. The server is contacted, and your synced scripts should be updated within moments. In this case, you should now see the *Delivery Date* script on the Scripts page.

Note: As Figure 13.19 shows, the Scripts home screen lists the last modification date for a script, along with its status as a synced or nonsynced script.

Syncing from Celtx Studios

Chapters 14 ("Celtx Studios: Creation and Administration") and 15 ("Celtx Studios: User Inter-action") explore Celtx Studios, a shared collaborative pre-production environment. Syncing between Celtx Studios and the Script app is also enabled, further expanding distribution and collaboration possibilities for scripts. See Chapter 15 for a discussion of this specific feature.

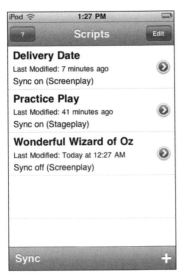

Figure 13.19 The updated Script Index page showing three scripts and latest modification dates for each.

Emailing and Duplicating Scripts

You can email scripts in text format from the Script app home screen. To email *Delivery Date*, tap the blue outlined arrow to the right of its name.

Figure 13.20 shows the triggered screen with emailing and duplicating buttons.

Figure 13.20 Emailing/Duplicating screen, triggered by tapping a script's arrow from the Scripts home screen.

Selecting the Email as Text button opens a Mail dialog box (as shown in Figure 13.21). A text version of the script has been embedded in the email body, and the script name has been placed in the subject line. You can insert an email address for the receiver, add CCs if necessary, compose a message, and then tap Send to transmit the email. (For practice, try sending the script to your personal or workplace email account.)

Figure 13.21   Mail message with text version of script embedded.

Figure 13.22 shows what happens if you tap Cancel instead: a menu pops up with choices for Delete Draft, Save Draft, and Cancel.

Figure 13.22   Menu triggered when you select Cancel from the mail message.

Duplicating a script is just what it sounds like, allowing you to "clone" a script so you can maintain alternate versions, or retain the original and experiment with revisions.

Get back to the Emailing/Duplicating screen shown in Figure 13.20, and tap the Duplicate button.

Figure 13.23 shows the Duplicate screen, with the word Copy appended to the title of the duplicate script file. You can modify this name as necessary (for example, appending Revisions or Alternate to the script name).

Figure 13.23 The Duplicate screen.

You can also elect to turn Sync on or off.

Tap Done and your new script is added to the Script Index home screen.

Deleting Scripts

From the Scripts home screen, tap the Edit button.

Notice that red outlined buttons pop up next to script names.

Tap the red button in front of *Practice Play*. The red button activates, and as Figure 13.24 shows, a Delete button appears to the right of the script name.

Tap Delete, and a confirmation screen pops up, confirming that the script and its synced copy on the server should be deleted. Tap Delete to finalize the deletion.

Caution: Scripts that are not synced do not get the confirmation screen. A Delete tap immediately executes the file erasure.

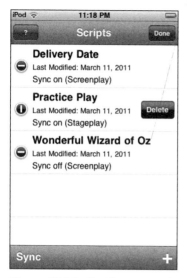

Figure 13.24   Red button activated and Delete button next to file name.

Summary

This chapter looked at the following:

- Acquiring Celtx Script from the iTunes App Store

- Viewing and editing scripts using the Script app

- Composing new scripts

- Downloading the sync add-on for desktop Celtx to enable script syncing

- Syncing scripts from mobile device to desktop and the reverse

- Emailing and duplicating scripts

- Deleting scripts

The next two chapters explore the use of Celtx Studios from both an administrator's and a user's perspective. Celtx Studios is a low-cost subscription-based platform that provides project management and collaboration features along with "cloud" storage. The platform can be ideal for building and managing a production unit's pre-production workflows, as well as for use in classroom and corporate environments.

14 Celtx Studios: Creation and Administration

Celtx Studios is a completely separate application from Celtx, although it is designed to aid the use of Celtx, especially within a production team. (Celtx Studios also happens to be useful if you're teaching scriptwriting at the high school, college, or college extension levels—for management of class project submissions and revisions.)

Celtx Studios is a browser-based application that provides the following features to Celtx users subscribed to the studio:

- Secure "cloud" storage of all projects

- Access to all projects from any computer

- Easy sharing of projects

- 5GB of storage space (more is available on request)

- Automatic versioning and backup and revision control of all drafts and revisions

- Easy monitoring and management of team workflow

- Live chat between studio users

- Web preview of projects for studio users

- Collaborative report information (when using the Performance Tracker add-on, discussed in Chapter 15, "Celtx Studios: User Interaction")

For a minimal cost, Celtx Studios eliminates questions on a production team like these:

- Who has the project file? Who's currently revising it?

- What computer is the project file on?

- Who has access to the project file? Who *should* have access to the project file?

- Can you find an earlier version of the script or storyboard?

- What revisions have been done, and by whom?

Project management. Revision control. Cloud storage. Celtx Studios is the portal for all these features and more.

This chapter looks at Celtx Studios from the viewpoint of a studio administrator and from a studio user. If your assigned role in a Celtx studio is that of a user, and if someone else is serving as administrator, you can skip the remainder of this chapter and move to Chapter 15.

Note: Celtx Studios is slated for further development in Fall 2011. The user interface may undergo some changes then.

Celtx Studios: Requirements

Although Celtx is free, Celtx Studios requires a monthly subscription fee. At the time of publication, the fee to set up and use a studio was $1 per user per month, with a minimum of 5 users. Thus, a 5-member ad-hoc production team could set up a private studio for 3 months for all of $15—about the cost of a meal-for-two at a fast-food establishment. A 14-student class or workshop could set up a private studio for 4 months for $60.

Note: Celtx offers a 15-day fully featured free trial of Celtx Studios (for five users). Signing up for a free trial can be a good way to try the platform and see if it works for your production team or classroom.

Celtx Studios requires no software downloads. Access and functionality are 100% browser based, meaning that any system using Windows, the Mac operating system (OS), or Linux can interact with a studio. (However, see Appendix F, "Setting Up Linux for Celtx Studios and Celtx Add-Ons," for some additional setup instructions for Linux users.)

The only local application requirement for effective use is that users have Celtx installed on their local hard drives or flash drives. (Users can access a studio without Celtx on their system, but Celtx is necessary for opening or reviewing a project file.)

Creating and Accessing a Celtx Studio

The administrator of the Celtx studio should be the one to set up and subscribe to the studio. This may be a showrunner, a project manager, a creative director for a production team, or the instructor for a class. Some of the one-time and ongoing tasks for the administrator include these:

- Setting up the subscription payment source and designating the number of users for the studio

- Customizing the onscreen studio look

- Adding and modifying user accounts

- Having viewing, editing, and deletion privileges for all project files in the studio

To begin setting up a studio, point your browser to Celtx.com, and select the Studio tab. Alternatively, the direct URL is https://studio.celtx.com.

Note: If someone (a project manager, a production coordinator, or an administrative assistant) has already set up a Celtx studio for you to administer, you can skip this section and move to the next.

The Celtx Studios Home Page

Figure 14.1 shows a typical Celtx Studios web entry screen at https://studio.celtx.com, with an option on the left to log in to a studio if you already have a user ID and password set up. The right side of the page provides an invitation (to anyone interested) in starting a subscription and setting up a studio. The lower portion of the page has several clickable navigation tabs to explore features, benefits, pricing tiers, and frequently asked questions.

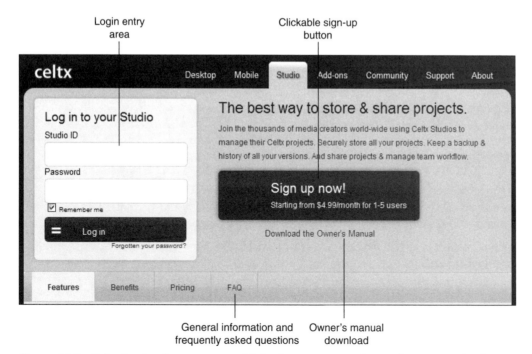

Figure 14.1   Celtx Studios home page, with login entry area, sign-up button, and informational links.

Caution: If someone else has been using your computer to log in to Celtx Studios, you might be able to immediately enter a studio and bypass this home page. If you're not the indicated user, you should log out and then either begin the subscription process or log in with your own user ID (and in some cases, you may need to notify your instructor or system administrator if the user ID is unknown to you, just to avoid login confusions).

Creating Your Studio

Click on the Sign Up Now button. You're taken to the Celtx Studio Registration page, where you're asked to establish several pieces of information for your new studio, as spelled out in the next sections.

Studio ID

You'll want to establish a unique (and ideally, easy-to-remember) name for your studio. For example:

- If your company name is Dark Hope Productions, then `darkhopeprod` might be a good ID.

- If your production team is working on the 2012 promotionals project, then `2012promo-project` might be a good ID—although an organizational acronym might also be incorporated into the ID (for example, `ibm2012promoproject`).

- If you teach a scriptwriting class or seminar designated as Film 2217, then `film2217-f11` could serve for the Fall 2011 term. (Your school acronym might front-end that ID, such as `uclafilm2217-f11`.)

A studio ID needs to be one word. It can be upper- and lowercase, but using all lowercase frequently makes entry easier for users.

Tip: Your studio ID should instantly identify your project or team. This is likely to make it easier to remember and easier to refer technical support to, if that's ever necessary. `Project` or `promo2011` is probably too generic. However, a studio ID that's too long will become clumsy or frustrating to use, because it may be necessary at times to type in the full ID. Thus, `acmeproductionsfall2011slateofapprovedclientprojects`—although unique—is probably not the most practical ID.

Each studio ID is unique; there is no chance that you'll create an ID that someone has previously used. You can immediately check the availability of a studio ID, and if you find your preferred ID is already in use, you can modify the ID until you create a unique one.

Caution: It never hurts to write down an ID or place it as a note that you can refer to on your smartphone (BlackBerry, Droid, iPhone).

Password

This is the administrator password. Ideally, you've already set up many passwords during your life as an Internet user, and the usual cautions apply.

Note: Both studio IDs and passwords are case sensitive. As the administrator, you may decide to restrict IDs and passwords to lowercase text strings in the interest of simplifying user support.

Email Address

This is the administrator's email address, and it should be an account that the administrator (you, or whoever is serving in the role) regularly uses, to receive updates and other emails about the studio.

Select Number of Users

A drop-down menu box allows you to designate how many users will have accounts (or "seats") in the studio. You can start with as few as 5 users and increment upward to a maximum-sized studio of 45. Be sure to count the administrator as one of the users.

Note: You can also add users later in the pre-production or production phase, if you need to.

If you are signing up for the free trial, you're restricted to five users, but you can change this once you begin a paid subscription.

Once you've selected your number of users, the page instantly refreshes to indicate the price per month or year. You may want to maintain a permanent studio for your organization's or team's projects, in which case a discounted annual payment may make the most sense for you. But because many projects span a brief period (three months, six months, and so on), you may decide that a continuing monthly subscription is the best option.

Choose Payment Method

You can elect to pay using either PayPal or a VISA or MasterCard credit card. If you don't have a PayPal account, you're prompted to set one up when you complete the Celtx Studios order. If you select credit card payment, an entry screen appears where you can input the necessary credit card data.

Completing the Order

Figure 14.2 displays a sample completed registration order form. Once you've completed yours, you can select the Complete Order button to submit the form. (Be sure you've checked your agreement with the Terms of Use and Sales Policy.)

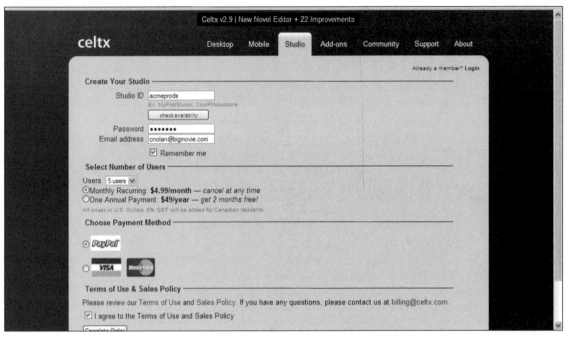

Figure 14.2   A sample, filled-out Celtx Studios registration order form.

Entering and Administering Your New Celtx Studio

Once you establish your Celtx studio, you are prompted to enter the studio right away. You can always reach the studio any time by going to Celtx.com and activating the Studio tab or by going to the direct URL at https://studio.celtx.com.

Note: Chapter 15 discusses additional ways to reach the studio.

Entering the studio triggers the opening of a new browser window; all interactions with the studio occur in that window. Typically, you are greeted with an informational welcome screen. When you're ready, you can close that window.

Figure 14.3 shows the Celtx studio administrator screen. Note the studio ID in the upper-right corner of the screen, and the logout link.

In the bottom right of the screen is the Celtx logo. Note, too, the diagonally tiled image of a film slate as the background for your Celtx studio window.

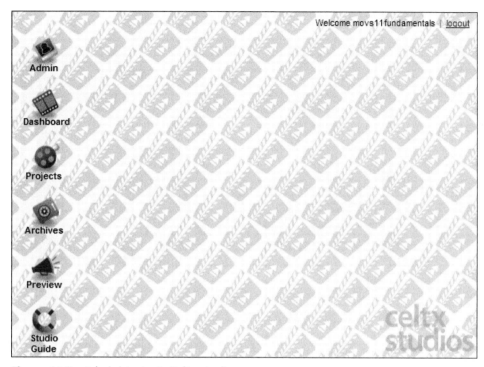

Figure 14.3   Administrator's Celtx studio screen.

A group of icons appears on the left edge of the screen:

- Admin (handles administrative tasks)
- Dashboard (tracks access and activity in the studio)
- Projects (the portal for accessing studio projects)
- Archives (contains version history and version access for all studio projects)
- Preview (a web preview tool for projects)
- Studio Guide (an online guide to Celtx Studios functions and features)

This chapter looks at the Admin and Dashboard features of Celtx Studios. Other features are accessible to all users and are discussed in Chapter 15.

Admin

Double-click the Admin icon to open its window. Figure 14.4 shows the window and its three functions:

- Accounts
- Theme
- Cancel Account

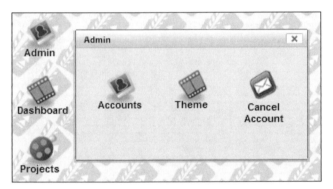

Figure 14.4   Celtx studio Admin window.

Accounts

Double-click the Accounts icon to open the Account Management window. Figure 14.5 shows the window, with a multicolumn table reflecting the current users in the studio (currently, just the administrator), and above it, a toolbar allowing you to edit, add, and delete users, along with an icon for upgrading the number of seats.

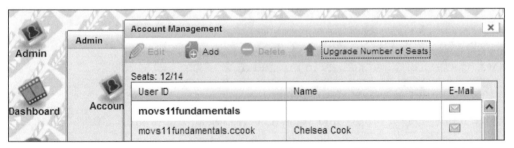

Figure 14.5   Celtx studio Account Management window, opened from Admin. (In this illustration, users have already been added to the studio.)

Click Add to begin adding users. Figure 14.6 shows the Add User window, before fields have been filled in.

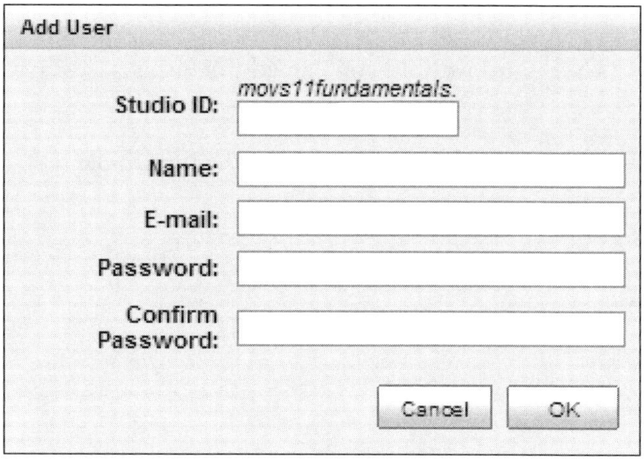

Figure 14.6   Celtx studio Add User window, opened from Account Management.

User records require the following fields:

- **Studio ID.** The user ID for the studio. For a small team, first names are probably sufficient; if it's a small team that prefers call signs or nicknames, those certainly work as well. For larger user groups, you may want to standardize on a formulation like `firstinitiallastname` (example: `rsmith`), or `firstnamelastinitial` (example: `rachels`). The ID is case sensitive: some administrators prefer keeping all IDs lowercase to avoid confusion about entry.

- **Name.** The full user name, which further helps identify project owners. Here, a standard uppercase/lowercase formulation is probably best (example: `Rachel Smith`).

- **E-mail.** The email address for the user. (Users often have several email accounts; you may need to find out the email account they're most likely to check on a regular basis for updates and news about the studio.)

- **Password.** A unique password for the user.

- **Confirm Password.** Reconfirming a unique password for the user.

Once you've entered a user record, click OK. You see the record added to the account table. You can continue adding records as necessary.

Tip: User records are sortable by either of the columns (User ID or Name).

Editing user records is a two-step process:

1. Select the record to be edited.

2. Click Edit.

The Edit User window is identical to the Add User window, and you can edit fields as necessary.

Tip: You can swap out users simply by editing a user record and changing the user studio ID, name, and email address.

Deleting user records is a three-step process:

1. Select the record to be deleted.

2. Click Delete.

3. A Delete Account window pops up, requesting confirmation of the action. Click either the Delete or the Cancel button, as appropriate.

To increase the number of users in the studio, click the Upgrade Number of Seats button. Figure 14.7 shows the new browser window—Celtx Studio Upgrade—that opens. You can fill out the order form (which is largely identical to the initial studio order form) to complete the upgrade.

Note: If you aren't already logged into your Celtx studio, you can go directly to https:// studio.celtx.com/upgrade to complete the same order form. You are then prompted to log in to your current studio.

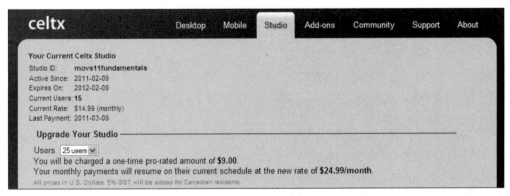

Figure 14.7   Celtx Studio Upgrade order form (triggered by the Upgrade Number of Seats button).

Theme

Closing the Account Management window returns you to the main Admin window. Figure 14.8 shows the dialog box that opens when you double-click the Theme icon.

Figure 14.8 Celtx studio Theme dialog box, opened from the Admin window.

The Theme dialog box allows you to set three screen design options:

- **Logo.** This allows you to place an organizational logo in the bottom-right corner of the screen (replacing the default Celtx logo) so you can better brand the studio.

- **Background.** This allows you to replace the default background image with one of your own. You can choose to either tile or center your uploaded image.

- **Preview Banner.** This allows you to place an organizational banner at the top of a web preview page that you can create for your project. (The Preview feature is discussed in Chapter 15.)

Clicking the Upload button for any of the options opens a File Upload dialog box. The Reset button allows you to return the studio to the default setting.

Cancel Account

Double-clicking the Cancel Account icon opens your email account and starts a mail message to Celtx's billing department, notifying them of your desire to cancel the Celtx studio account. You can cancel your account at any time.

Dashboard

Double-clicking the Dashboard icon opens a window displaying recent activity in the studio. The Recently Updated Projects table includes the following fields:

- **Project.** Project name.

- **Owner.** Owner name; studio ID used.

- **Version.** The total number of versions.

- **Last Modified.** The most recent revision of the project file.

- **Modified By.** Particularly useful when a project file has been shared among multiple team members, or when the administrator is actively revising others' projects.

- **Shared.** A simple yes/no as to whether the project has been shared with other studio users; however, all projects are shared with the studio administrator by default. Project sharing is discussed in Chapter 15.

- **Preview.** A simple yes/no on whether a web preview has been set up for this project. Web preview is discussed in Chapter 15.

Figure 14.9 displays a typical Dashboard window.

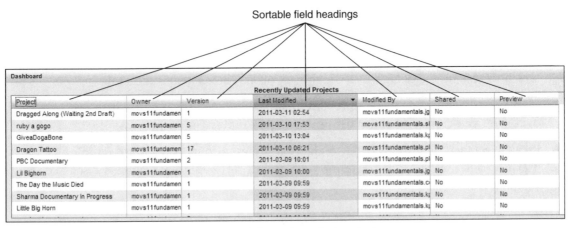

Figure 14.9 Celtx studio Dashboard, opened from the Admin window.

Tip: The Dashboard window, like all windows in your Celtx studio, is resizable and repositionable. Moving your pointer inside the window's title bar allows you to drag the window anywhere within the browser window. Clicking and dragging on a window corner allows you to resize the window.

You can sort the table by any of its fields. One click on the column heading sorts in A–Z (or most recent date) order, and a second click reverse-sorts the columns (Z–A order).

The Dashboard provides the studio administrator with an easy way to monitor progress and recent activity.

Note: Studio administrators are automatically shared on project files saved to the studio. File sharing in the studio is discussed in Chapter 15.

Summary

This chapter looked at establishing and administering a Celtx studio. Celtx Studios provides project versioning, storage, collaboration, and management features—useful for small production shops, ad-hoc production teams, and project-oriented media classes.

To set up a Celtx studio, visit Celtx.com's Studio page (reachable from the home page) and follow the instructions for creating your own unique studio.

Once your studio is set up, you can log in as administrator and begin exploring Celtx Studios' features. You can begin to add and edit users, customize the visual studio theme, and track studio activity.

The next chapter looks at Celtx Studios from the user perspective.

15 Celtx Studios: User Interaction

This chapter looks at how users can interact with Celtx Studios: using its storage, sharing, versioning, and collaboration features. You'll see how Celtx Studios can maximize your production team's productivity and progress.

If you're a studio administrator, be sure you read Chapter 14, "Celtx Studios: Creation and Administration," which discusses the Admin and Dashboard features of Celtx Studios. This chapter focuses on features available to *all* Celtx Studios users, including the administrator.

Note: This chapter assumes that you have access to a studio. If you don't currently have access, studying this chapter still provides you with a basic understanding of a studio's key features.

Note: Celtx Studios is slated for further development in fall 2011. The user interface may undergo some changes at that time.

Entering the Studio

Celtx provides several ways of opening a studio project:

- Starting the Celtx application to enter the studio

- Entering the studio from a web browser

- Entering the studio from an open Celtx project

Note: Linux users should review Appendix F, "Setting up Linux for Celtx Studios and Celtx Add-Ons," and confirm they've made a one-time configuration of browser values to use Celtx Studios successfully. If you're not sure if these configuration changes have been made, consult your system administrator.

Starting Celtx to Enter the Studio

Open Celtx from your program menu, program shortcut list, program dock, or application folder. As Figure 15.1 shows, the splash screen includes an Open from Studio button.

Figure 15.1   Celtx splash screen, with the Open from Studio button located just below the Recent Projects scrollable menu.

Click the button to open the Celtx Studios login webpage (https://studio.celtx.com). Enter your complete studio ID and password (as supplied by your studio administrator) in the text boxes, and select Log In.

Caution: Both studio IDs and passwords are case sensitive. Check the case of text strings before trying to recover a password or contacting your administrator.

Note: Administrators only need to enter the studio name as their ID. Users will find that their studio ID is composed like this: *studioname.userID* (for example: darkhopeprods. jsmith).

Your studio's home page now opens.

Entering the Studio from Your Browser

If you already have a browser window open, you can directly access the Celtx Studios login page. Enter https://studio.celtx.com into your browser's address bar. Once at the site, you can then enter your studio ID and password to log in.

Entering the Studio from Within a Celtx File

To practice this approach, you need an open Celtx file. And although you may not currently have access to a studio, keep a project open to study menu options in this chapter.

Almost any open Celtx file will do, but if you don't have one immediately accessible, download the `DeliveryDate-Breakdown&Storyboard` project file from the book's Online Companion website at www.courseptr.com/downloads, and then open the file. (If you have completed Chapter 8, "Storyboards," you may already have this file on your local drive.)

Figure 15.2 shows the open project. If you study the main toolbar, you see My Studio as the last icon on the right. Click the icon to launch the Celtx Studios login page, where you can enter your studio ID and password.

Figure 15.2   The My Studio icon in the Celtx toolbar.

Logging In and Out of Celtx Studios

A Logout link is always available on the Celtx Studios home page, which returns you to the Studios login page.

You can also sign in and out of studios using the status bar at the bottom of the Celtx window. Figure 15.3 shows the Celtx Studio Authentication dialog box, triggered when you click on the Sign In button at the right edge of the status bar.

Enter your user name and password to log in to your studio.

The Sign In on Startup check box, when checked, tells Celtx to automatically log in to the studio in the future.

Click OK to log in to your studio.

Note: The Celtx Studio Authentication dialog box also allows you to recover a password or create a studio account.

Figure 15.3   Celtx Studio Authentication dialog box triggered when you click the Sign In/Sign Out button.

As Figure 15.4 shows, once you're logged in, the Celtx status bar reflects your studio user ID in the Sign In/Sign Out button.

Figure 15.4   The Sign In/Sign Out button now labeled with the user ID name, after you have signed in.

Once you're logged in, clicking the Sign In/Sign Out button triggers a menu that includes the Sign Out option.

> **Note:** The status bar also contains a Chat button, which is discussed later in this chapter in the section titled "Chatting in the Studio."

Using the Studio

Figure 15.5 shows the icons on your studio's home page:

- **Dashboard.** Tracks your access and activity in the studio
- **Projects.** The portal for accessing user-owned and user-shared projects
- **Archives.** Contains version history and version access for all user-owned and user-shared projects
- **Preview.** A web preview tool for user projects
- **Studio Guide.** An online guide to Celtx Studios functions and features

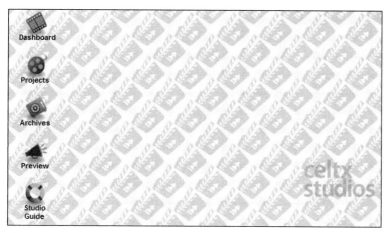

Figure 15.5 A studio's user home page.

Double-clicking an icon launches the feature. This chapter will look at each of these user features shortly. But how do you place a file into the studio?

Saving Projects to the Studio

Return to your open Celtx project (and if one isn't open, go ahead and open one).

Tip: If you're the studio administrator or if the studio administrator approves, try using the `DeliveryDate-Breakdown&Storyboard` project file that you've been practicing with in earlier chapters. You may already have it available on your local drive, or you can download it from the book's Online Companion website at www.courseptr.com/downloads. You can then open the file to follow the tutorials in this chapter.

Pull down the File menu in the open Celtx project and choose Save to Studio. If you're not logged in to your studio already, Celtx asks for your studio ID and password information.

Figure 15.6 shows the Studio Projects dialog box that opens when you're saving to the studio. This lists current studio projects and provides a text box for the name of your studio project. The current local project name is already entered into the text box, but you can change it if necessary.

Clicking OK triggers a Save Comment dialog box. You can enter a comment to better identify the current draft. For example, enter `Complete 1st draft of script with outline`.

A check box asks whether to prompt for save comments. Entering comments on each studio save may seem like "busy work" or otherwise unnecessary, but during the deployment of a studio,

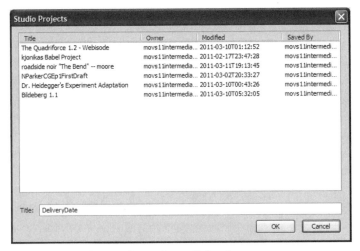

Figure 15.6 The Studio Projects dialog box.

the consistent entering of comments is useful. A detailed comment aids in building a trackable revision history and becomes invaluable if you ever need to roll back to an earlier version of a project. See the "Archives" section later in this chapter for further discussion of revision history.

Figure 15.7 displays the Save Comment dialog box, with the prompt checked and a comment entered.

Figure 15.7 The Save Comment dialog box: the last step in saving a project to the studio.

Click OK to complete saving the project to the studio. This returns you to the open Celtx project file. Saving the project file to the studio designates you as the owner of the project, which will be important as you manage projects (as either user or studio administrator).

Note: Projects saved to the studio are automatically shared with the studio administrator. The administrator has full editing privileges.

Click My Studio to return to your studio's home page.

Opening Projects from the Studio

If you are already working within Celtx solely from your local drive and need to open a project from your studio, follow these steps:

1. Pull down the File menu.

2. Select Open from Studio from the menu.

3. If you're already signed into the studio, you immediately enter its home page. Otherwise, you trigger the Celtx Studio Authentication dialog box, where you can enter your user ID and password, as shown in Figure 15.3.

4. To open a studio project, open Projects, as discussed in the next section.

Where Are My Studio Projects Going?

Celtx Studios uses *cloud storage* for saved projects: all data is saved to Amazon's proven and secure storage network infrastructure, so you can access the project from any computer, iPad, or iPhone that has Celtx or the Celtx app installed.

You are certainly able to maintain local copies of the Celtx project file as well. Any time you have a project open, you can pull down the File menu and choose Save Project As to store the project to a flash drive or a local drive folder. This may be useful if you plan to work on a computer that won't have a reliable Internet connection (a remote location, an airplane, a secured site).

You can then save the revised file to the studio when you're next logged in.

Projects

Double-click the Projects icon to open the Projects window. Figure 15.8 shows a sample Projects window, which displays all studio projects the user currently has access to. (Administrators have access to *all* studio projects.)

Selecting a project icon displays important data about the project. Figure 15.9 shows file ownership and history information displayed in the right frame of the window:

- File name

- Last modification date- and time-stamp

- Version number

- Sharing status

- Owner

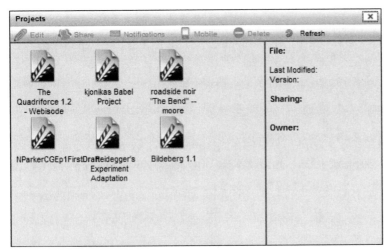

Figure 15.8 The Projects window, showing all user-accessible studio projects. (Administrators see all projects in the studio.)

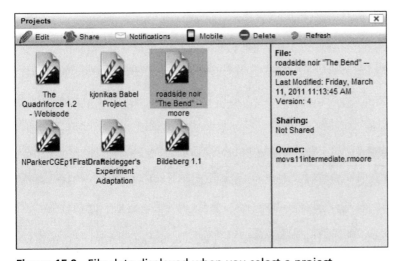

Figure 15.9 File data displayed when you select a project.

The Projects toolbar provides the following features:

- Edit
- Share
- Notifications
- Mobile
- Delete
- Refresh

Edit

Clicking the Edit button opens the selected file in Celtx, where you can begin editing the file.

Note: Double-clicking a project icon also opens the project in Celtx.

Share

Figure 15.10 displays the Sharing dialog box, triggered when you click on the Share button in the Projects toolbar.

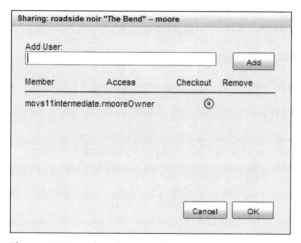

Figure 15.10   The Sharing dialog box for studio projects.

If you own a project, you can share it with one or more studio users. Current sharers (if any) are already displayed in a data table.

If you'd like to share the project with new or additional users, type in a full user studio ID in the Add User text box; then click the Add button.

Tip: As you begin typing in the text box, you see Celtx try to anticipate the user ID. Once Celtx determines the studio ID, it lists the first 10 users in your studio, and you can click on the full studio user ID as soon as you spot it.

Figure 15.11 shows a new user added to the share list table. A drop-down list box provides two choices for sharing:

- **Limited.** The user can view the project and print scripts and reports, but he can't save edits back to the studio.

- **Full.** The user has complete access to the project and can add, edit, and delete as necessary.

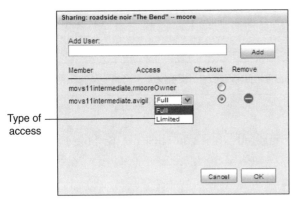

Type of access

Figure 15.11   New user added to the share list table, and access drop-down list box displayed.

The share list table contains four fields:

- **Member.** This is the user ID with file access.
- **Access.** This is the type of access the user has (owner, full, limited).
- **Checkout.** If a user has checkout privileges, only that user can edit the file.
- **Remove.** Clicking this removes the user from the share list.

You can add as many users as you'd like to share your file.

When you've completed adding or removing users or adjusting the access level, click OK to lock in the changes.

Tip: Users don't need to go to the trouble of sharing their projects with studio administrators. All user projects are automatically shared with the administrator.

Tip: In general, give users full access to the project only when they need to edit the project themselves. Often, users only need viewing access; if given unnecessary editing access, users may make inadvertent changes to a project file.

Notifications

Figure 15.12 displays the Email Notifications dialog box, triggered when you select a project and click on the Notifications button in the Projects toolbar.

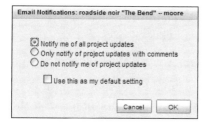

Figure 15.12   The Email Notifications dialog box for studio projects, with full notifications selected.

Three notification settings are available:

- **Notify me of all project updates.** Full notification of changes
- **Only notify of project updates with comments.** Limited notification of changes
- **Do not notify me of project updates.** No notification of changes

A check box allows you to select a notification level and declare it as a default setting for future projects.

When you've set the level and default preference, click OK to lock in the changes.

Different projects may require different levels of notification. You may update some projects infrequently, so the first selection may make the most sense. You may update other projects constantly, and continual notifications may be self-defeating. You can try out settings and adjust when necessary.

Mobile

Figure 15.13 displays the Mobile dialog box, triggered when you select a project and click on the Mobile button in the Projects toolbar.

Note: See Chapter 13, "Celtx Script," for a discussion of the Celtx Script app for mobile devices like iPhones and iPads.

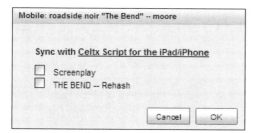

Figure 15.13   The Mobile dialog box for studio projects, showing a project file containing multiple scripts.

Most project files, of course, contain only one script. However, as Figure 15.13 shows, you can choose which script or scripts to sync with your mobile device via check boxes.

Check the script(s) to sync, and click OK. A "mobile" icon becomes part of the file name icon.

The next time you sync Celtx Script on your mobile device, you should find the script in your index. Edit the script on the mobile device, sync within the app, and the script updates in the studio.

Caution: If you're using a Google or Facebook account with Celtx Script logins but also have a separate studio login, you are likely to encounter trouble with the sync. Be sure that you're logging into both the studio and Celtx Script with the same user name and password, and this should resolve any issues you have. See Chapter 13 for information about Celtx settings.

Delete

The Delete button begins deletion of a selected project. Figure 15.14 shows the dialog box triggered when you click Delete. You're given the following reminder: `Deleting a project will delete all archived versions of the project`. Be sure that's what you want to do, and if it is, click the Delete button in the dialog box to confirm.

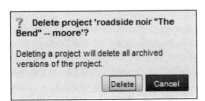

Figure 15.14   Clicking the Delete button in the Projects toolbar triggers this dialog box. Read the warning carefully! There is no undo of a delete file action.

Refresh

While you're working in your Celtx studio, other studio users may be busy updating, adding, or deleting projects. To make sure the Project window is reflecting the current status of projects, click the Refresh button.

Tip: In a classroom situation where many students may be creating new projects and sharing with each other in a single class session, frequent Refresh actions may be necessary.

Archives

The Archives feature is the repository for project version history.

Double-click the Archives icon to open the Archives window. Figure 15.15 shows a sample Archives window, which displays folders for all studio projects the user currently has access to.

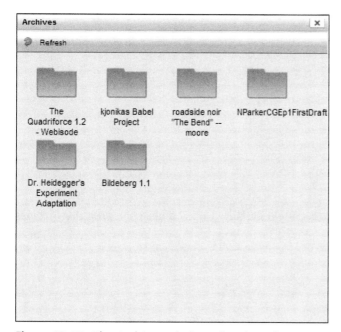

Figure 15.15   The Archives window, showing all user-accessible studio projects. (Administrators see all projects in the studio.)

Note: You can have multiple studio windows (such as Projects and Archives) open at the same time, and you can move and resize the windows as necessary if you want to control their layout (overlapping them or tiling them, for example).

Double-clicking a project folder icon displays the version history for the project in an upper frame, as well as icons for all Project Library items in a lower frame. Figure 15.16 shows a sample version history window.

Version History Table

The version history table has four columnar fields:

- Version (number)

- Date (date- and time-stamp of last save)

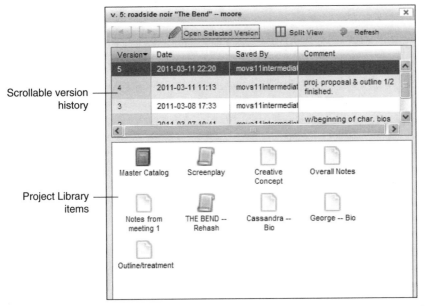

Scrollable version history

Project Library items

Figure 15.16   The version history window reached by double-clicking a project folder in the Archives window.

- Saved By (user who made revision)
- Comment (comment attached to saved version)

> **Note:** You can now see the value of a detailed comment attached to every update to the studio.

The version history table is sortable by column and can be sorted and reverse-sorted by clicking the column header. You can also scroll through version records.

When you find a version you want to examine, you can click the Open Selected Version button in the toolbar. This opens the version in Celtx.

If you want to revert to this version, save the version to the studio and add a comment about the reverted version. You can also save the older version to a new project name in the studio, creating a new project.

Project Library Items

For any selected version, you can quickly view items in the project's library. (All items are displayed in the lower frame.) Viewing an item in a specific version requires two steps:

1. Select the preferred version in the version history table. Project Library icons populate the lower frame.

2. Double-click an item's icon. The item's contents display in the lower frame.

Figure 15.17 shows the library content frame with a script draft displayed.

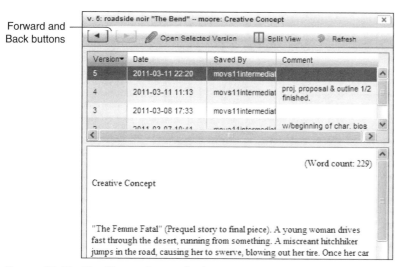

Forward and Back buttons

Figure 15.17 The library frame displaying contents of a selected library item.

Notice that you have Forward and Back buttons in the Version History toolbar. Particularly if you have items nested inside of folders (and even subfolders), you can drill down to a particular item in the library content frame and then move backward and forward through the structural hierarchy, so you can continue to inspect items in the frame.

Split View

Clicking the Split View button in the Version History toolbar lines up two version history windows, so you can compare different versions side by side.

Figure 15.18 shows Split View selected, with different versions of a project selected in each window. Notice that the button has now toggled to Single View to provide the option for reverting to the default single view window.

Clicking Single View returns to the default version history window.

Refresh

The Refresh button in the Version History toolbar updates the version history, which becomes necessary if one or more users are updating a project while you're simultaneously inspecting its versions.

Split view/Single
view toggle button

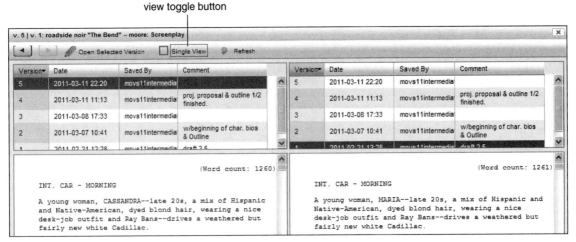

Figure 15.18   Split View selected for inspecting project versions side by side.

Preview

The Preview feature allows you to publish a professional-looking browser-based preview of your project. This preview does not require that Celtx be installed on a local drive. It's great for delivering a project to studio user(s) who fall into any of the following categories:

- May not normally use Celtx

- Are unfamiliar with the specific project and just need a quick look at project progress (without drilling down into a Project Library to dig up catalogs, research, and so on)

- Are with a client, a producer, or an investor and need to show project scope and status (without worrying about whether Celtx is installed at a remote site)

Click on the Preview icon to begin studying its features. Figure 15.19 shows an opened Preview window, currently empty, with the toolbar running at the top of the window.

Figure 15.19   An empty studio Preview window and toolbar.

The toolbar provides the following features:

- Create

- Update

- Delete (grayed out when no project previews exist)

- Refresh

Create (Preview)

To begin setting up a browser-based preview (retrievable on any computer with an Internet connection), click the Create button in the toolbar. Figure 15.20 displays the Create dialog box that opens up.

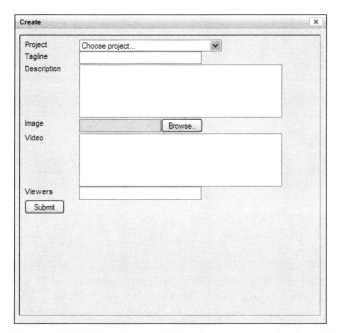

Figure 15.20 The Create dialog box, triggered when the Create button in the Preview toolbar is clicked.

The Create dialog box contains the following entry fields:

- **Project.** A drop-down list box containing all projects that you own

- **Tagline.** A text box for you to enter a tagline or logline about the project

- **Description.** A text box for a lengthier synopsis or summary about the project

- **Image.** A file browser to locate a key "front page" image (possibly a logo or poster shot)

- **Video.** A text box for embedding "front page" HTML video code (such as YouTube or Vimeo code)

- **Viewers.** A text box for subscribing Celtx Studios users to the published web preview

> **Caution:** You need to choose *either* an image *or* a video as the "front page" graphic. If you browse for an image *and* embed HTML video code, the video is granted first priority.

Figure 15.21 displays the Create dialog box with entry fields filled out.

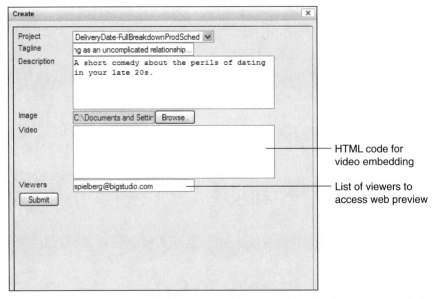

Figure 15.21   The Create dialog box, with entry fields filled out and ready for submission.

Taglines, descriptions, and a graphic are not required elements, but a tagline and description do help to quickly orient the viewer in the preview, and the graphic (whether a still image or a video) can add some appealing "eye candy" to a project's presentation.

> **Tip:** You can include studio users who are subscribed to a different studio than your own, but make sure you have their complete studio user ID to do so. Only Celtx Studios users can access published web previews; the previews are not available to nonstudio users. Subscribed viewers are automatically emailed with a link to the project preview.

Click the Submit button in the dialog box to publish the preview.

Figure 15.22 displays the Preview window with a published project.

Figure 15.22   The Preview window with a published project.

To test the web preview and see what subscribed users will see, double-click the Project Preview icon. As Figure 15.23 shows, a new browser window opens with the preview.

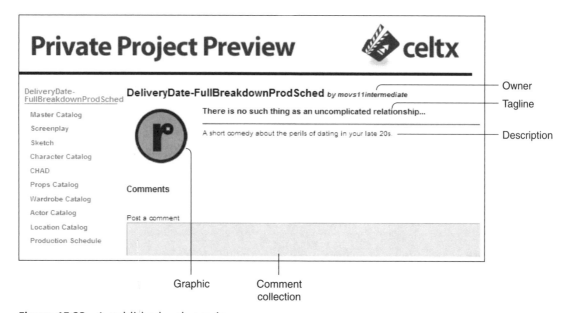

Figure 15.23   A published web preview.

The web preview has structured the project and created a hierarchical navigation menu on the left side of the webpage, based on items in the Project Library. Catalogs, folders, storyboards, scripts, and outlines are accessible via standard web links.

Figure 15.24 shows a script displayed within the preview (after the Screenplay link was selected).

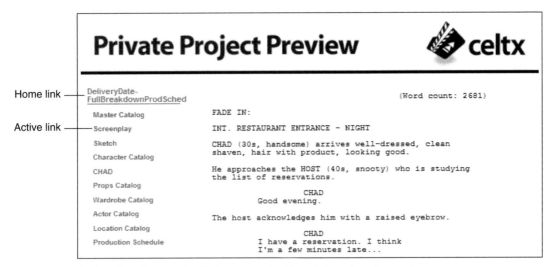

Figure 15.24   A script displayed within the project's published web preview.

Posting Comments on a Web Preview

Web previews include a comment collection feature on the project's home page. This is a useful way to collect quick comments from team members, top-level management, clients, and other viewers.

To post a comment, simply begin typing in the Post a Comment text box. Your user ID is appended to the comment, and push buttons to Post or Cancel immediately become available.

When you've completed composing your comment, click the Post button to post the comment. Preview viewers see all posted comments; because there is no option to undo a comment, make sure your comment is something you're comfortable having public (within the assigned viewer pool).

When you're finished browsing a preview, simply close the preview's browser tab to put it away.

Update (Preview)

The Update button in the Preview toolbar allows you to edit the settings for your project's web preview. Figure 15.25 shows the Update dialog box, triggered when you click the Update button.

Note: The Update dialog box is similar to the Create dialog box and contains all the same entry fields, but it displays a clickable direct URL for the project's web preview.

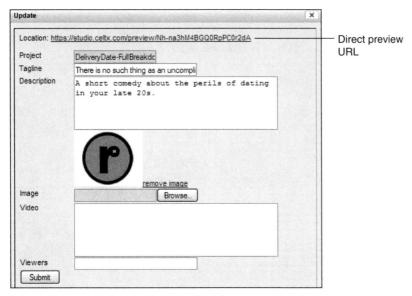

Figure 15.25   The Update dialog box for project previews.

The dialog box allows you to modify these preview features:

- Tagline
- Description
- Image or Video (replace or remove)
- Viewers (add or remove)

Delete (Preview)

The Delete button in the Preview toolbar allows you to delete the currently selected project preview.

Caution: There is no delete confirmation dialog box triggered when you click the Delete button in the Preview toolbar. Clicking Delete instantly erases the project preview.

Refresh

While you're using the Preview features in your Celtx studio, other studio users may be busy publishing new project previews. To make sure the Preview window is reflecting the current availability of web previews, click the Refresh button.

Tip: In a classroom situation where many students may be collaborating and publishing new project previews, frequent Refresh actions may be necessary.

Studio Guide

Figure 15.26 shows the Studio Guide window, triggered when you double-click the Studio Guide icon.

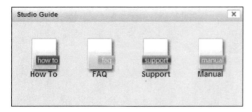

Figure 15.26   The Studio Guide window in Celtx Studios.

The Studio Guide offers the following features:

- **How To.** Clicking this icon opens a webpage that walks through key studio features with text and screenshots.
- **FAQ.** Clicking this icon opens a Studio FAQ (frequently asked questions) webpage.
- **Support.** Clicking this icon opens a Studio Support webpage.
- **Manual.** Clicking this icon opens an online PDF version of the studio manual, which you can download or print.

Figure 15.27 shows the How To window, opened when you select the How To icon.

Figure 15.27   The How To window, available in the Studio Guide.

The How To window provides numerous screenshots illustrating features and execution in Celtx Studios. It is a quick way to get a visual reminder about a step to take or an icon to click.

The Studio Guide window remains open in your Celtx studio so that you can continue trying out its features.

Figure 15.28 shows the FAQ window, opened when you select the FAQ icon.

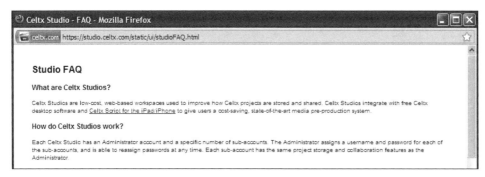

Figure 15.28 The FAQ window, available in the Studio Guide.

The Studio FAQ (Frequently Asked Questions) is a simple Q&A text window. Like any browser window, it is searchable for text.

Figure 15.29 shows the Studio Support window, opened when you select the Studio Support icon.

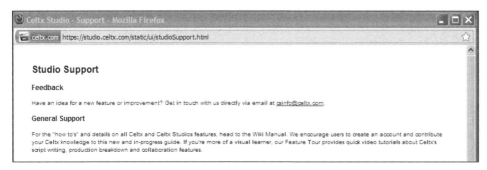

Figure 15.29 The Studio Support window, available in the Studio Guide.

The Studio Support window provides some basic support and billing information.

Figure 15.30 shows the Celtx Studios Owner's Manual, opened when you select the Manual icon.

The Celtx Studios Owner's Manual is a PDF that opens in your browser, providing detailed information about Celtx Studios features. The PDF can be printed or saved to your local drive for reference.

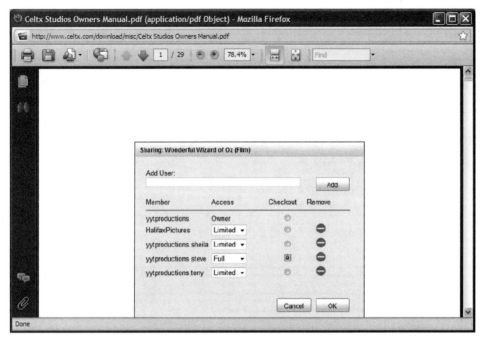

Figure 15.30   The Celtx Studios Owner's Manual, available in the Studio Guide.

Chatting in the Studio

Need to quickly message a fellow studio user while working on a project? Celtx Studios provides a live chat feature for studio users.

The chat client needs to be triggered from within Celtx (not your studio's browser window).

Buddy List

Figure 15.31 shows the Buddy List window opened in Celtx when the Chat button is selected.

The Buddy List shows all the projects you own and have shared with one or more users. Each project provides a bulleted list of all shared users. The bullets are green if users are currently logged into the studio; otherwise, the bullets are grayed out.

Note: Like any browser window, the Buddy List can be moved, resized, or maximized. Its default placement is the left edge of the screen, overlaying the primary Celtx window.

Conversations Window

To chat with an in-studio user, double-click on the user ID. Figure 15.32 shows the Conversations chat window that opens.

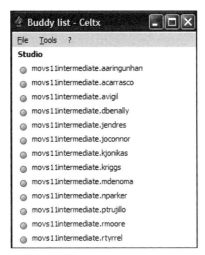

Figure 15.31   Buddy List, triggered when you click the Chat button in the Celtx status bar.

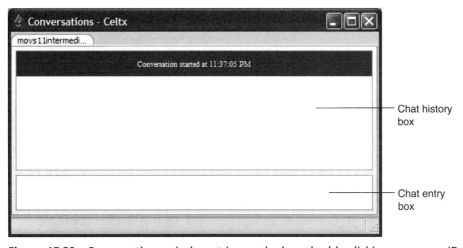

Figure 15.32   Conversations window, triggered when double-clicking on a user ID in the Buddy List.

Note: Double-clicking an inactive user ID also opens a Conversations window. Although the window is fully functional, you can only conduct one-sided chats.

Celtx's chat feature works like most other chat applications.

To begin a two-way chat with the selected user, type in the chat entry box at the bottom of the Conversations window. Pressing the Return or Enter key on the keyboard completes the message and displays it in the history box above, along with an indicator of the sender and a date- and time-stamp for the message entry.

The receiver can then reply, and a chat dialog can be sustained for as long as necessary. Figure 15.33 shows a typical chat session in the Conversations window.

Figure 15.33 Sample chat session in the Conversations window.

To start up a second, concurrent two-way chat session:

1. Return to the Buddy List.

2. Double-click a second user ID. (Remember to look for the green button indicating the user is currently logged in to the studio.)

You now see two tabbed chat sessions in the Conversations window. Clicking a tab makes the current session available for your interaction with it.

Figure 15.34 shows a Conversations window with two concurrent chat sessions running.

You can continue opening chat sessions as necessary and moving between them by selecting tabs.

Tabbed chat
sessions

Figure 15.34 Two concurrent chat sessions in the Conversations window.

Note: Currently, the chat client doesn't support three-way, four-way, or five-way chats. Each chat session is between two users.

Tip: Chat histories can be selected, copied, and then pasted into a text editor or word processing program for preservation.

Buddy List Menu Bar

The Buddy List menu bar contains two active pull-down menus:

- **File.** Accesses notification and exit features

- **Tools.** Accesses messaging style, sounds, and emoticons

File Menu

Figure 15.35 displays the Buddy List's File menu choices:

- **Away.** This triggers an "away from computer" message for chat participants when the choice is checked. Unchecking the selection clears the message.

- **Exit.** This closes out the Buddy List window.

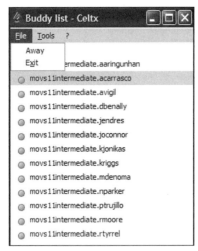

Figure 15.35   File menu pulled down from Buddy List menu bar.

Tools Menu

Figure 15.36 displays the Buddy List's Tools menu choices, which include Sounds, Message Styles, and Smileys.

Sounds. This menu item toggles audio cues during chats. Most users prefer Sound checked in the menu to provide audible feedback while interacting with another user.

Message Styles. Figure 15.37 displays the Message Styles dialog box, which contains a preview window for chat histories, and settings to customize the message style.

The settings follow:

- **Theme.** Four themes are available: Default (a plain text layout); Blackened (a light text on dark background history screen); Depth (a more compressed display using a smaller font and highlighting for the current message); and Minimal (black-on-white with colored fonts to distinguish chat participants).

- **Variant.** For the Minimal theme only, dozens of "variant" color combinations are available.

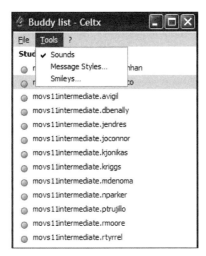

Figure 15.36   Tools menu pulled down from Buddy List menu bar.

Figure 15.37   Message Styles dialog box, selected from the Tools menu.

- **Show Header.** For the Minimal theme only, a chat header can be displayed (marking the chat's start time).

Smileys. Figure 15.38 displays the Smileys dialog box, which allows you to set two different emoticons themes (default or MSN)—or disable emoticons completely. Aside from the drop-down menu box to set the theme, most of the dialog box contains a two-column table displaying emoticons (the smileys) and their text equivalents.

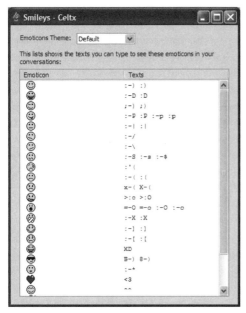

Figure 15.38 Smileys dialog box, selected from the Tools menu.

Summary

This chapter looked at the following:

- Logging in to the studio (in a variety of ways)

- Saving projects to the studio and opening projects from the studio

- Using Projects features such as editing, sharing, and deleting

- Using Archives features to look up a project's version history, step through library items for each version, and generate side-by-side views of project versions

- Using Celtx Studios' web Preview feature, which gives studio users a way to build professional-looking internal websites for easy perusal of project content

- Using the Studio Guide to answer frequently asked questions, find demonstration screenshots, and read the owner's manual

- Using Celtx Studios' real-time chat client and initiating multiple chat sessions with fellow studio users

The next chapter looks at Celtx add-ons and additional sketch images to see how they can add further value to Celtx usage.

16 Celtx Add-Ons, Utilities, and Sketch Images

Celtx offers a number of free and low-cost add-ons for project building and editing. In addition, Celtx offers low-cost sketch images to more fully exploit the Sketch tool discussed in Chapter 9, "Sketches."

The categories of Celtx add-ons covered in this chapter include

- Free downloadable utilities that can help with script composition, script breakdowns, iPhone/iPad syncing, and project management

- Free localized spell check dictionaries

- Low-cost add-ons focused on the composition and editing process

- Low-cost add-ons focused on learning the craft of screenwriting and project development

- Low-cost sketch images

Free Downloadable Utilities

Celtx's two free downloadable utilities—iPhone/iPad Desktop Sync and Session Timer—sync files between device systems and help perform project management and client billing.

Celtx's free utilities are available on the Celtx website (www.celtx.com). Once there, click on the Add-Ons tab in the nav-bar. The direct URL is http://celtx.com/addons.html.

Note: Linux users should review Appendix F, "Setting Up Linux for Celtx Studios and Celtx Add-Ons," particularly if they haven't previously used Celtx Studios. (See Chapter 14, "Celtx Studios: Creation and Administration," and Chapter 15, "Celtx Studios: User Interaction," for full discussion of this Celtx application.) A one-time configuration of browser values is necessary to install and use add-ons. If the configuration has already been executed for Celtx Studio, there is no need to repeat when using add-ons. If you're not sure if these configuration changes have been made, consult your system administrator.

Once you're at the Add-Ons page, scroll down to find tabs for different kinds of add-ons. Choose Free Utilities. Figure 16.1 shows the Free Utilities page.

Figure 16.1 The Free Utilities webpage, accessible through the Add-Ons page of the Celtx website.

Figure 16.2 shows the Toolbox window, which opens when the add-on is downloaded. An informational reminder in the toolbox advises that you close and restart Celtx to complete the installation.

Tip: You can always reach the Toolbox window in Celtx by pulling down the Tools menu and selecting Toolbox. There, you can identify currently installed add-ons.

---

iPhone/iPad Desktop Sync

The Desktop Sync add-on enables you to sync your scripts between mobile devices and desktop/laptop Celtx (including any Celtx studios you might be using). This add-on is only useful if you're already using the Celtx Script mobile app.

Once installed, the add-on works transparently. Chapter 13, "Celtx Script," describes the downloading, installation, and usage of the iPhone/iPad Desktop Sync add-on, and the section titled "Syncing Scripts Between Mobile Devices and Desktop/Laptop Devices" discusses how to sync between devices.

Session Timer

The Session Timer add-on manages and tracks writing time, break time, and words written during a writing session. This can be useful in any of the following ways:

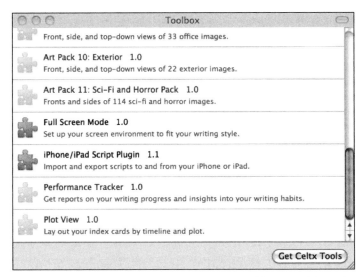

Figure 16.2   The Toolbox window, triggered by an add-on download.

- Setting your own personal goals and tracking your performance

- Tracking project commitment time for a client, a supervisor, or an instructor

- Discovering optimum productivity periods during the course of the day

Installation of the Session Timer add-on adds a digital timer button to the lower-right corner of a script editing window, just below the right sidebar.

Select the timer to view the pop-up menu.

The pop-up menu provides the following choices:

- **Timer.** Starts/pauses/resumes the timer

- **Show Remaining.** Displays the remaining time to the next break

- **Session Summary.** Displays the summary writing time, break time, and words written

- **Start Break.** Starts a session break

- **Reset Timer.** Resets the timer

- **Settings.** Allows you to view and change the settings

Figure 16.3 shows the Settings dialog box.

The Settings dialog box lets you do the following

- Automatically start the timer when the script opens

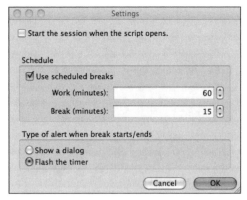

Figure 16.3   The Settings dialog box, triggered when you select Settings from the Session Timer pop-up menu.

■ Set work and break times for a writing session. The default setting is 60 minutes of work followed by a 15-minute break. Based on the time you set, you are prompted to take a break and to continue your writing.

■ Select the type of alert when your break starts/ends. Show a Dialog pops up a dialog box when your break starts and ends. Flash a Timer means the timer flashes several times when your break starts and ends.

> **Caution:** Deselecting Use Scheduled Breaks means that all session time is considered writing time and you are not prompted to take a break. Alerts only appears if Use Scheduled Breaks is selected.

You can start the Session Timer in three ways:

■ Hover your mouse pointer over the Clock icon. The Clock icon changes to a Play button. Click on the Play button to start the Session Timer.

■ Select Start Timer from the Session Timer pop-up menu.

■ In the Settings dialog box, select Start the Timer When the Script Opens, which automatically starts the timer.

> **Note:** Automatic timer starts may be particularly useful if you have to submit a report to a professor or client noting how many hours you worked on a project file. Of course, you may find it helpful for your own progress to force yourself to work 30 minutes or 5 hours a day on a project!

There are two ways to pause the Session Timer:

- When the timer is active, hover your pointer over the Clock icon. The Clock icon changes to a Pause button. Click the Pause button to pause the Session Timer.

- Select Pause Session from the Session Timer pop-up menu.

Free Localized Spell Check Dictionaries

Localized dictionaries can better customize the Celtx user experience. As of publication, some two dozen localizations had been developed, and more are sure to come. Setting up your preferred dictionary involves two steps:

1. Once you install a dictionary and restart Celtx, pull down the Tools menu and select Check Spelling.

2. Then, from the drop-down menu at the bottom of the Check Spelling dialog box, select the dictionary you want to use as the spell check default.

Add-On Bundles

Celtx bundles collections of add-ons for discounted purchase. Bundles include a writer's pack (the writing add-ons), a learning pack (the learning series), and the entire collection of Sketch images.

Writing Add-Ons

Celtx provides several low-cost add-ons focused on increasing writing productivity:

- **Plot View.** Lay out your index cards by timeline and plot to get a clear picture of how your story is taking shape.

- **Full Screen Mode.** Set up your screen environment to fit your writing style.

- **Performance Tracker.** Get reports on your writing progress and insights into your writing habits.

You can buy these add-ons separately or bundled together. This section looks at the purchase and installation process, and then the individual add-ons.

Paid Add-Ons

Clicking the Buy button for an add-on triggers a typical online purchase process. Once the transaction has been approved, you are presented with a Download link. You're also sent an email confirmation, which provides a direct Download link.

Selecting the Download link opens the Toolbox dialog box to show you that your add-on has been properly downloaded. Close the dialog box, and then restart Celtx to complete the installation process.

Full Screen Mode

Many writers prefer a minimum of clutter when they are composing or revising scripts. The Full Screen Mode add-on does exactly that, adding three buttons to the script editing toolbar:

- Full Screen Mode

- Text Color

- Background Color

Figure 16.4 shows the new color selectors and Full Screen Mode toolbar. This will be appended to the script editing toolbar when the add-on has been installed.

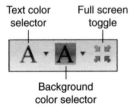

Figure 16.4 Color selectors and Full Screen Toggle button. These will be added to the script editing toolbar.

Clicking the Full Screen button switches the script editor to Full Screen Mode; clicking it again returns to the default view with sidebars.

Tip: You can also use keyboard shortcuts to enter and exit Full Screen Mode. For the Mac, press Cmd+Option+F; for Windows and Linux, press Ctrl-Alt-F.

Clicking the Text Color or Background Color button provides a palette of color swatches to select from.

Tip: In general, combining two high-contrast colors is best when enhancing text composition and editing. Some writers prefer dark text against a light background (dark blue or black on white or ivory, for example). Others prefer bright text against a dark background (bright green or amber on black, for example). Low-contrast combinations don't work effectively for most people.

Plot View

The Plot View add-on lays out your index cards by timeline and plot to give you a clear picture of how your story is taking shape. Plot View also displays your index cards using an attractive paper card and corkboard theme.

To access Plot View, first select the Index Cards tab in the script editing window. As Figure 16.5 shows, Plot View adds a Show Plot View button to the Index Cards toolbar.

Figure 16.5   The new Show Plot View button in the Index Cards toolbar.

Clicking the Show Plot View button triggers a corkboard display with index cards laid out left to right. Figure 16.6 shows the main window with the cork background, along with the lower plot line panel, which contains the following:

- Plot line names, such as Plot A and Plot B, or Action Plot and Thematic Plot. (See Chapter 2, "Getting Familiar with Celtx," for the discussion on tagging index cards with plot names.) Plot lines can be selected and deselected to focus on specific narrative arcs within the script.

- A gray highlight box representing the current view of index cards shown in the main window. You can drag the highlight box around to review a different set of index cards. (Think of the highlight box as a sort of magnifier for the main window view.)

- Narrow rectangles representing index cards. You can drag and drop the rectangles, reshuffling index cards in a particular plot line or across plot lines. (For example, you can move a Plot A index card into Plot B.)

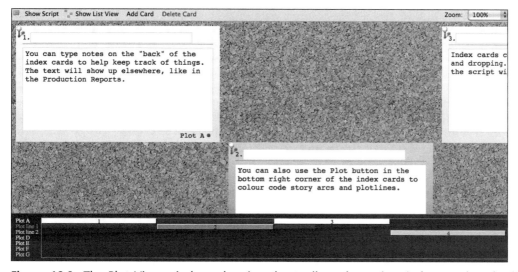

Figure 16.6   The Plot View window, showing the toolbar, the main window, and a plot line panel below the main window. (This sample is taken from *The Wonderful Wizard of Oz* project file included with Celtx.)

Tip: Decreasing the zoom allows you to display more index cards in the main window.

The Plot View toolbar includes the following buttons (and one drop-down list box):

- **Show Notes.** Displays complete index cards (headings and full content)
- **List View.** Provides a list view of the index card headings
- **Add Card.** Adds a new index card
- **Delete Card.** Deletes the currently selected index card
- **Zoom.** Controls the zoom level

Performance Tracker

The Performance Tracker add-on provides session and summary reports on every writing session and script, including these:

- Number of words written
- Time spent writing and on break
- Element and dialog word breakdown

The Performance Tracker also analyzes the following:

- Best writing days of the week
- Contribution of each writer on multiwriter projects
- Achievement of session, daily, and script goals

In addition, the Performance Tracker allows you to publish your progress through Twitter, which can be useful either in a classroom situation or to provide breathless progress reports as part of the momentum-building for future crowd-funding or other promotional activities.

Once installed, the Performance Tracker shows up as a Timer button in the lower-right corner of the script editing window. Figure 16.7 shows the Timer location in relation to the script editing subtabs.

Figure 16.7   Performance Tracker timer button, installed in the script editing window on the right of the subtabs and below the right sidebar.

Note: If you've previously installed the Session Timer, you may find two separate timers installed below the right sidebar once you install the Performance Tracker. To remove the

Session Timer, pull down the Tools menu and select Toolbox. Scroll and find the Writing Session Timer. Select the tool and click on the Disable button. Restart Celtx when you're instructed to onscreen, and you will now have a single timer while working.

As Figure 16.8 shows, clicking the Performance Tracker timer pops up the session menu, providing the following features:

- **Start Session.** Begins the Session Timer (once selected, this feature toggles to End Session

- **Show Remaining.** Displays the remaining time to the next scheduled break

- **Reports.** Displays your writing session report

- **Start Break.** Starts a session break

- **Reset Session.** Resets the session

- **Settings.** Allows you to view and change the settings

Figure 16.8   The Performance Tracker session menu, triggered when you click the timer.

Reports

Figure 16.9 shows the Reports window that opens when you select Reports from the session menu.

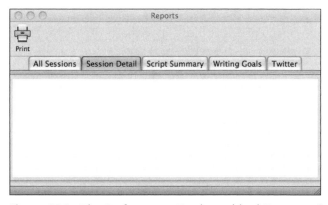

Figure 16.9   The Performance Tracker tabbed Reports window.

Reports tabs include the following:

- All Sessions
- Session Detail
- Script Summary
- Writing Goals
- Twitter

All Sessions. This tab shows your cumulative project writing time and words written.

In addition, the report gives session-by-session breakdowns of writing time and words written, and notes the date each session was started.

If the writer is signing in to Celtx Studios (see Chapters 15 and 16 for a full discussion of this feature), the report also displays the session author.

Session Detail. This tab displays a session-by-session breakdown and analysis of your writing, including the following:

- Session number
- Session start date
- Session start time and end time
- Session writing time and break time
- Number of words written
- Number of new scenes, action words, and dialog added
- New characters added

The report also analyzes your word contribution and provides illustrative charts of how you split your writing among different elements and dialog each character speaks.

Script Summary. This tab displays a total project breakdown and analysis of your writing, reporting on

- Longest and shortest session length, and average duration
- Most and fewest words written per session, and overall average

If Celtx Studios is being used and a project is being shared, this report also provides a chart of each writer's word contribution toward the project.

This report also provides charts illustrating the following:

- Total number of words written, by element

- Total number of words of dialog for each character

- Your most productive writing days of the week, by session and by total words written

Writing Goals. This tab sets and tracks your progress toward session, daily, and script goals.

Twitter. This tab allows you to tweet your progress to your Twitter followers. You can pre-populate tweets with goal messaging and writing hash tags.

Tip: Using hash tags enables your tweets to show up in popular threads.

Settings

Clicking the Settings selection on the session menu opens the Settings dialog box, which is identical to the free Session Timer Settings dialog box shown in Figure 16.3. Inside the dialog box, you can do the following:

- Automatically start the timer when the script opens.

- Set work and break times for a writing session. The default setting is 60 minutes of work followed by a 15-minute break. Based on the time you set, you are prompted to take a break and to continue your writing.

- Select type of alert when break starts/ends. Show a Dialog pops up a dialog box when your break starts and ends; Flash a Timer means the timer flashes several times when your break starts and ends.

Caution: Deselecting Use Scheduled Breaks means that all the session time is considered writing time and you are not prompted to take a break. Alerts only appear if Use Scheduled Breaks is selected.

You can start the Session Timer in one of three ways:

- Hover your mouse pointer over the Clock icon. The Clock icon changes to a Play button. Click on the Play button to start the Session Timer.

- Select Start Timer from the Session Timer pop-up menu.

- In the Settings dialog box, select Start the Timer When the Script Opens, which automatically starts the timer.

There are two ways to pause the Session Timer.

- When the timer is active, hover your pointer over the Clock icon. The Clock icon changes to a Pause button. Click the Pause button to pause the Session Timer.

- Select Pause Session from the Session Timer pop-up menu.

There are three ways to end a session:

- Select End Session in the Session menu.

- Close the Script tab.

- Close the project.

Sketch Images

Celtx's Sketch tool increases tremendously in value when low-cost image bundles are downloaded and installed. Installation automatically places the images in the Sketch palette. As of our publication date, Celtx had more than 600 images available for purchase. Image bundles include

- Characters

- Animals

- Vehicles

- Sound FX and Speech Bubbles

- Equipment

- Arrows

- Kitchen

- Bedroom & Bathroom

- Living Room

- Office

- Exterior

- Sci-Fi & Horror

See Chapter 9 for a full discussion of the Sketch tool and its use. Building out the Sketch tool with additional images makes the tool useful for pre-visualizing camera placement, lighting setups, shot selections, and character blocking within scenes.

To illustrate this, Figure 16.10 shows the same overhead shot sketch demonstrated in Figure 9.14, but now with a greater array of objects using the purchased sketch images.

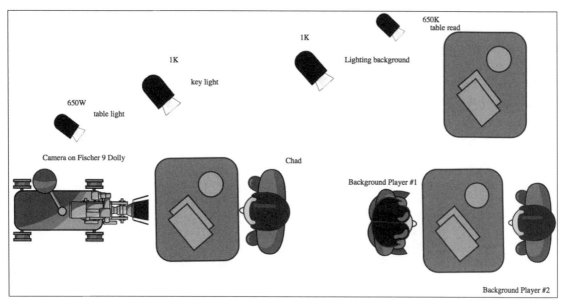

Figure 16.10   Shot 5.1 of *Delivery Date*, using additional purchased sketch images.

Learning Series

Celtx offers several low-cost projects designed to instruct users in aspects of project development and composition:

- *Welcome to Machinima.* A deconstruction of a chapter from an online machinima series, created by Phil Rice

- *Writer's Development Kit.* Lessons on document workflow, developed by story analyst Karel Segers

- *Beginner's Guide to Comic Books.* Demonstration on comic book development by comic book author Wallace Ryan

Summary

This chapter looked at the following free and low-cost add-ons Celtx provides:

- Free downloadable utilities, including the Session Timer and iPhone/iPad sync.

- Free localized spell check dictionaries.

- Low-cost writer's add-ons, including Full Screen Mode, Plot View, and Performance Tracker.

- Low-cost sketch images that upgrade the Sketch tool to a full-fledged pre-visualization solution.

- Low-cost learning series tutorials for machinima, comic book, and film/video script creation.

The next chapter looks at the growing Celtx community, where you can continue to find support and new ideas for applications in creating media.

17 The Celtx Community

Hundreds of thousands use Celtx around the world, and a fervent and active community has grown up around the screenwriting and pre-production software.

This chapter looks at the Celtx forums, maintained on the Celtx website; the Celtx blog; Celtx on Facebook and Twitter; the Celtx wiki; and third-party sites devoted to fostering the Celtx community.

Celtx Forums

Celtx forums provide a hub for Celtx's worldwide community of users. If you have a question about Celtx use, capabilities, or troubleshooting, the forums are the place to post your question and study other users' experiences and information.

Figure 17.1 shows the entry page for the Celtx forums (http://forums.celtx.com/).

The forums are divided into two categories: community and support.

Community forum topics include these:

- **General Discussion.** Posts revolve around scripts, films, and writing.

- **Script Reviews & Collaboration.** Posts revolve around feedback and assistance for your Celtx project.

- **Script Competitions.** Posts revolve around screenwriting contests.

- **Celtx International.** Posts revolve around localizations and building communities in users' countries.

Support forum topic threads include these:

- News and Announcements

- Celtx Q&A

- Celtx Studios

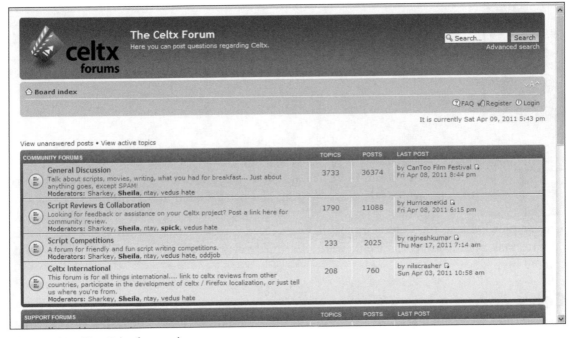

Figure 17.1 The Celtx forums home page.

- Mobile Apps
- Features Suggestion
- Modifying Celtx
- Report a Bug
- Attachment Testing

Any visitor can read postings on the forums, but to post, you need to register.

Celtx Blog

The Celtx blog (http://blog.celtx.com) allows the Celtx team to go in depth on new developments and observations. Posts discuss Celtx's place in media industries and appearances at trade shows, news about media conferences and competitions, and more.

Celtx on Facebook and Twitter

The Celtx Facebook page rounds up Celtx Facebook users around the world for social networking and to publicize announcements and relevant news for the Celtx community.

Keeping tabs on the Celtx Facebook page may be a great way to network with fellow professionals or media enthusiasts and to find out about new releases and tutorials, contests, user projects, and more.

The Celtx Twitter feed also networks thousands of Celtx enthusiasts for real-time information on new Celtx developments, screenwriting news and announcements, event blasts, and more.

Both the Twitter feed and the Facebook page are resources for seeing what twenty-first century media practitioners are creating, often using Celtx.

Celtx Wiki

The Celtx wiki (http://wiki.celtx.com) is a user-generated user manual that can usually answer any question you might have about how the software works.

As Figure 17.2 illustrates, the wiki is available in a number of languages, including German, French, Slavic, Spanish, Swedish, Turkish, and Hungarian.

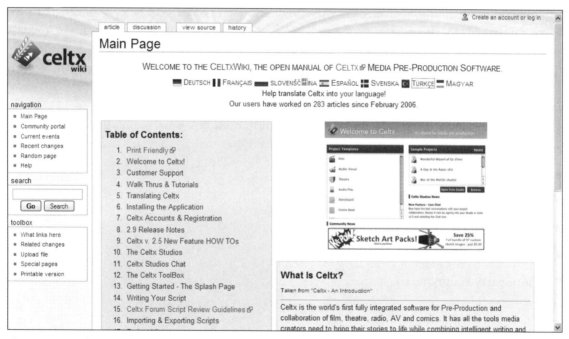

Figure 17.2   The Celtx wiki home page, showing links to localized versions of the wiki.

Caution: As a user-generated resource, sections of the wiki are sometimes out of date. Although the wiki is one useful resource, be sure to consult the forums for additional or updated information.

Third-Party Community Resources

Celtx users have created dozens of 2–3 minute screen-capture video tutorials to walk through various Celtx features. (Texas videographer Drew Noah is one source for these videos.) Many of these are found on the how-to site ehow.com, as well as on YouTube.

In addition, filmmakerIQ.com has curated more than 100 free online Celtx tutorials.

Celtx is also discussed in an online video series called *Motion Sketches*, which explores twenty-first century approaches to media production and workflow. You can find the video series at Vimeo.com (www.vimeo.com/celtx) and blip.tv (http://celtx.blip.tv).

The Celtx forums and Facebook page can keep you abreast of new third-party community resources.

You Are Part of the Celtx Community

If you've worked through most or all of this book, you are now a part of the Celtx community and can contribute to the continued growth and development of Celtx. Celtx continues to evolve based on user feedback and emerging needs. Get on the forums, make some tutorials, request features you'd like to be added, and see if you can find hidden nooks and crannies in the software that this book hasn't covered!

Summary

This chapter looked at the following Celtx community resources, some maintained and nurtured directly by Celtx, and others created by Celtx enthusiasts:

- Celtx forums
- The Celtx blog
- Celtx on Facebook and Twitter
- The Celtx wiki
- Third-party community resources

Appendix A: Understanding Script Formats

Script formats have evolved over many decades, and the more you understand the purposes behind the layouts and the formats of scripts, the easier they become to write.

Master Scene (Screenplay) Format

The master scene format has evolved from the earliest days of "talking pictures" and is what media nonprofessionals generally recognize as "screenplay format." You should select this format whenever audio and video capture is largely simultaneous, such as when you're shooting scenes with actors speaking dialog. The *Delivery Date* script used as an example throughout the book is an instance of a screenplay written in the master scene format.

In feature film screenplays from the 1930s, screenwriters were asked to provide relatively explicit camera directions (such as CLOSE-UP ON MARLOWE, ANGLE ON SCARLETT). However, cinematographers and directors rarely paid attention to these camera directions. With the passing of the old "studio system" in the 1960s, the master scene format gradually simplified to function more effectively as a film "blueprint" that would read well for investors, executives, talent, and crew.

Single-camera episodic television adopted the same format, while three-camera television (typically situation comedies) made some alterations due to their unique production workflow.

This first section of Appendix A looks at the key elements in the master scene format.

Left-Justified Elements

Elements that are left-justified using this format include the following:

- **The scene heading.** Often called the slug line, this appears in all capital letters and demarcates the commencement of a scene. It typically includes the following:

  1. An indication of an interior (INT.) or exterior (EXT.) setting

  2. The location

  3. An indication of either a day shoot or a night shoot (with occasionally more explicit time-of-day indications). Example: INT. HIGH SCHOOL CLASSROOM—DAY

- **The action description.** Often called stage direction, this indicates what the characters may be doing and what other sights, actions, or events are occurring within the frame of the shot.

- **The shot.** This appears in all capital letters and sometimes indicates a momentary change of focus or interaction within a single (often large) location, such as a warehouse that includes an UPPER CATWALK. Figure 2.4 in Chapter 2, "Getting Familiar with Celtx," shows an example of how to use the Shot element within a screenplay.

Indented Elements

Master scene format elements that are left-justified include:

- **Character name.** This appears in all capital letters and directly precedes dialog the character speaks. The element is consistently indented nearly halfway across the page.

- **Dialog.** This is indented one inch from both the left margin and the right margin, and it follows the line immediately after the character name element.

- **The parenthetical.** This is sometimes inserted on a single line between the character name and the dialog to indicate how a line of dialog is read. This is consistently indented.

- **The transition.** This demarcates the end of a scene and describes how one scene ends and a new scene begins, such as a cut or fade or dissolve into the next scene. The transition element is right-justified and is something of a holdover from the early days of the master scene format, when screenwriters were asked to compose more technical directions. Many contemporary professional screenwriters argue that the transition element is unnecessary, because the majority of scenes conclude with a simple cut—and worrying about transitions is really a post-production, not a pre-production issue.

How Master Scene Format Elements Help in Pre-Production

The format of a screenplay has remained largely unchanged for 80+ years because of its functionality. Indentation and capitalization make the document easily scannable for any reader. Think about how these elements assist cast and crew in pre-production—with the script serving as both database and instruction manual.

- A location scout or location manager just needs to read the scene headings to know what locations to begin looking for (and whether they're interior or exterior locations and night or day locations)—and how many locations exist of various kinds.

- An assistant director can look at the scene headings, character names, and overall scene lengths to begin constructing schedules.

- A casting director just needs to look at scene headings and character names to know how big the cast is and how many scenes characters are in.

- An actor just needs to look at scene headings, character names, and dialog to find out how many scenes he is in and how many lines he has to memorize or read from a prompter.

- A propmaster just needs to look at scene headings and action descriptions to find out what and how many props are in a scene.

- A director can read action descriptions to determine when a prop needs to show up; a cinematographer can read them to determine when a composited shot may be necessary.

A/V Script Format

The A/V (audio/visual) script format is commonly used when separate audio and video assets are pieced together to assemble a narrative.

An example would be a documentary combining audio-only interviews, archival video and stills, silent dramatic re-creations, voiceover narration, and animation of charts and graphs.

Television and web commercials, training and marketing films, documentaries, and episodic reality TV are examples of projects that typically require A/V formatted scripts.

The A/V format is commonly known as the two-column or dual-column format, because this is its salient feature. Somewhat confusingly given the name audio/video, the video portion of the script goes on the left side of the page, and the audio portion goes on the right side. Figure A.1 shows a typical A/V script.

Most of the A/V format elements are identical to master scene format elements, but the two-column arrangement continuously segregates the audio and the video and emphasizes the shot more than the scene. All elements are left-justified within the column.

Video Elements

The A/V format includes the following video elements:

- **The scene heading.** Often called the slug line, this appears in all capital letters and demarcates the commencement of a scene. It typically includes the following:

  1. An indication of an interior (INT.) or exterior (EXT.) setting (if necessary)

  2. The location or "event"

  3. An indication of a day or night setting (if necessary). Example 1: INT. HIGH SCHOOL CLASSROOM—DAY. Example 2: MONTAGE OF ARCHIVAL YEARBOOK PHOTOS.

- **The shot.** This appears in all capital letters and describes the central visual focus of the action. Example 1: THE SPORTS CAR TOOLS DOWN THE HIGHWAY. Example 2: CAT AND FOOD DISH.

- **The action description.** This indicates the current visual action. It could be a re-creation of Egyptian slaves building a pyramid, or a slideshow of historic images.

1

VIDEO	AUDIO
TITLE: Acme Learning Systems tag and logo Fade to Black: then up on...	NARRATOR (V.O.) The following is a college course, based on the textbooks, "Marketing" and "Marketing: It's Cool," written by Warren, Goodrich and Hazard and published by Big Time Case Study Publishers.
MONTAGE: Las Vegas. Include places highlighted throughout program.	(Ambient audio - slot machines, poker, casino patron buzz, etc.) NARRATOR Las Vegas. At one time, it was the only city in America that offered legal casino gaming. Today, there's some form of gambling throughout the United States, as well as many parts of the world. People don't need to visit Las Vegas to indulge in this particular form of entertainment. Yet, they do -- in increasing numbers. There are many reasons for the success of this City of Lights. And it's a sure bet marketing has a lot to do with it.
TITLE: PRINCIPLES IN MARKETING An Introduction to Marketing Case Study LAS VEGAS	(Series Theme Music)
MEDIUM: GREG DONNER SUPER: Greg Donner, Corporate Director of Marketing, Acme Gaming Corp. MONTAGE: Consumers in the buying process, i.e. purchasing products, checking ads, comparing prices, etc. Include Las Vegas vacationers and gamblers. (Stock footage.)	DONNER Marketing to me is the enticement of people to, uh, look at purchasing your goods or services. Uh, and a lot of times it's an intangible.

Figure A.1 A page from a typical A/V script.

Audio Elements

The A/V format includes the following audio elements:

- **Character name.** This appears in all capital letters and directly precedes dialog the character speaks.

- **Dialog.** This follows on the line immediately after the character name element. Frequently, this dialog may be extracted from audio-only or audio/video interviews, and it may include time code from the interview recording.

- **The parenthetical.** This is sometimes inserted on a single line between the character name and the dialog to indicate how a line of dialog is read.

Two-Column Layout

Audio and video elements need to be parallel with each other. For example, if a piece of audio time code or voiceover narration needs to overlay a shot of a car pulling into a driveway, the two elements need to line up, so people understand the time relationship between them. Figure A.2 shows this parallelism.

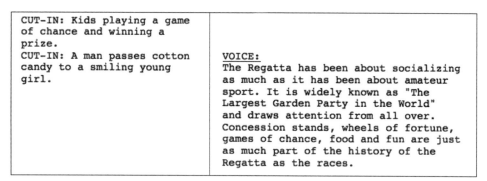

CUT-IN: Kids playing a game of chance and winning a prize. CUT-IN: A man passes cotton candy to a smiling young girl.	VOICE: The Regatta has been about socializing as much as it has been about amateur sport. It is widely known as "The Largest Garden Party in the World" and draws attention from all over. Concession stands, wheels of fortune, games of chance, food and fun are just as much part of the history of the Regatta as the races.

Figure A.2   Video and audio shown in parallel in A/V format.

How A/V Format Elements Help in Pre-Production

Reading scripts in A/V format is often more challenging than scripts using the master scene format; however, the two-column layout increases the naked-eye scannability of the document.

Think about how these elements assist cast and crew in pre-production—with the script serving as both database and instruction manual.

- Artists can focus solely on the video-only column to create storyboards.

- Voiceover actors can focus on the audio-only column to concentrate on lines.

- Cinematographers can isolate product "beauty shots" in the video-only column.

The A/V format may also force a media creator to think more about the blend and balance between audio and visual elements—while avoiding tendencies toward writing static filmed mini-plays.

Stageplay Format

The printed stageplay format as it's known today was largely ratified by the publishings of William Shakespeare's and Ben Jonson's plays in the seventeenth century and has evolved modestly in the centuries since. Because playwrights often wrote the first "talkie" screenplays, the stageplay worked as a model for the master scene formatted screenplay that developed in the 1930s.

Indentation of key elements can vary modestly, depending on the playwright's or the publisher's preference. Consistency of the indentation is critical. Figure A.3 shows how a stageplay looks using Celtx.

ACT I

Scene 1

Morning-room in Algernon's flat in Half-Moon Street. The room is luxuriously and artistically furnished. The sound of a piano is heard in the adjoining room. Lane is arranging afternoon tea on the table. The music ends and, after a moment, Algernon enters.

ALGERNON
Did you hear what I was playing, Lane?

LANE
I didn't think it polite to listen, sir.

ALGERNON
I'm sorry for that, for your sake. I don't play accurately - anyone can play accurately - but I play with wonderful expression. As far as the piano is concerned, sentiment is my forte. I keep science for life.

LANE
Yes, sir.

ALGERNON
And, speaking of the science of life, have you got the cucumber sandwiches cut for Lady Bracknell?

LANE
Yes, sir.

Hands them on a salver.

Figure A.3 Stageplay page in Celtx.

Key Elements

Stageplay format elements include the following:

- **The Act heading.** This demarcates the start of a new act on the stage—typically centered, usually at the top of the page.

- **The scene heading.** This is usually numbered, underlined, and centered, and sometimes it includes a brief location indicator. Example: <u>Scene 1—Living Room</u>

- **Stage direction.** This is usually italicized and often substantially indented on the page. Typically more minimal than screenplay action (after all, there aren't going to be crashing cars or characters jumping off buildings), stage directions usually set the time and place and handle entrance and exit cues. In addition, they may provide minimal character blockings, set design suggestions, and other information about what's seen on stage.

- **Character name.** This appears in all capital letters and directly precedes dialog the character speaks.

- **Dialog.** This follows immediately after the character name element (usually on the line below).

- **The parenthetical.** This is sometimes inserted on a single line between the character name and the dialog to indicate how a line of dialog is read. This is indented consistently.

How Stageplay Elements Help in Pre-Production

The format of a stageplay has remained largely unchanged for hundreds of years because of its functionality. Layout and italicization make specific elements easily scannable. Think about how these elements assist cast and crew in pre-production—with the script acting as both database and instruction manual.

- An actor just needs to look at character name and dialog to find out how many lines he has to memorize.

- A stage manager just needs to look at scene headings and stage directions to learn about entrance and exit cues, props, and costume requirements. A set designer studies the same elements for an understanding of set needs.

Audio Play Format

The audio play format was developed during the heyday of radio, from the 1920s to the 1940s. Audio scripts are still useful for broadcast radio/Internet radio/podcast commercials, public service announcements, and the occasional audio-only drama or comedy that's written and produced. Figure A.4 shows a typical page from an audio script.

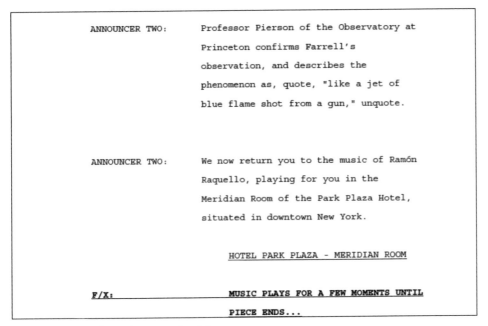

Figure A.4 Audio script page in Celtx.

Key Elements

Key elements have been standardized for most of a century, with minor variations in layout and print attributes. They include the following:

- **The scene heading.** This is usually underlined and centered and may be numbered or indicate a location.

  Example: <u>Los Angeles—Staples Center</u>

- **Character name.** This appears in all capital letters and directly precedes dialog the character speaks.

- **Dialog.** This follows immediately after the character name element. (In the two-column audio play format, this will be just to the right of the character name.)

- **The parenthetical.** This is sometimes inserted on a single line between the character name and the dialog to indicate how a line of dialog is read. This is consistently indented.

- **Sound.** All uppercase and underlined, this indicates a sound effects (SFX) cue.

- **Voice.** All uppercase and underlined, this indicates a voiceover cue.

- **Music.** All uppercase and underlined, this indicates a music cue.

- **The production note.** Often placed in parentheses and indented, this is used for any necessary production information or instructions (not unlike a stage direction for visual work).

How Audio Play Elements Help in Pre-Production

The layout and case of audio play text make specific elements easily scannable. Think about how these elements assist cast and crew in pre-production—with the script acting as both database and instruction manual.

- An actor just needs to look at character name and dialog to find out how many lines he has to read from a script or prompter.

- A narrator just needs to look for voice cues to find out how many lines he will have to read from a script or prompter.

- The Foley artist (who creates sound effects) just needs to review sound cues to know what audio and sound-making equipment are needed.

- A music arranger just needs to review music cues to know what music needs to be licensed or composed.

Comic Book Format

Comic books are narratives that advance via image and text, so it isn't a stretch to say that a comic book is scripted. The comic book also has a rigorous format, established in the early days of printed comics.

Key Elements

Key elements have been standardized for more than three-quarters of a century. They include the following:

- **The page.**
- **The panel.** If you are "scripting" the comic book, you would want to describe the visuals contained within the panel. Most traditional comic book pages contain two or four panels.
- **The panel caption.** This typically describes the narrative advancement within the panel.
- **A character.** This is someone who may be speaking or thinking within the panel.
- **The balloon.** This contains either the thoughts or the words of a character within the panel.
- **The balloon type.** This may indicate either an internal monologue (thinking) or spoken dialog (speaking).
- **The scene heading.** This is usually underlined and centered and may be numbered or indicate a location.

  Example: <u>Los Angeles—Staples Center</u>
- **The character name.** This appears in all capital letters and directly precedes dialog the character speaks.
- **Dialog.** This follows after the character name element (usually on the line below).

Figure A.5 shows a typical comic book script page.

```
Page 1    (4 Panels)
```

Panel	Description	Dialog
1.1	Wide, top-down exterior view of an average two-story house in suburbia. We see the house and the surrounding property.	Caption: It was on this occasion in that grand year of 2004 that the subject of our story, Aaron, sat down to toil over his overdue homework. This was a real chore at the best of times.
1.2	Medium, top-down exterior view of just the upper windows of the house. In the background you can see the adjoining property across the fence, which is partially obscured by a tree.	Caption: School is not one of Aaron's strong suits. He especially didn't like the little punks that made it a living hell.
1.3	Close, exterior view of an open window on the second floor of the house. Through the window we see from back on, Aaron sitting in front of his computer. Aaron is 11-12 years old and is overweight. He has blond curly hair and thick round glasses.	Caption: But at home, Aaron was in his own private shell, and the gang's cruel taunts would fade into the din of the outside world.

Figure A.5 Comic book script page in Celtx.

How Comic Book Elements Help in Pre-Production

Although no standardized comic book "script" layout exists, you can borrow from the A/V script format to facilitate a typical comic book production workflow (where an artist creates panels, and a letterer creates captions and balloons).

If you place panels on the left and captions on the right in a two-column format, an artist can focus solely on the left column, while the letterer can focus on the right column.

Appendix B: Script Template Typeset/ PDF Format Options

Each script template provides different format options for rendering the finished distribution script on paper or in a PDF. This appendix surveys these options. See Chapter 2, "Getting Familiar with Celtx," for an initial discussion of using the Format Options toolbar button in the Typeset/PDF window.

Master Scene (Screenplay) Format Options

Master Scene format options are contained on two separate tabbed dialog boxes: General, and Mores and Continueds.

General

General format options include the following:

- **Paper Size.** Choose North American letter size or European A4 size paper.

- **Show Scene Numbers.** This option is normally toggled on only when your script is locked and headed for pre-production. The default setting during script composition is None. Once your script is locked, you want to show scene numbers. The most common layout for scene numbers is "both" the left and right margin, but some productions are satisfied with right margin numbers only.

- **Lines Between Scenes.** You can increase or decrease the number of blank lines between scenes. Some screenwriters prefer 1, whereas others prefer 2. A setting of 3 would be used only rarely.

- **Page Break After Each Scene.** This option is normally not used, unless you're printing out "sides" for auditioning actors.

- **Show Title Page.** This option ensures that the title page is printed whenever hard copy or a PDF is output.

Mores and Continueds

The Mores and Continueds dialog box provides a number of options, as indicated in the list that follows. Turn on all these options when scripts go to production, but you can skip them for script composition and revision. You can safely uncheck all the options if you find that they clutter the script page while writing.

- **Show Dialogue Breaks.** Typically used for production scripts, this option is usually unchecked for script composition purposes to reduce distraction and clutter.

- **Show Character Continueds.** Some productions like this indicator for successive dialogs from the same character; other productions (and actors) prefer to avoid this. It is typically used for production scripts only.

- **Show Scene Breaks.** This option is common for production scripts, but it's typically unchecked for script composition purposes to reduce distraction and clutter.

- **Show Continued Page Count.** This option lets the reader know when a scene page has part of a scene on an earlier page. Typically used for production scripts, this setting is usually unchecked for script composition purposes to reduce distraction and clutter.

See Figure B.1 (which duplicates Figure 4.6 in Chapter 4, "Creating and Editing Production Film Scripts"), for an example of Mores and Continueds turned on in a production script.

A/V Script Format Options

A/V script format options are contained on two separate tabbed dialog boxes: General and Script Header.

General

General format options include the following:

- **Paper Size.** Choose North American letter size or European A4 size paper.

- **Format (Two Columns).** This lays out the standard A/V format. Figure A.1 in Appendix A, "Understanding Script Formats," shows a typical sample.

- **Format (Shot List).** This setting generates an A/V script shot list. This may be particularly useful if you like using standard shot indicators like CUTAWAY and MEDIUM SHOT. (When composing the script, use a colon after the shot indicator to help Celtx identify the shot in the shot list: for example, MONTAGE: or WIDE:) Figure B.2 shows the layout of a typeset shot list.

- **Show Scene Headers.** This shows scene headings in the A/V two-column script. Some projects and team members may prefer these shown; some may not. Figure B.3 shows scene headers in use.

- **Show Title Page.** This option ensures that the title page is printed out whenever hard copy or a PDF is output.

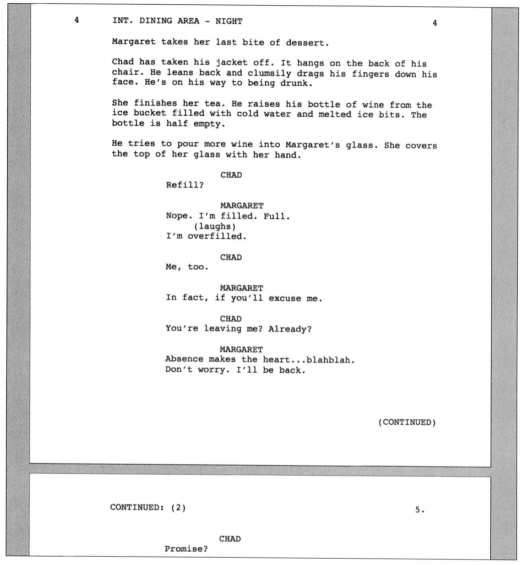

Figure B.1 Scene numbers, Mores and Continueds inserted into script.

Script Header

Particularly in advertising, corporate communications, and any other applications where you may be serving clients, A/V scripts include a script header. Celtx provides the following header fields:

- Project
- Title

Save PDF   Format Options   (H) (4) 1 of 1 (5) (H)   Zoom: [120%]

SHOT	TYPE OF SHOT	DESCRIPTION
1.1	TITLE	Acme Learning Systems tag and logo
1.2	Fade to Black	then up on...
2.1	MONTAGE	Las Vegas. Include places highlighted throughout program.
3.1	TITLE	CONCEPTS IN MARKETING An Introduction to Marketing Case Study LAS VEGAS (Series Theme)
3.2	MEDIUM	GREG DONNER
3.3	SUPER	Greg Donner, Corporate Director of Marketing, Acme Gaming Corp.
3.4	MONTAGE	Consumers in the buying process, i.e. purchasing products, checking ads, comparing prices, etc. Include Las Vegas vacationers and gamblers.
3.5	Marketing Montage of IMAGES	illustrating goods, services, places, ideas.

Figure B.2   Shot list from a typical A/V script.

Scene header

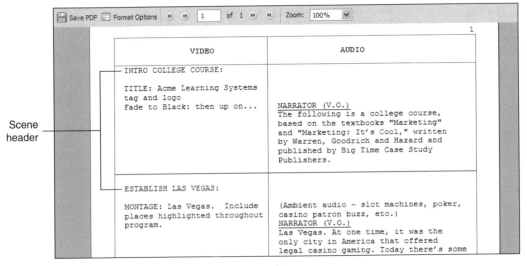

Figure B.3   Scene headers displayed in an A/V script.

- Subject
- Comment
- Writer

- Producer
- Director
- Contact

The Show Script Header check box offers the writer control over whether a header should be printed.

Figure B.4 illustrates this header in use.

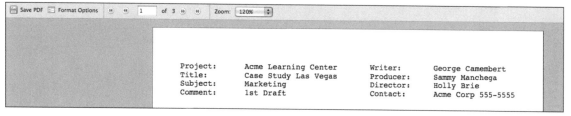

Figure B.4 Typical A/V script header.

Stageplay Format Options

Stageplay format options are contained on two separate tabbed dialog boxes: General, and Mores and Continueds.

General

General format options include the following:

- **Paper Size.** Choose North American letter size or European A4 size paper.

- **Format (International).** This selection formats the stageplay in an international layout, italicizing stage directions and indenting them one inch from the left margin. Character names are set flush left, and dialog is indented one-half inch from the left margin. Scene headings are indented 2 1/2 inches from the left margin. Transitions are set flush right.

- **Format (American).** This selection formats the stageplay in an American layout, dispensing with italics. Stage directions are kept flush with scene headings, character names, and transitions 2 1/2 inches from the left margin. Dialog is flush left.

- **Show Scene Numbers.** This is normally toggled on only when your script is locked and headed for pre-production. The default setting during script composition is None. Once your script is locked, show scene numbers. The most common layout for scene numbers is selecting Both for the left and right margin, but some productions are satisfied with right margin numbers only.

- **Show Title Page & Cast.** Cast lists are typically included with a stageplay. Figure B.5 illustrates a cast list inserted on the page directly following the title page.

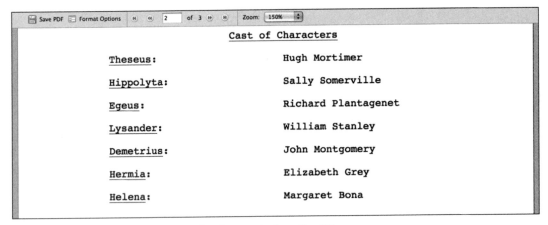

Figure B.5 Typical stageplay cast list, inserted after the title page.

The cast list is created in the stageplay editing window, when you activate the Cast tab. Figure B.6 displays stageplay editing tabs, and Figure B.7 displays the Cast list being filled out.

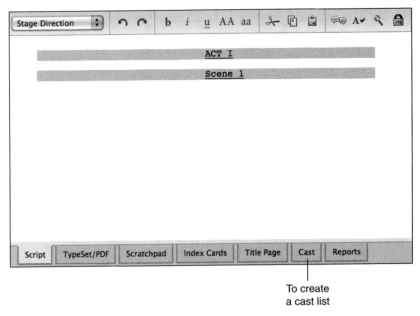

Figure B.6 Script editing window, including Cast tab.

Mores and Continueds

This dialog box offers identical selections to the screenplay Mores and Continueds dialog box. Refer to Figure B.1 for an illustration of usage.

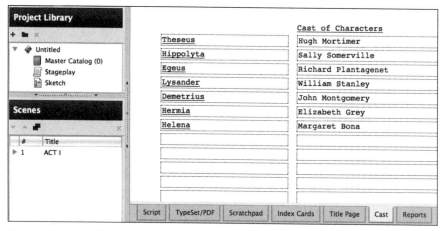

Figure B.7   Cast list being filled out, once you activate the Cast tab.

Audio Play Format Options

Audio play format options are contained on two separate tabbed dialog boxes: General and BBC Options.

General

- **Paper Size.** Choose North American letter size or European A4 size paper.

- **Show Title Page & Cast.** Cast lists are typically included with an audio play. Audio play cast lists work just like stageplay cast lists: see Figures B.5, B.6, and B.7 for usage illustrations.

- **Show ID numbers.** This option assigns a number to every dialog line. The number is displayed in the Standard Format only (see the next bullet). Figure B.8 displays ID number usage.

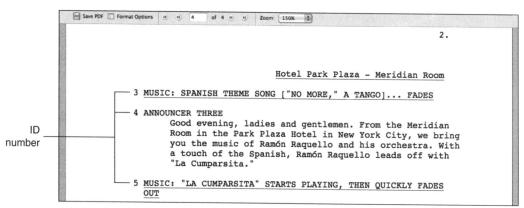

Figure B.8   ID numbers displayed in a standard format.

- **Format (Standard).** This selection formats the audio play in a "standard" layout, placing stage directions and transitions in all uppercase and indenting them 1 inch from the character names. Character names are set flush left (but use of ID numbers indents them slightly), and dialog is left-indented 1/2 half inch from the character names. Scene headings are indented 2 1/2 inches from the character names. Figure B.9 illustrates the standard format in an audio play (with ID numbers turned off).

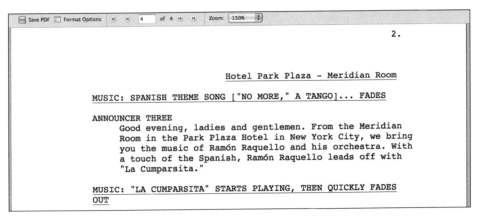

Figure B.9 The standard audio play format (without ID numbers selected).

- **Format (BBC Cue).** This selection formats the stageplay in a preferred BBC format emphasizing cues; this is intended primarily for comedic "sketch" material. (The BBC is one of the prime producers of audio plays in the world.) Stage directions and transitions get an Action cue flush left on the page; the actual text is rendered all uppercase, indented 2 1/2 inches from the left margin. All action cues and directions are bolded and underlined. Character names are flush left, and dialog begins on the same line as the character name, indented 2 inches from the left margin. Scene headings are also indented 2 1/2 inches from the left margin and are rendered all uppercase and underlined (but not bolded). Figure B.10 illustrates the BBC cue format in an audio play.

- **Format (BBC Scene).** This selection formats the stageplay in a preferred BBC format emphasizing scenes (more often used for dramatic content). Scene headings, stage directions, and transitions are rendered uppercase, underlined, and indented 2 1/2 inches from the left margin. Character names and dialog are rendered identically to the BBC Cue format. Figure B.11 illustrates the BBC scene format in an audio play.

BBC Options

This dialog box embeds additional information only in the BBC cue format. The show title, sketch title, and comments display as a header on every page. Figure B.12 illustrates usage of these options on a typeset page.

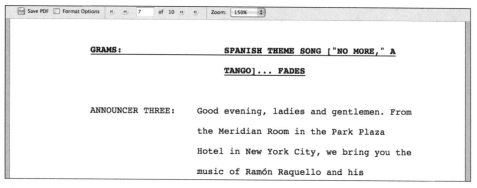

Figure B.10   The BBC cue audio play format. (ID numbers will not appear even if they're selected.)

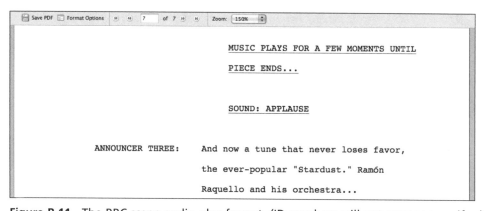

Figure B.11   The BBC scene audio play format. (ID numbers will not appear even if selected.)

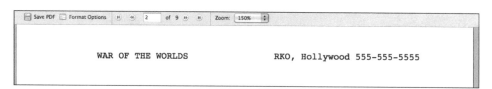

Figure B.12   Optional BBC data displayed as a header in a BBC cue format.

Comic Book Format Options

The comic book template offers simple format options in a single dialog box:

- **Paper Size.** Choose North American letter size or European A4 size paper.

- **Show Title Page.** This option ensures that the title page is printed out whenever hard copy or a PDF is output.

Appendix C: Breakdown Item Data Fields

Actor

For any actors tagged in a script, breakdown items include the following:

- Actor
- Tags
- Description
- Media
- Availability—Start Date and End Date
- Contact Information—Name, Email Address, Phone #, Cell #, Address, Comments, URL
- Detailed Physical Description—Height, Weight, Eyes, Hair, Date of Birth, Sex
- Wardrobe Sizes—Shirt, Pants, Dress, Hat, Shoes, Jacket

Additional Labour

For any additional labor (or labour, in Celtx) tagged in a script, breakdown items include the following:

- Additional Labour
- Tags
- Description
- Media
- Details—Scene Used In and Comments

Animal Handler

For any animal handler(s) tagged in a script, breakdown items include the following:

- Animal Handler
- Tags

- Description
- Media
- Details—Scene Used In and Comments

Animals

For any animals tagged in a script, breakdown items include the following:

- Animals
- Tags
- Description
- Media
- Details—Scene Used In and Comments

Camera

For any camera(s) tagged in a script, breakdown items include the following:

- Camera
- Tags
- Description
- Media
- Details—Scene Used In and Comments

CGI

For any CGI (computer-generated imagery) tagged in a script, breakdown items include the following:

- CGI
- Tags
- Description
- Media
- Details—Scene Used In and Comments

Character

For any characters tagged in a script, breakdown items include the following:

- Character

- Tags
- Full Name
- Actor
- Description
- Media
- Schedule ID
- In Scenes
- Detailed Physical Description—Height, Weight, Eyes, Hair, Date of Birth, Sex
- Character Traits—Key Character Traits, Principal Function
- Motivation—Goal and Plan
- Character Background—Family Background, Habits/Vices, Education, Personality, Likes, Dislikes
- Wardrobe Sizes—Shirt, Pants, Dress, Hat, Shoes, Jacket

Construction

For any construction tagged in a script, breakdown items include the following:

- Construction
- Tags
- Description
- Media
- Details—Scene Used In and Comments

Crew

For any crew tagged in a script, breakdown items include the following:

- Crew
- Tags
- Full Name
- Department
- Title

- Media
- In Scenes
- Availability—Start Date and End Date
- Contact Information—Name, Email Address, Phone #, Cell #, Address, Comments, URL

Electrics

For any electrically related items tagged in a script, breakdown items include the following:

- Electrics
- Tags
- Description
- Media
- Details—Scene Used In and Comments

Extras

For any extras tagged in a script, breakdown items include the following:

- Extras
- Tags
- Description
- Media
- Details—Scene Used In and Comments

Greenery

For any greenery tagged in a script, breakdown items include the following:

- Greenery
- Tags
- Description
- Media
- Details—Scene Used In and Comments

Hair

For any hairstyles and other hair-related issues tagged in a script, breakdown items include the following:

- Hair
- Tags
- Description
- Media
- Details—Scene Used In and Comments

Lights

For any lights tagged in a script, breakdown items include the following:

- Lights
- Tags
- Description
- Media
- Details—Scene Used In and Comments

Livestock

For any livestock tagged in a script, breakdown items include the following:

- Livestock
- Tags
- Description
- Media
- Details—Scene Used In and Comments

Location

For any location tagged in a script, breakdown items include the following:

- Location
- Tags

- Description

- Media

- Address (an adjacent link immediately creates an onscreen Google map of the location)

- Scouting and Selection—Selection for Scenes, Scouted for Scenes

- Contact Information—Name, Email Address, Phone #, Cell #, Comments

- Facility Information—Dates Available, Square Footage, Rental Cost, Elevator, Power Capabilities, Light Sources, Noise Issues, Washroom Locations, Parking Information, Comments

Makeup

For any makeup tagged in a script, breakdown items include the following:

- Makeup

- Tags

- Description

- Media

- Details—Scene Used In and Comments

Mechanical FX

For any mechanical effects tagged in a script, breakdown items include the following:

- Mechanical FX

- Tags

- Description

- Media

- Details—Scene Used In and Comments

Miscellaneous

For any miscellaneous elements tagged in a script, breakdown items include the following:

- Miscellaneous

- Tags

- Description

- Media
- Details—Scene Used In and Comments

Music

For any music cues or notes tagged in a script, breakdown items include the following:

- Music
- Tags
- Description
- Media
- Details—Scene Used In and Comments

Optical FX

For any optical effects tagged in a script, breakdown items include the following:

- Optical FX
- Tags
- Description
- Media
- Details—Scene Used In and Comments

Painting

For any painting tagged in a script, breakdown items include the following:

- Painting
- Tags
- Description
- Media
- Details—Scene Used In and Comments

Production Notes

For any production notes tagged in a script, breakdown items include the following:

- Production Notes
- Tags

- Description
- Media
- Details—Scene Used In and Comments

Props

For any props tagged in a script, breakdown items include the following:

- Props
- Tags
- Description
- Media
- Details—Scenes Used In, Characters Used By, Size, Color, Era
- Procurement—Type of Procurement, Cost, Dates Needed, Return Date
- Contact Information—Name, Email Address, Phone #, Cell #, Address, Comments

Scene Details

For any scene details tagged in a script, breakdown items include the following:

- Scene Details
- Tags
- Alternate Name
- Description
- Media
- Scene Details—Central Event, Impact, Characters, Setting, When, Mood
- Protagonist/Antagonist—Identify Protagonist, Identify Antagonist, Protagonist Goal, Antagonist Goal, How Does Protagonist Achieve Goal, How Does Antagonist Achieve Goal

Security

For any security tagged in a script, breakdown items include the following:

- Security
- Tags
- Description

- Media

- Details—Scene Used In and Comments

Set

For any set elements tagged in a script, breakdown items include the following:

- Set

- Tags

- Description

- Media

- Details—Scene Used In and Comments

Set Dressing

For any set dressing tagged in a script, breakdown items include the following:

- Set Dressing

- Tags

- Description

- Media

- Details—Scene Used In and Comments

Sound

For any sound tagged in a script, breakdown items include the following:

- Sound

- Tags

- Description

- Media

- Details—Scene Used In and Comments

Sound FX

For any sound effects tagged in a script, breakdown items include the following:

- Sound FX

- Tags

- Description

- Media
- Details—Scene Used In and Comments

Special Equipment

For any special equipment tagged in a script, breakdown items include the following:

- Special Equipment
- Tags
- Description
- Media
- Details—Scene Used In and Comments

Special FX

For any special effects tagged in a script, breakdown items include the following:

- Special FX
- Tags
- Description
- Media
- Details—Scene Used In and Comments

Stunts

For any stunts tagged in a script, breakdown items include the following:

- Stunts
- Tags
- Description
- Media
- Details—Scene Used In and Comments

Vehicles

For any vehicles tagged in a script, breakdown items include the following:

- Vehicles
- Tags

- Description
- Media
- Details—Scene Used In and Comments

Wardrobe

For any wardrobe tagged in a script, breakdown items include the following:

- Wardrobe
- Tags
- Description
- Media
- Worn By—Character and Scenes Used In
- Details—Size, Color, Era
- Procurement—Type of Procurement, Cost, Dates Needed, Return Date
- Contact Information—Name, Email Address, Phone #, Cell #, Address, Comments

Weapons

For any weapons tagged in a script, breakdown items include the following:

- Weapons
- Tags
- Description
- Media
- Details—Scene Used In and Comments

Appendix D: Menu Bars and Icon Toolbar

This appendix surveys pull-down menus from the menu bar in Celtx.

File

The File menu contains many options common to virtually all programs, along with options unique to Celtx.

- **New Project.** Begins a new project
- **Open Project.** Opens an existing project
- **Open Recent.** Opens recently opened projects
- **Save Project.** Saves the project with the current name
- **Save Project As.** Saves the project in a different location or with a different name
- **Create Template.** Creates a customized script template you design, for use with future projects
- **Close Tab.** Closes one of the currently opened Project Library items
- **Open from Studio.** Opens a project from a Celtx Studio
- **Save to Studio.** Saves a project to your Celtx studio
- **Add Item.** Adds an item to the Project Library
- **Add Folder.** Adds a folder to the Project Library
- **Delete Item.** Deletes a currently selected Project Library item
- **Page Setup.** Controls page orientation (portrait, landscape); print scaling; margins; and header and footer
- **Print Preview.** Displays the printout view
- **Print.** Prints the project

- **Show Project File.** Displays the folder the project file resides in
- **Exit.** Exits Celtx

Edit

Celtx's Edit menu is nearly identical to that of most text editing programs.

- Undo
- Redo
- Cut
- Copy
- Paste
- Select All
- Find
- Replace
- Find Next
- Find Previous

View

Toolbars is the only option on this menu. It will allow you to control whether to solely display text or icons (or both) in the icon toolbar, or dispense with the toolbar altogether.

Script

The Script menu varies slightly across templates. When you're using the Novel template, the menu is replaced by a Novel pull-down.

- **Import Script.** Allows for importing of ASCII-formatted (text-formatted) scripts, which initially may have been created in Final Draft, Movie Magic Screenwriter, Microsoft Word, or any program that can export to a text-with-layout file. Additionally, if the Sync plug-in has been installed, you can import scripts from an iPhone or iPad.

- **Export Script.** Allows for exporting of the opened script to a text-with-layout file that is readable in Final Draft, Movie Magic Screenwriter, Microsoft Word, and almost any other text editing program. Additionally, if the Sync plug-in has been installed, you can export scripts to your iPhone or iPad.

- **Adapt To.** Allows you to instantly create a new type of script format for your current script. For example, you can convert your film script to a stageplay format with this menu.

- **Revision Mode.** This feature is specific to the film script template and converts a script to a production script with additional formatting and tracking features.

- **Add Characters to Catalog.** This is a handy way to automate adding characters to the catalog; Celtx picks up all speaking roles and lists them in the Master Catalog. This is particularly useful for scripts you've imported into Celtx from other programs.

- **Format Options.** See Appendix B, "Script Template Typeset/PDF Format Options," for a thorough discussion of this feature.

- **Show Breakdown in Script.** This is a toggle that shows or hides color-coded breakdown elements in the script. If you find multiple text colors distracting when you're editing, uncheck this feature to return all text to black. (Checking the feature returns the breakdown colors.)

- **Sidebar.** This is another way to remove or reveal the right sidebar.

The Novel template has a reduced feature set based on the preceding list:

- **Import.** Allows for importing of ASCII-formatted (text-formatted) text, which may have been initially created in Final Draft, Movie Magic Screenwriter, Microsoft Word, or any program that can export to a text-with-layout file.

- **Export.** Allows for exporting of the opened text material to a text-with-layout file that is readable in Final Draft, Movie Magic Screenwriter, Microsoft Word, and almost any other text editing program.

- **Show Breakdown.** This is a toggle that shows or hides color-coded breakdown elements in the novel. If you find multiple text colors distracting when you're editing, uncheck this feature to return all text to black. (Checking the feature returns the breakdown colors.)

- **Sidebar.** This is another way to remove or reveal the right sidebar.

Tools

The Tools menu handles the spell checker, the add-on toolbox, and other Celtx options.

- **Check Spelling.** Runs the spell checker.

- **Inline Spell Checking.** A toggle that marks incorrect or unrecognized spellings as you type. Some writers like this; others find this distracting. You can check or uncheck the feature. The default setting is On.

- **Toolbox.** Opens the Toolbox dialog box where you can view current add-ons and enable or disable them if necessary.

- **Options.** Controls a variety of Celtx features. These include:

  1. **General.** Automates Celtx Studio sign-in if desired; automates file saves; controls Studio comment feature.

  2. **Categories.** Enables or disables breakdown categories. (For many projects, a reduced number of categories is preferable.)

  3. **Script.** Allows you to add additional location, time-of-day, and shot designations, or alternatively, to reduce the recognized designations.

  4. **Production Schedule.** Allows you to control workweek days, default scene lengths, and perform other schedule functions.

  5. **Privacy.** Controls whether Celtx pings the Celtx server on launch; the information is only used to count Celtx users, but you can turn this ping off if desired.

  6. **Network.** Allows the setup of network proxies.

Help

The Help menu provides help-related options, along with access to the Celtx splash screen, which is the portal to template selection for new project files, recently opened projects, and sample projects.

- **About Celtx.** Displays the Celtx version you're using

- **Splash Screen.** Opens the splash screen, enabling easy access to sample files, recently opened files, and the full selection of templates

- **Online Support.** Opens a default browser window and directs to Celtx's support page

- **Celtx Wiki.** Opens the wiki within your default browser

- **Video Tutorial.** Connects to Celtx's video tutorial

- **Report a Bug.** Allows you to report a program bug

Appendix E: Keyboard Shortcuts

For users who don't want their fingers to leave the keyboard, Celtx has built-in keyboard shortcuts for a variety of functions.

Script Template Element Select Shortcuts

Table E.1   Screenplay

Command	Windows	Mac OS
Scene Heading	Ctrl+1 or Ctrl+Enter	Command+1
Action	Ctrl+2	Command+2
Character	Ctrl+3	Command+3
Dialog	Ctrl+4	Command+4
Parenthetical	Ctrl+5	Command+5
Transition	Ctrl+6	Command+6
Shot	Ctrl+7	Command+7
Text	Ctrl+8	Command+8

Table E.2   Stageplay

Command	Windows	Mac OS
Act	Ctrl+1	Command+1
Scene Heading	Ctrl+2	Command+2
Stage Direction	Ctrl+3	Command+3
Character	Ctrl+4	Command+4
Dialog	Ctrl+5	Command+5
Parenthetical	Ctrl+6	Command+6
Transition	Ctrl+7	Command+7
Text	Ctrl+8	Command+8

Table E.3   Audio Play

Command	Windows	Mac OS
Scene Heading	Ctrl+1	Command+1
Production Note	Ctrl+2	Command+2
Character	Ctrl+3	Command+3
Dialog	Ctrl+4	Command+4
Parenthetical	Ctrl+5	Command+5
Sound	Ctrl+6	Command+6
Voice	Ctrl+7	Command+7
Music	Ctrl+8	Command+8

Table E.4   A/V

Command	Windows	Mac OS
Scene Heading	Ctrl+1	Command+1
Shot	Ctrl+2	Command+2
Character	Ctrl+3	Command+3
Dialog	Ctrl+4	Command+4
Parenthetical	Ctrl+5	Command+5

Table E.5   Comic Book

Command	Windows	Mac OS
Page	Ctrl+1	Command+1
Panel	Ctrl+2	Command+2
Caption	Ctrl+3	Command+3
Character	Ctrl+4	Command+4
Balloon Type	Ctrl+5	Command+5
Balloon	Ctrl+6	Command+6

General Editing Keyboard Shortcuts

Table E.6   Keyboard Shortcuts

Command	Windows	Mac OS
Select all	Ctrl+A	Command+A
Cut	Ctrl+X	Command+X
Copy	Ctrl+C	Command+C
Paste	Ctrl+V	Command+V
White Space	Shift+Enter	Shift+Return
Bold	Ctrl+B	Command+B
Italic	Ctrl+I	Command+I
Underline	Ctrl+U	Command+U
Undo	Ctrl+Z	Command+Z
Redo	Ctrl+Y	Command+Y
Find & Replace	Ctrl+F	Command+F
Find Next	Ctrl+G	Command+G
Find Previous	Shift+Ctrl+G	Shift+Command+G
New Project	Ctrl+N	Command+N
Open Project	Ctrl+O	Command+O
Save	Ctrl+S	Command+S
Print	Ctrl+P	Command+P
Tab Switching	Ctrl+Tab	Command+option+left/right

For even more keyboard shortcuts, head to http://wiki.celtx.com/index.php?title= Keyboard_shortcut.

Appendix F: Setting Up Linux for Celtx Studios and Celtx Add-Ons

Linux needs a little extra care if you're using Celtx Studios or Celtx add-ons under this operating system. You need to make a one-time configuration of browser values so that Linux can handle the use of Celtx Studios (discussed in Chapters 14, "Celtx Studios: Creation and Administration," 15, "Celtx Studios: User Interaction," and 16, "Celtx Add-Ons, Utilities, and Sketch Images").

A complete collection of screenshots to walk you through this process is available on the Celtx wiki (http://wiki.celtx.com/index.php?title=Using_Studio_on_Linux). The basic steps in Firefox are as follows:

1. **Open about:config in Firefox.** Input `about:config` into the address bar in Firefox to see advanced options.

2. **Add a new preference.** Right-click in the preferences area and choose to add a new boolean.

3. **Enter the preference name for the `celtx` protocol.** Input `network.protocol-handler.expose.celtx` into the dialog box, and click OK.

4. **Select false.** Select False in the dialog box, and click OK.

5. **Add another new preference.** Right-click in the preferences area and choose to add a new boolean.

6. **Enter the preference name for the `celtx` protocol.** Input `network.protocol-handler.expose.celtxs` into the dialog box, and click OK. This is the same as step 3, except the protocol is `celtxs`, not `celtx`.

7. **Choose False.** Choose False in the dialog box, and click OK.

8. **Confirm that both entries show up correctly.** You may need to click the Show All button to refresh the list. If you followed the steps correctly, you will see two new lines in the network section, corresponding to the preferences you just added.

9. **Add settings with `gconftool`.** Open a terminal window (Applications, Accessories, Terminal on most distributions) and enter the following, where `/path/to/celtx` is the full

path to the file called celtx inside the celtx folder (for example, /usr/local/celtx/celtx or ~/Desktop/celtx/celtx):

```
gconftool -s /desktop/gnome/url-handlers/celtx/command -t
string "/path/to/celtx %s"
```

```
gconftool -s /desktop/gnome/url-handlers/celtxs/command -t
string "/path/to/celtx %s"
```

```
gconftool -s /desktop/gnome/url-handlers/celtx/enabled -t bool true
```

```
gconftool -s /desktop/gnome/url-handlers/celtxs/enabled -t bool true
```

These are all the changes you need to make if you're just using add-ons and not Celtx Studios. On the other hand, it may not hurt to prepare for the use of a studio, even if it's not part of your plans just yet.

To finish preparing Linux for Celtx Studios usage, do the following:

1. Edit a project in your Celtx studio. Visit your Celtx studio, open the Projects window, select a project, and click the Edit button. A dialog box should show up asking you to pick an application to handle the link. Click on the Choose button.

2. Enter the path to the Celtx application. In the location bar of the open dialog that shows up, enter the path to the Celtx application and click Open. The path is usually /usr/local/celtx/celtx.

3. Select Celtx as the handler. Then select the new Celtx option that shows up. Click the Remember My Choice for Celtxs Links check box, and then click OK.

Note: You only need to carry out these steps once.

Glossary

ADR (automated dialogue replacement, or additional dialog recording). Also known as a looping session or postsynchronization, ADR is a rerecording of original captured dialog in the studio to improve sound clarity, diction, and timing. Most feature films and television shows use at least some ADR.

animatic. A series of still images edited together and played in sequence to create a simple mock-up of a scene's visual flow.

blocking. The movement and positioning of actors within a scene.

breakdown. A script analysis extracting production elements that will be assembled into lists and simple databases for purposes of scheduling and budgeting. An example would be identifying and inventorying all props in a script to have that list available for prop acquisition.

call sheet. A sheet of paper issued to the cast and crew of a film production informing them where and when they should report for a particular day of shooting. Call sheets also include other useful information such as contact information (for example, phone numbers of crew members and other contacts), the day's schedule, shooting scenes, shoot location address, and weather forecast.

CU or C.U. Close-up camera shot.

Foley artist. The reproduction of ambient sound in filmmaking. Classic examples are the use of coconut shells to create the clip-clop of horses' hooves, and the slicing of frozen lettuce to create head injury sounds.

locked script. A script that has had its page numbers and scene numbers set ("locked") to avoid confusion when script revisions are made. Scene 6 remains Scene 6 even if other scenes are added or subtracted before it.

machinima. The process of using real-time computer graphics rendering engines (typically video game engines) to create animated films.

mise-en-scene. A French term describing the design aspects of a stage or film production, including composition, sets, props, costumes, and lighting. Terry Gilliam's *Brazil* and David Fincher's *Seven* are two examples of films with highly distinct mise-en-scene.

non-linear editing (NLE). Editing that allows random access to any film image frame; often used as a substitute for digital editing, because all digital editing (Final Cut Pro, Avid Media Composer, iMovie) is non-linear.

pre-production. The preparation done for film or video production. This includes script writing, crew hiring, talent casting, production office staffing, location scouting and selection, prop and costume acquisition, equipment rentals, budgeting, scheduling, and numerous other activities.

pre-visualization. Also known as "previz," pre-visualization describes any attempt to anticipate the visual flow of a film sequence. Storyboards, animatics, cinematics, and digital 3D visualizations are examples of pre-visualization.

POV or P.O.V. An acronym for a point-of-view camera shot.

sides. Sample scenes or scene excerpts that casting directors use to audition actors.

time-based media. Any media that progresses over a period of time. Newspapers and photographs are media that don't rely on time passage; films, TV commercials, and video games are examples of time-based media.

trans-media. A narrative-driven experience that is built to span multiple media platforms for full delivery of the story world.

workflow. An established sequence of job processes and executable tasks designed with a single end goal: usually the creation of a product or delivery of a service. Creation of video game assets or delivery of a finalized distributable film requires a specific workflow for success.

Index